JAPAN

Profile of a Postindustrial Power

NATIONS OF CONTEMPORARY ASIA
Mervyn Adams Seldon
Series Editor

†*Japan: Profile of a Postindustrial Power,* Ardath W. Burks

Nepal: Profile of a Himalayan Kingdom, Leo E. Rose and John T. Scholz

Sri Lanka: Profile of an Island Republic, Tissa Fernando and Robert Kearney

Mongolia: A Profile, William R. Heaton

†Available in both paperback and hardcover editions

JAPAN

Profile of a Postindustrial Power

Ardath W. Burks

Westview Press / Boulder, Colorado

All photographs courtesy of Japan Information Center, Consulate General of Japan, One Citicorp Center, New York, New York.

Nations of Contemporary Asia

Published in 1981 in the United States of America by
Westview Press, Inc.
5500 Central Avenue
Boulder, Colorado 80301
Frederick A. Praeger, Publisher

Library of Congress Cataloging in Publication Data
Burks, Ardath W.
Japan.
(Nations of contemporary Asia)
Bibliography: p.
Includes index.
1. Japan. I. Series.
DS806.B85 952 80-14183
ISBN 0-89158-786-1
ISBN 0-86531-040-8 (pbk.)

Printed and bound in the United States of America

Contents

Figures and Tables

Figures

Tables

Photographs

Preface

Japan may well be the most progressive nation in the world. And indeed, if Japan does not offer "lessons for America," its intricately wrought and efficiently functioning society at the least deserves close attention. For some forty years, through travel and residence, research and teaching, it has been my privilege, and occasionally frustration, to study Japan and the Japanese. Upon reflection, I have detected several subtle shifts in my own emphasis in scholarship and teaching. A decade ago when I team-taught an introductory course on South and East Asia's great traditions and predominantly agrarian lifestyles, Japan already proved the interesting exception because a majority of the country's residents had begun to migrate to the large industrial cities.

More recently the concept of the postindustrial society has been the focus of my attention. As is explained in the text to follow, Japanese society is one in which the majority of the labor force is not only removed from primary (chiefly agricultural) pursuits, but also removed from secondary (industrial) employment and engaged in tertiary (service) activities. I have found it increasingly useful to relate metropolitan Tokyo to the greater metropolitan New York area: both are postindustrial societies. Most of today's students know little about rural America and even less about village Japan. In this context, the Japanese experiment is eminently worthy of study, not because any of the social formulas are directly transferable, but because Japanese attempts to come to grips with often intractable problems sometimes resemble, and sometimes contrast with, our own efforts.

Anyone who works in, or does research on, Japan quickly accumulates a stock of obligations to cooperative Japanese. The author is no exception. During some ten trips to Japan in the postwar period, a large number of Japanese gave me and my family help, encouragement, and flawless hospitality. I wish to recognize my debt specifically to the members of the International House of Japan, Inc.: chairman of the board, Dr. Matsumoto Shigeharu; executive officer, Tanabe Tatsuro; librarian, Fujino Yukio; and the ever cheerful and helpful staff. In Tokyo, I. House has always been my second home. To Professor Emeritus Sakata Yoshio of Kyoto University, my *sensei,* and to other members of the Kindaika ("modernization") Seminar, I owe a debt for their patient attempts to introduce me to the views of Japanese scholars.

At the National Institute for Educational Research (NIER, Kokuritsu Kyōiku Kenkyūjo), my former student, research assistant, and colleague Kaneko Tadashi provided me as regularly as the Japanese seasons with up-to-date statistical data for my annual contributions to encyclopedias, as well as with information for this volume.

Here in the United States, I have received regular monthly inoculations of inspiration and enthusiasm from my colleagues in the University Seminar: Modern Japan, hosted generously by the East Asian Institute, Columbia University. Consul Sugano Yukio of the Japan Information Center, New York, has given generously of his and his staff's time to provide data, the Japanese viewpoint on issues, and the splendid illustrations in this volume. As a member of the Japan Society, I have profited from proximity to the Japan House in New York, where I have attended well-organized programs, discussions, and seminars.

Several neighbors and colleagues have read parts of chapter drafts. Professor Marius Jansen of Princeton University was remarkably patient with my mere social scientist's attempt to encapsulate the Japanese tradition (in Chapter 2). Mr. and Mrs. David Cayer, who claim to be only amateur collectors of Japanese art, read the section on art and culture (Chapter 3). Dr. Richard Wilson, director of International Programs at Rutgers University and a specialist on China and political socialization, read over and commented on the section on national character (Chapter 8). For this section I am also indebted to Professor Nobuo Shimahara, my colleague in the Rutgers Graduate School of Education. Although, unfortunately, I am not a neighbor of Professor David Kornhauser, Department of Geography, University of Hawaii, our long and fruitful exchange of ideas (reflected in Chapter 1) has served to strengthen my grasp of Japan at ground level, so to speak. Professor Leon Hollerman of Claremont Men's College was patient and helpful in his comments on my treatment of Japan's postwar economy (Chapter 6). I am grateful to a former colleague, Professor Charles Ogrosky, for his care in rendering maps and charts.

Several generations of students at Rutgers, at Columbia, and at the University of Hawaii have listened attentively, challenged poorly framed concepts, and helped me clarify what is presented below.

Members of the efficient editorial staff of Westview Press—Vicki Groninger, Deborah Lynes, and especially Mervyn Adams Seldon—have been indefatigable in trying to improve the final draft of the manuscript. In particular, Mrs. Seldon has, quite simply, been the best consulting editor with whom I have ever worked.

Dr. Wilson's staff at the International Center at Rutgers has lent strong support. Finally, at home, Jane Burks—"good wife and wise mother"—has subtly suggested improvements while pretending to do only typing and to be patiently proofreading the manuscript. In spite of all this help, which I will try to repay during the rest of my life, some misinterpretations and errors undoubtedly remain in the text. For these I, of course, assume full responsibility.

In any book on Japan, the author and the reader encounter the problem of style in handling Japanese proper names. In most cases, as a courtesy to the Japanese, names are given according to their custom; that is, the surname first, with the given name following. In rare cases, the documentation of works by Japanese that have been translated into English and published in the West will show the name as it is listed in these works (given name first, followed by family name). Most Americans of Japanese ancestry (*nisei* and *sansei*) prefer the Western style (given name first, followed by family name) and in these cases, their preference was honored in this book.

I have tried (for the general nonspecialist reader) to keep the use of Japanese words to a minimum. Even the casual reader, however, may wish to master some of the vocabulary and others (for example, advanced students in area language studies) will wish to note the Japanese terms for social phenomena.

Ardath W. Burks
Rutgers University

Introduction

This is a book about a land that was once—and indeed on occasion is still—regarded as exotic and "Oriental," Japan; and about a remarkably homogeneous people, the Japanese.

The Japanese no longer really live in the "Far East"; the term is an ethnocentric invention of the Europeans. Today Japanese reside in an area Americans might well call the "Middle West." In fact, Japanese now live throughout the world, in Southeast Asia, in Europe, in Latin America, and in the United States. For example, it is estimated that there are some 30,000 Japanese nationals working and residing in the metropolitan New York area. There may be even more in California. By one count there are about 80 Japanese firms located in New Jersey. Throughout the New York area there must be at least 500 Japanese restaurants.

If today's Japanese, unlike their ancestors who visited us in the nineteenth century, are not considered exotics, neither may they be considered familiar friends. As someone said, Americans and Japanese look at each other through opposite ends of a cultural telescope. This book is an attempt to bring Japan and the Japanese into sharper focus.

A description of the Japanese landscape is a logical beginning. Despite the depredations of industrialization and pollution, the proximity of mountains and sea still makes for startlingly beautiful scenery. The island nation is resource-poor, however, almost completely dependent on the outside world for resources and particularly for energy. Most Japanese live not in the celebrated villages, nor even in the cities, but in vast conurbations. Movement to the megalopolis in recent generations marks one of the significant migrations of our day. Yet the Japanese have a sense of continuity, the baggage of a long-lived tradition. Within that tradition is a finely tuned aesthetic sense, which, in turn, has guided the wonderful Japanese art.

In describing the Great Tradition and the Little Tradition of Japan, one encounters problems. Throughout there is need to balance culture change (the persistence of a Japanese Way, yet its imperceptible alteration at home) with culture contact (the regular and dramatic confrontation with powerful influences from abroad). For example, how does one handle what has been called Japanese "feudalism"? Is it to be regarded as an isolated, backward, oppressive stage in the history of Japan? Are there "feudal residues" in Japanese society even today? Or, as former ambassador to Japan Edwin Reischauer and others do, should we think of the long period of Tokugawa peace (1600–1868) as in fact "post-feudal" or even "proto-modern," in short, as a preparation to withstand the impact of the nineteenth century and the West? Finally, how useful is the conceptual framework of modernization in explaining the social, economic, and political development directed first by the Meiji modernizers (1868–1912) and then by the aliens during the Occupation (1945–52) of Japan?

In any case, our contemporary neighbors, the Japanese, are themselves obsessed with a veritable fad of introspection. "Who are we Japanese?" they ask. There are various answers (some enlightened by scientific insight, some dangerous generalizations), replies that sometimes explain and sometimes exaggerate the complex social structure, intricate political culture, and vigorous economic behavior of the Japanese. The highly literate, well-informed Japanese are nonetheless not quite worldly. Acculturated within a unique society and facing formidable language barriers, they demonstrate an insularity that makes it difficult for them to do business abroad. Similarly, non-Japanese (*gaijin* or "outsiders") find it equally hard to do much more than tour Japan.

The cultural gap is most clearly revealed in the world's response to Japanese activities in foreign trade, investment abroad, and establishment of multinational branch plants outside Japan. Japan's need to trade for the sake of growth, its aggressive export policy, and its success, as measured by towering balance-of-payments surpluses, all create *real* economic issues between Japan and the other industrial democracies. The Japanese unusual capacity for work, unique commercial organization, and decision-making style, on the other hand, often create *unreal* fears about "the ugly Japanese," the superpower status of "Japan, Inc.," and the revival of Japanese imperialism.

Japan and the United States, for example, are now engaged in the largest bilateral cross-ocean trade in the history of the world. The Tokyo-Washington axis is marked by regular ministerial consultation, integrated security policies, and massive cultural and educational exchange. And yet Americans persist in thinking of Japanese as strange and exotic. To be fair, Japanese, too, carry around only caricatures of American life.

The Japanese experience is, on the one hand, a classic example of the movement from a primitive to a settled, agrarian—if preindustrial—lifestyle. On the other hand, it represents a unique example of conversion from the traditional agrarian to the modern industrial style. Japan has been one of the first of the handful of countries to be "beyond modern." A majority of its labor force is now employed in the service, or tertiary, sector. This sector generates a larger proportion of the gross national product than do the primary (agricultural) and secondary (industrial) sectors. Finally, Japan's levels of capital accumulation and mass consumption now make possible a move from a labor-intensive or even capital-intensive stage to a knowledge-intensive stage. Politics, political institutions, and political parties; economics, economic institutions, and labor-management negotiations; the society, social institutions, and social issues—all these display a cultural lag. Whether rooted firmly in nineteenth-century economic "struggle" or uprooted in the overwhelming "growth" of the 1960s, traditional Japanese organizations confront new problems as they face the costs of growth and new modes of citizen participation. Whether the disengaged in Japanese politics symbolize the end of ideology in this mass society remains an open question, but even tentative Japanese solutions should be of interest to citizens everywhere, especially to those who perceive the promise and peril of the technetronic age.

1

Sansui: The Landscape and Its Settlement

In Japanese art there is a venerable tradition called *sansui.* This term, which literally means "mountain and water," refers both to a style and to the visible, pleasing proximity of rounded hills, jagged peaks, calm bays, and tempestuous seas. Originally used to describe an inspiration for monochrome landscape painting, the term is also useful in summarizing the structure of the island nation.

STRUCTURE

The combination of mountains and sea in Japan has profoundly affected the historic development of the country and has contributed to the problem of human settlement faced by the Japanese even today. In brief, Japan is scenery-rich and resource-poor.

The Mountains

Geologists view the Japanese archipelago not so much as islands as immense mountains on the globe. These ranges rise 20,000 to 30,000 feet from the floor of the Pacific Ocean. Just east of, and close to, Japan is a deep trough, the Japan Trench, which at bottom reaches 36,198 feet below sea level. Just to the south is another trough with a depth of more than 13,000 feet. On shore, Japan's mountains are sharply ridged; many of the peaks in central Honshū rise more than 10,000 feet above sea level. Since glacial effects were not felt in this area, mountain slopes are quite steep and the valleys narrow, yet most of the terrain is forested hills.

Division of the country into relatively small plains (except where noted) may have contributed to the early clannishness of the Japanese and probably set the boundaries for old provinces. The topography, according to former ambassador Edwin O. Reischauer, may have also helped to shape the decentralized feudal pattern of medieval Japan. Until modern engineering enabled the building of rail lines, their cuts, bridges, and tunnels, and toll roads, lateral connections between the valleys were few. And sometimes, even today, topographical barriers have proved to be formidable. For example, in January 1979 the national railway system completed the world's longest tunnel on the Jōetsu superexpress line, beneath Mt. Tanigawa on the Gumma-Niigata prefectural border. At 13.7 miles in length, the Daishimizu Tunnel just surpassed the length of the Simplon Tunnel (12.3 miles) on the Swiss-Italian alpine border.

Geographers do, of course, describe Japan as a series of festoon islands, stretching some 1,300 miles from the Chishima (Kurile) island group in the northeast to the Nansei (Ryūkyū, including Okinawa) group in the southwest. In between, the archipelago consists of the four main islands–Hokkaidō, Honshū, Shikoku, and Kyūshū (97 percent of the total land area)–and of some 3,300 islets and rocks, many uncultivatable and uninhabited. Even when one thinks of Japan as an island-nation, it is difficult not to think of mountains.

Circum-Pacific crustal movements have formed and continue to shape the land, which is torn into bewildering fractions along fault lines, some heaped above and some sunk below the water. The resultant islands lie between a shallow submerged valley, the Sea of Japan, and a deep submerged depression, the Japan Trench.

Another explanation, borrowed from both geologists and geographers, has the Japanese islands poised precariously on a ring of fire. This zone of instability runs clear around, and borders on, the Pacific basin. In this sense, the islands are laid out in arcuate patterns, a series of convex bows. At the nodes in which the arcs intersect, there is direct or indirect evidence of volcanic activity. The four bows are

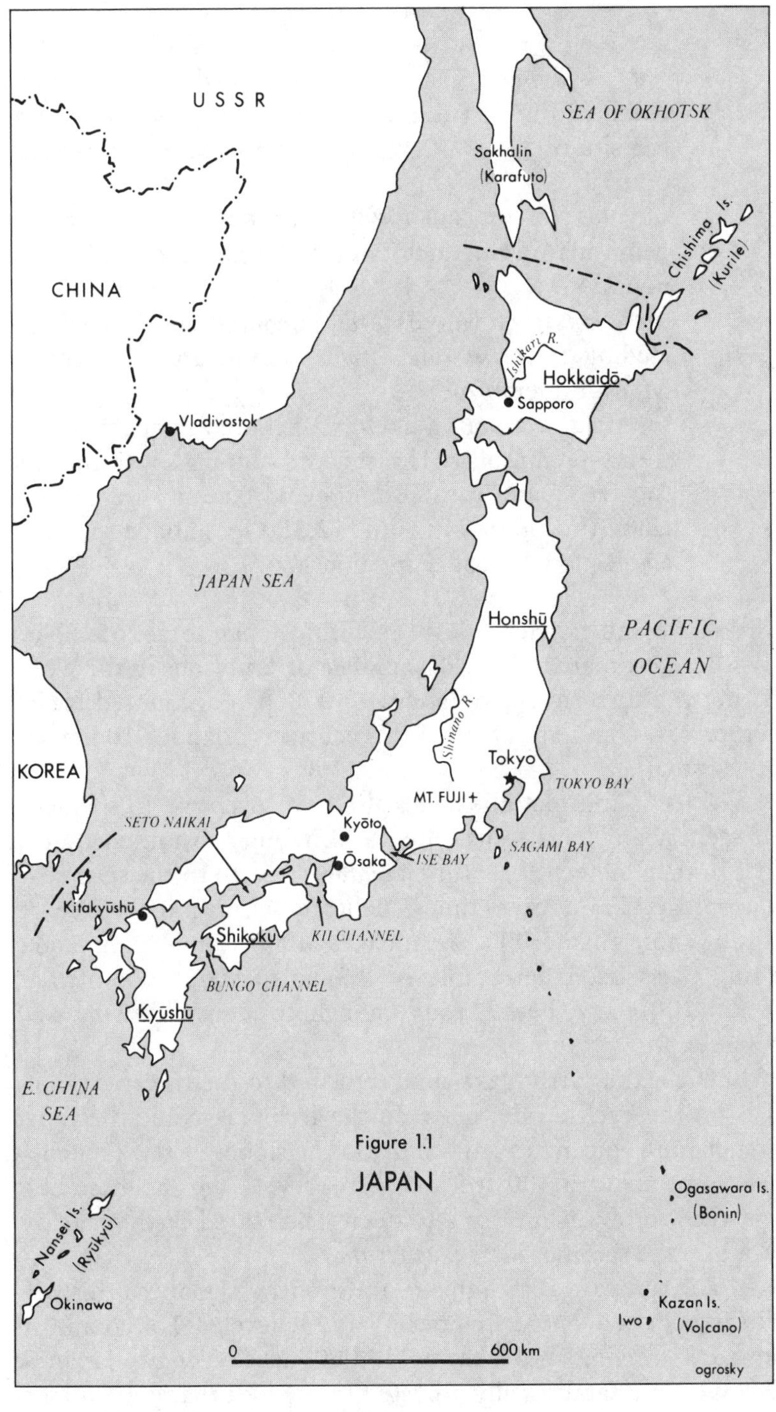

Figure 1.1

JAPAN

1. *the Chishima* (Kurile) *arc:* anchored in the central Hokkaidō node (recent volcanic eruptions occurred at the site of the 1972 Winter Olympic games, near Sapporo)
2. *the Honshū arc:* anchored in the north on the western peninsula of Hokkaidō and in the south in the Kyūshū node
3. *the Nansei* (Ryūkyū) *arc:* anchored in Kyūshū (including Mt. Aso, an active volcano and the world's largest caldera type)
4. *the Ogasawara* (Bonins) *arc:* anchored in the north on the Izu Peninsula of Honshū and running south through the Izu, Ogasawara (Bonin), and Kazan (Volcano) islands (including Mt. Fuji, 12,389 feet above sea level, a volcano that last erupted in 1707)

The active and extinct volcanoes within Japan total 265. Scientists have estimated the total number of eruptions in the world during the historic age at about 540. Japan accounted for 30 before 1900, and about 20 in this century (or about 10 percent of the total).

Cross-island tectonic zones also have given rise to spectacular scenery and have contributed to instability. Another result is that in the nineteenth century Japan gave birth to the science of seismology. In modern times, delicate seismographs have recorded more than 5,000 earthquakes annually in Japan. About 1 in 5 has been detectable by humans. About one-fifth of these (200) have been strong enough to stop the swing of a pendulum.

The major earthquake zone is related to the volcanic nodes. It is on the Pacific side, between the archipelago and the Japan Trench, and epicenters tend to be on the slopes of the Trench at depths of about 3,300 feet below sea level. The Japanese have lent the world a name for a frequent and feared earthquake byproduct, the seismic tidal wave (*tsunami*).

The greatest earthquake in modern Japanese history, which occurred on September 1, 1923, leveled Tokyo and its environs, leaving more than 130,000 dead. Today, Japanese have become fatalistically adjusted to the idea that great quakes will occur. In 1975, an earthquake forecast council estimated that a Richter-scale-5 quake would cause suffering for more than 133,000 citizens in the southwestern wards of Tokyo; water supply to some 420,000 houses in Tokyo would be interrupted; and some 15,000 citizens would be killed in Kawasaki City, just south of Tokyo. In spite of these forecasts, with the most up-to-date engineering and a considerable dose of faith, Tokyoites have continued to erect towering office buildings and have expanded vast underground networks of subways, pedestrian malls, and shops.

Indeed, the Japanese have become so inured to nature's might that in the 1970s a novel titled *Nihon chimbotsu* (Japan sinks)[1] was widely read with fear and fascination. The work, actually a *social science* fiction, described the effect on society if the whole archipelago was doomed to slide into the ocean after a tectonic shift.

This is not to say that natural disasters have offered no blessings. As a result of volcanic activity and earthquakes, Japan has magnificent natural scenery: the perfect cone of Fuji-*san*, the cauldron of Aso, volcanic bays in Hokkaidō, and the hot springs that dot the islands.

The Seacoast

The coasts of Japan are also, in effect, mere adjuncts to the mountainous structure. Capes, headlands, peninsulas with their lighthouses, and the bays between are either protrusions of, or submerged valleys between, the pervasive mountains. Japanese tend to think of their country as "a small, narrow, island nation." In fact, no part of Japan is more than seventy miles from a coast, and all of the country lies in the shadows of mountains.

For the total area of the four main islands (about 140,000 square miles), there is a total length of shoreline of about 9,800 miles. Japan thus has 1 linear mile of coast per 14 square miles of land (as compared to Britain's ratio of 1:8).

The magnificent Setonaikai (literally, "sea within channels," or the Inland Sea) is actually a submerged shallow structural depression nestled between the mountains of Shikoku and the less rugged highlands of western Honshū. The line of fracture is fringed by a chain of volcanoes (all extinct except Mt. Aso on Kyūshū) and more than 950 islands. Some one-half million acres of shores surrounding the Inland Sea have been declared national park in hopes of protecting the legendary beauty of the region. The main western water highway is well known to the Japanese, historically having served as the connection between the parts of Kyūshū that were points of contact with the continent of Asia and the oldest settled culture in the Yamato Basin, around Nara. As geographer David Kornhauser has described them, the coastal plains on Honshū face south and west just like the porch and sliding doors of a classic Japanese farmhouse. Shifting the image, the Setonaikai is Japan's Mediterranean with a pleasingly mild climate.

Today one can easily forget the long and relatively quiet coastline facing north and west over the Japan Sea. Japan's "backside" (*ura Nihon*), it has quite different topography and sharply different climate. It can therefore be a delight to the infrequent tourist who travels west to Matsue, where Lafcadio Hearn lived and died, or who journeys northwest to the undisturbed "Little Kyoto," Kanazawa. Older Japanese remember pre–World War II days, however, when this coast linked Japan with its interests on the continent—in Manchuria, Korea, and North China. There are still important ports in the area. One is Niigata, which was used in the 1950s to repatriate Koreans.

Geography, climate, and recent history have made the Pacific, or eastern and southeastern, coasts vastly more important. The major bays, really submerged valleys, used for shipping Japan's exports are here. They are (ranging southwest) Tokyo (including the port of Yokohama), Sagami, Ise, and Ōsaka, including the port of Kōbe. Mention must also be made of the portals of the Setonaikai, the Bungo Channel to the west, and the Kii Channel to the east. There are new port cities all along the Setonaikai and harbors serving the modern industrial complex located on northern Kyūshū. Perhaps more important in history are the other large bays in Kyūshū, serving Nagasaki, Sasebo, and Kagoshima.

The peninsulas that jut into, and the bays that welcome, the Pacific Ocean enjoy the warm flow of the Kuroshio (the

Black, or Japan, Current). It serves the same function as does its sister stream along the California coast, namely, to moderate the climate of all neighboring areas. Thus, climate and accessibility have encouraged the growth of great cities and the expansion of ports (and consequently the mainstream of history) to be on the Pacific side. The post–World War II development of Japan to superpower status, linked through the Pacific basin to the Americas and to Western Europe, has accelerated the trend, making this region domestically a great urban corridor and internationally Japan's window to the world.

The Plains Between

In Japan, then, the seacoast is nearby, and throughout almost all the land mountains are visible. The compact character of the habitable remainder is possibly the explanation for the Japanese love of landscapes and the tendency to reproduce them on a small scale, for example, in tiny trees (*bonsai*) and in miniature gardens.

It follows that level land has always been at a premium: traditionally, as a base for rice culture; currently, as a base for industrial and postindustrial cities. *Only about one-quarter of the total area of Japan has land with slopes less than fifteen degrees;* only 24 percent of Honshū, the most populated island, is so constructed. Lowlands make up only about one-eighth of the total area, and a large proportion of these are eroded deposits from the highlands. Thus, Japan's lowlands, too, are mere adjuncts to the mountains.

There are only a few relatively large plains, and these, of course, loom large in Japan's history. They include the Kantō, which hosts the modern Tokyo metropolitan area; the Nobi, which is occupied by Nagoya and its industrial environs; the Tsukushi, which holds the manufacturing cities of northern Kyūshū; and the Ishikari and the Tokachi, which contain Sapporo and the developing regions of Hokkaidō. None of these, it should be noted, is anywhere near the size of the immense North China Plain.

As a result of the topography, Japan's rivers tend to be short and, in rainy season, fast flowing. There are only two rivers over 200 miles in length: the Ishikari in Hokkaidō and the

Shinano in central Honshū. Fourteen rivers are between 100 and 200 miles in length; eight, less than 100 miles long. None of the rivers plays a role in Japanese life equivalent to that of the Yangtse in China, the Mississippi in the United States, or the Amazon in South America.

Japanese tend to think of their country as being quite small. Japan is about 10 percent smaller than the U.S. state of California, with which it is most often compared. The country is larger in area, however, than any of the European nations except Sweden, France, and Spain. In latitudinal spread it is quite elongated, stretching (in the American imagination) from Hokkaidō (between Montreal and Boston) in the north through northern Honshū (Philadelphia), Tokyo (North Carolina), Ōsaka (South Carolina), and southern Kyūshū (the Florida panhandle), to Okinawa (Gulf of Mexico) in the south. A south to north journey between Fukuoka and Sapporo takes more than twenty hours by rail, even with the advantage of the speedy sector on bullet trains of the New Tōkaidō Line (six hours from Fukuoka to Tokyo). By jet aircraft, if schedules were so fitted, it would still take three hours to fly from Kyūshū to Hokkaidō. In longitudinal width Japan is narrow, but cross-Honshū travel is hindered by the fact that lateral rail connections are widely spaced. Central Honshū terrain is rugged, and rail traffic across it is slow because most of the connections are single-track lines. (In October 1978, the government approved plans for completion of five new superexpress rail lines over the next decade, which will increase both vertical and lateral connections.)

Distances and space are relative, of course, to the state of the art in transportation technology. Sometimes (as will be seen in an examination of human settlement below), social change and government decree set the boundaries of districts. Nonetheless, the Japanese have tended to think of certain regions in rather traditional fashion. Viewed geographically and in terms of early history, such regions still make sense in light of the placement of mountain barriers, stretches of seacoast, and narrow valleys. They include

Northeast Japan: *Hokkaidō* ("northern sea road")
Tōhoku ("northeast")

Central Japan: *Kantō* ("east of the pass")
Tōkai ("east, or Pacific, coast")
Hokuriku ("north, or Japan Sea, shore")
Tōsan ("eastern highlands")

Southwest Japan: *Kinki* ("near boundaries," or old home provinces; also *Kansai*, "west of the pass")
Chūgoku ("middle realm")
Sanin ("shady, or north, side of mountains")
Sanyō ("sunny, or south, side of mountains")
Shikoku ("four provinces" [island name])
Kyūshū ("nine provinces" [island name])

CLIMATE

The mountains, the seas, and the relative location of the plains between them do, of course, work their effects on Japan's climate. And naturally, the latitudinal range is influential. Thus, Hokkaidō's climate is boreal, Tokyo's is temperate, and Okinawa's is subtropical. The major sources of the country's weather cycles, however, are really external. In the broader sense, they are continental and maritime in origin. There are three major air masses to which, over the years, Japanese have become acclimated.

The first is the Siberian polar continental high, or northwest monsoon, of winter. This air mass supplies initially cold and dry winds that are modified into warmer, moist, and unstable currents, particularly over the Japan Sea coast. The result is exactly like that found in the snow shadow east of the Great Lakes of North America. In fact, there is probably more snow cover on the northwest Japan Sea coastal region than is found in any equally populous area of the world. The environment's "atmosphere" has been captured by Nobel Prize winner Kawabata Yasunari in his novel *Yukiguni* (Snow country).[2]

For the rest of Japan, during winter the northwest monsoon provides dry weather and bright sunshine during the day and snapping cold, owing to radiation, at night. Even high areas in

Snow Country: Prefectures on Japan Sea, famous for winter snows.

Kyūshū may see some snow, but it melts promptly. Some yearly averages include 3 days of snow for Ōsaka; 8 days, Tokyo; 42 days, Sendai; 82 days, Niigata; and 132 days (December through early April) for Sapporo on Hokkaidō. The heaviest fall of all occurs around Takata, directly north of Tokyo on the Japan Sea coast, with as much as 26.5 inches (70 cm.) on a single day.

The second major air mass that profoundly affects Japan is the Ogasawara tropical oceanic low, or southeast monsoon, of summer. This generates southeasterlies and pours heat and humidity over Tokyo Bay and into Tokyo, just as the summer circulation around Bermuda pumps humid heat over Chesapeake Bay and into Washington, D.C. There is considerably less difference in climate between the two sides of Honshū in summer than in winter. Summers on the Japan Sea coasts can be quite warm but are less humid than those on the Pacific side.

The third major system is the Okhotsk polar oceanic high, which in the June-July period flows down from the north and confronts the Ogasawara system coming up from the south. The result is that for about thirty days (in most areas except for Hokkaidō) there is a front of stagnation, with soft winds and high humidity, gloomy skies, and rainy weather. Dense clouds filter the sunshine, and Japanese refer to this period as "the season of mold." Ample precipitation, called "plum rains" (*baiu*), comes precisely in the warm growing season and makes possible the traditional, intensive garden or hothouse agriculture.

Similar monsoonal shifts in the August-October period result in the other familiar natural disaster (besides earthquakes)—the typhoons (*taifū*, literally, "great winds"). These sweep up through "typhoon alley," Okinawa. If the Japanese are lucky, these storms only brush the southern and eastern Pacific coast; but on occasion they are accompanied by torrential rains and slam into the heavily populated regions of Kyūshū and Honshū.[3]

Since the changes in weather have been fairly regular, they have been translated by Japanese into traditional life cycles, planting and harvesting seasons, and religious rituals. These in turn mark subtle subdivisions of seasons. The old lunar calendar, which was used until 1872, recognized twenty-four subseasons in a year, including "beginning of spring," "appearance of worms," "opening of summer," "little heat," "great heat," "beginning of autumn," "cold dew," "opening of winter," "little cold," and "great cold."

Just as the mountain spine on Honshū divides Japan, so latitude provides a useful dividing line of the country. Above about 37° north latitude (and at higher elevations even in central Japan), winters are too cold and long for double cropping. Below this latitude there are usually two crops: irrigated rice in summer and a dry crop in winter. The growing season ranges from less than 150 days in Hokkaidō to as much as 300 days in the warmest parts of the south. Climate has been linked with the history of settlement: in the north, farms appeared later than in central and southern Japan. The north remains less densely populated, and farms there are much larger (10 to 12 acres in Hokkaidō) than those in the south since it takes more land to support one household.

Within moderate limits, Japan has a variety of climates; average temperature and humidity reflect latitude and the movement of air masses in fairly regular patterns (as shown in Table 1.1). Ordinary Japanese mark the change of seasons in a more mundane fashion: when to shed long (winter) underwear and put on short (summer) garments, and when to shift from drinking warm sake (winter) to drinking cold beer (summer). Another familiar sign (of spring) is the appearance of the beloved cherry blossoms. Any Japanese can tell you within a few days the traditional date when the blossoms appear for any region. In more scientific terms, the blooms—a symbol of Japan—appear when the average daytime temperature reaches 50° F. (10° C.). Thus, isochronal lines (as shown in Figure 1.2) reinforce tradition and clearly show the march of spring from southwest to northeast Kyūshū-Shikoku, end of March; central Honshū-Kantō, April 10; north-central Honshū, April 20; Tōhoku, April 30; and Hokkaidō, May 10.

A less aesthetic and more practical means by which Japanese mark the seasons is their use of either heating or cooling.

TABLE 1.1
Average Temperature (Celsius) and Precipitation (mm)

Place / Month	Sapporo	Tokyo	Kagoshima
January	-6°C 100mm	2°C 40mm	7°C 65mm
February	-5°C 70mm	3°C 70mm	8°C 110mm
March	-2°C 60mm	6°C 100mm	10°C 150mm
April	5°C 55mm	12°C 150mm	15°C 200mm
May	10°C 50mm	17°C 150mm	18°C 220mm
June	15°C 50mm	20°C 175mm	23°C 400mm
July	20°C 80mm	25°C 130mm	27°C 330mm
August	22°C 100mm	30°C 140mm	27°C 225mm
September	17°C 150mm	22°C 240mm	22°C 200mm
October	10°C 125mm	15°C 235mm	16°C 110mm
November	3°C 130mm	15°C 200mm	13°C 80mm
December	-3°C 110mm	10°C 80mm	8°C 80mm

Source: Ryuziro Isida, Geography of Japan (Tokyo: Kokusai Bunka Shinkokai, 1961), p. 28.

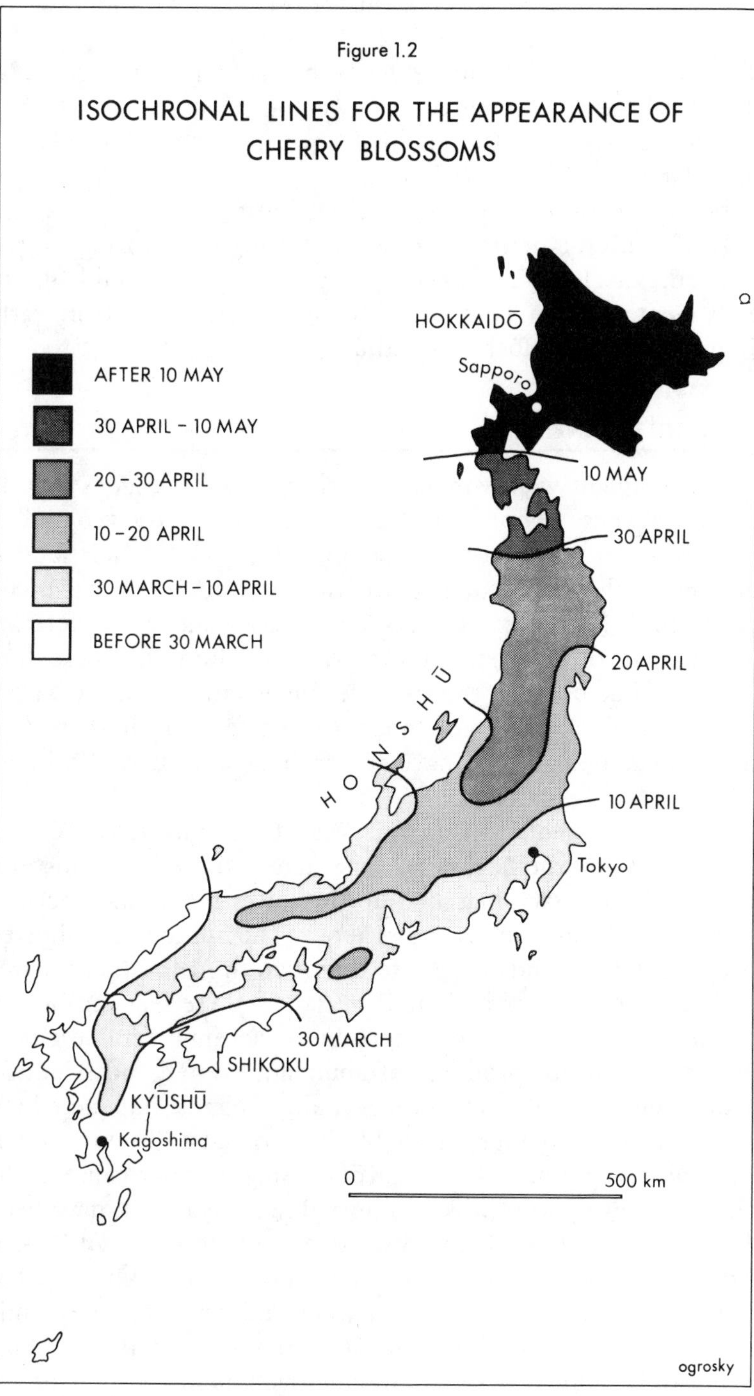
Figure 1.2
ISOCHRONAL LINES FOR THE APPEARANCE OF CHERRY BLOSSOMS
HOKKAIDŌ
Sapporo
AFTER 10 MAY
30 APRIL – 10 MAY
20 – 30 APRIL
10 – 20 APRIL
30 MARCH – 10 APRIL
BEFORE 30 MARCH
10 MAY
30 APRIL
20 APRIL
HONSHŪ
10 APRIL
Tokyo
30 MARCH
SHIKOKU
KYŪSHŪ
Kagoshima
0
500 km
ogrosky

The Japan Meteorological Agency has gathered statistics that indicate heating is required for dwellings from mid-October to the end of April in Hokkaidō; from the end of November to mid-March in Tokyo; and from mid-December to the end of February in southern Kyūshū. Air-conditioning is never needed in Hokkaidō. It is desirable for about twenty days during August in northeast Honshū; for about sixty-five days from mid-July to early September in Tokyo; and for seventy-five days from early July to mid-September in Kyūshū.

THE JAPANESE

One might well wonder why there should be a description of the Japanese people in a chapter devoted to basic geography. Yet the relationship of the people of Japan to their land is unique. Both are so intertwined that it is doubtful that a cultural group anywhere else has had such an impact on defining its own part of the earth. Moreover, although the Japanese, too, like to think back to their simple, rustic, and natural environment, scarcely a portion of Japan has not been subtly shaped by the human beings who have for so long inhabited the island nation.

Irrigated paddy fields for wet rice culture have been in existence since the Japanese came across the edge of history. Terraced plots have marched up the lower mountain slopes to catch water from the reservoirs above. The hillsides have hosted rice, vegetables, and tea. More than two-thirds of Japan's area is covered by forests and, at first glance, these seem to be primeval. In fact, the woods have been cut innumerable times. Present stands are products of abundant rainfall and scientific management by man. On level ground, of course, Japanese have used and misused every available inch of land. They have cut into the mountains in back of Kōbe, using the fill to extend the plain. Bodies of water, like Kojima Bay in Okayama, have been diked to make more land. Much of the western side of Tokyo Bay, from Tokyo through Kawasaki down to Yokohama, has been reclaimed from the sea. The Organization for Economic Cooperation and Development (OECD) has reported that Japan is the only country with comprehensive zoning nationwide. In

1968, the entire country was divided into three land use zones: agricultural, urban, and other. In Japan, people have long been part of the landscape.

People of the Plains

Although Japan's total population is dwarfed by that of China, India, the Soviet Union, or the United States, again the Japanese are not really a small group. In June 1979 a summit meeting of leaders of seven industrialized countries met for the first time in Tokyo. Of the nations represented, Japan was twice the size of each of the European partners in population (West Germany, France, Great Britain, and Italy), almost five times the size of Canada, and about one-half the size of the United States.

From the end of the sixteenth century up to the 1860s, the population remained fairly stable. Until modern times the total never exceeded 30 million; the standard Asian pattern of high birth but also high death rates set limits to growth. Even so, in the 1700s Japan's population (25 million) exceeded that of France, which had the largest population in Europe.

Beginning in 1868 with the modernization that marked the Meiji period, although the birthrate remained high, the death rate began to decline dramatically. By 1900 the total population had reached 44 million. Reliable census data compiled every five years thereafter revealed an annual increase of anywhere from 4 to 8 percent in the years 1900–35 and an estimated total population of 69.3 million in 1935. As might be expected, the *rate* of increase showed a drastic decline in Japan's war years (1935–40, 3.87 percent; 1940–45, 0.30 percent). Then the next five years brought the celebrated "baby boom" (1945–50, 15.32 percent), which resulted in a total population of 83.2 million by 1950. Thereafter, strong social measures (including legalized abortion) and a taste of affluence have slowed the growth rate to about 1 percent annually. Even such a low rate, however, has still produced a net yearly increase of more than 1 million because of the large total population base (estimated at 115 million on October 1, 1978). Experts have predicted that Japan will reach equilibrium in the year 2005 at about 129 million.

Indeed, it is now quite clear that the interesting population issues in Japan lie not in questions of quantity—sheer numbers—but of quality, the age structure, distribution of the total, and employment of the labor force. A good deal more attention will be devoted to these problems in Chapters 6 and 7. It will suffice here to cite a few illustrations.

For example, although the *rate* of increase in Japan's total population has declined steadily, on occasion certain sectors have increased dramatically. Thus, in the spring of 1978 an unprecedented total of more than 2 million first-grade pupils flooded the elementary schools. These were, of course, the children of the baby boom generation of thirty years before. In somewhat similar fashion, because of the very high health standards in Japan and concomitant longevity, the population has shown signs of aging rapidly. The "graying" of Japan had already resulted, in the late 1970s, in 8.6 percent of the total population being sixty-five years of age or older. Estimates have projected the percentage at 18 percent of the total in the year 2020, far surpassing the proportion reached in other advanced industrial nations. Finally, there has been, of course, a sharp shift in distribution of the population across the landscape of Japan, from rural areas (and primary pursuits in agriculture, forestry, and fishing) to metropolitan regions (secondary and tertiary pursuits in industry and services). This move has constituted one of the great migrations of modern times.

In this last sense, too, Japan is not among the small but among the large countries. Gross figures for population density tend to be misleading. The overall average is 710 people per square mile, less than that of the Netherlands, three times that of West Germany, and almost five times that of Great Britain. The only comparable figures are those for unusual neighbors of Japan, which are in fact city-states—Hong Kong and Singapore.

The Settlements

Geographers tend to use the term "settlements," but often find themselves puzzling (particularly since 1960) over how to explain the differences among governmental units, traditional and modern metropolitan regions, and actual (settled) areas in Japan. Let us sort these distinctions out in very general terms.

First, there are 47 major administrative divisions of the total area of Japan: 42 rural prefectures (*-ken*), including Okinawa; 2 urban prefectures (*-fu*), Ōsaka and Kyōto; the metropolitan-capital prefecture (*-to*), Tokyo; and 1 district (*-dō*), Hokkaidō. Thus one speaks of rural Shimane-*ken*; of the traditional capital, Kyōto-*fu*; of the modern capital, Tōkyō-*to*; and of the island-district, Hokkaidō. As of October 1960, the entire area of all of these major divisions was subdivided into 3,511 administrative units. These included 1,031 villages (*-mura*), 1,924 towns (*-machi*), and 556 cities (*-shi*).

It is perhaps easier to return to the concept of settlements. This is because the legal units, cities, towns, villages—even metropolitan Tokyo—have embraced, since 1953, farmlands, forests, mountainous areas, and even (in the case of Tōkyō-*to*) remote islets. In that year such areas were incorporated in an amalgamation of administrative units. Similarly, on the other extreme, within villages (*-mura*) there are still smaller, extralegal settlements called hamlets (*buraku*). These are basic collections of 10 to 100 farm households—functionally agrarian settlements built around the planting and harvesting of rice, the rice cooperative, and irrigation projects.

Although they encompass agricultural lands, the small towns are not completely artificial units in that their core populations (10,000 to 20,000) do constitute marketplaces for surrounding rural areas. The cities, with their core populations (20,000 to 50,000), also make up local centers for commerce, industry, and administration. Finally, even the largest legal units only roughly delineate the actual urban settlements. Modern demographers use another term, the "densely inhabited district" (DID), to arbitrarily demark areas containing 10,000 persons per square mile. Although in the 1970s such areas accounted for only 1.25 percent of Japan's total area, they housed more than 47 million persons, or almost half the total population of Japan.

This chapter will pay somewhat greater attention to the dwindling rural areas, closer to the original landscape, and somewhat less to the booming urban regions, imposed on the landscape by man. The latter will be discussed in greater detail in the chapters on modernization, the Japanese personality, the economy, and postindustrial society in Japan. To describe these two different kinds of human settlement, Fred Riggs has coined two descriptive terms, agraria and industria, which go beyond the obvious—agricultural as compared with industrial pursuits—and highlight variable lifestyles.

Agraria. Despite the fact that by 1965 the population in what might be called agrarian households had fallen below the 30 million mark, the rural origins of most people remained significant in the Japanese mental set. And although the proportion of labor force applied to agricultural work has declined below 15 percent, Japanese have persisted in emphasizing the rustic and traditional in their village background. The outlook is somewhat similar to that of Americans who persist in watching their late-night television dramas to harken back to a long-eliminated frontier.

To those who have never had to labor in the milieu—foreign tourists and city-bred Japanese—village Japan still holds great charm. Historians believe that rice culture, probably imported from South China, arrived at least as early as the second century A.D. The Japanese have been cultivating rice ever since.

Into the small dike-bordered paddy, as level as a pool table in order to distribute water evenly, rice has perennially been transplanted from carefully tended seedbeds near the farmhouse. This has traditionally been a labor-intensive project, small-scale horticultural agriculture. It was not efficient in terms of man-hour input, but in output per acre it has remained the most productive in the world. (Late in 1978, two months after Japan signed a treaty of peace and friendship with China, the former moved to repay an historic debt. Tokyo signed a further agreement in Beijing promising to send eight Japanese agricultural experts to North China to teach local farmers how to grow high-yield rice in cold climates.)

In modern times, production has been heightened by intensive application of fertilizer: at first, nightsoil from the urban areas, and later, chemicals. A steady decline in labor force was thus offset by an agricultural revolution, which also saw an invasion of the paddies by machines. In the 1950s in villages throughout Japan, Japanese began to use a one-cycle plow called the bean (*mame*) cultivator because of its size and shape.

Modern Mechanized Agriculture: The one-cycle bean (*mame*) cultivator.

Today, according to polls conducted by the Office of the Prime Minister, rice remains *the* staple food in Japanese diets: for 71 percent of the respondents at breakfast, for 77 percent at lunch, and for 96 percent at dinner. As a result, some 40 percent of Japan's total cultivated area is in rice; 99.5 percent of the rice fields is in wet paddies.

Noodles in a variety of styles have always been popular, and bread, in an increasingly mobile society, has grown in favor. The demand for wheat and barley has therefore increased, and more than four times the domestic wheat supply has to be imported.

Fruit as dessert appeals to Japanese and has become a premium cash crop, but costs have outpaced inflation of other food prices. Apples are grown in the north; pears, grapes, melons, and mandarin oranges in the south. Tea is grown mainly in Shizuoka, but many areas in the south and even in the mountains boast of local brands, which are prized as souvenirs by returning tourists.

Animal husbandry traditionally has not been a prominent

pursuit, except for cattle introduced into Hokkaidō in the nineteenth century and for the celebrated hand-tended Kōbe beef (with appropriately prohibitive prices). Chickens and pigs have constituted the main livestock supply. Goats have been practically household pets.

It is no surprise to learn that in recent times some members of rural households have left home entirely during slack seasons, seeking employment in seasonal deep-sea fishing, or, in light industry farther south. In such households the average total membership (5.1) simply cannot be supported by the average number engaged in agricultural work (1.8). Put another way, only about one in seven farmers cultivates plots of more than 3.5 acres (whereas 3.7 acres are required for a living). Finally, four-fifths of all Japanese farmers are engaged in supplemental occupations in nearby cities.

If the first historically visible settled Japanese were agriculturalists on the plains, the very first archaeologically identified Japanese were fishermen on the seas. With an unusual concurrence of warm and cool ocean currents just offshore, Japan has traditionally depended on products from the sea for a major portion of its protein. Rapid industrialization after the war, together with headlong neglect, has resulted in contamination of the Inland Sea. Its condition has become as bad as that of the eastern Great Lakes in the United States, and other nearby waters have also felt the effects of pollution. Despite the growing scarcity of nearby fish and the toll of inflation, the national taste for seafood continues unabated. Japanese commercial fishermen have therefore roamed the seas widely. Japanese have led the world in range of operations, variety of fish taken, and total catch (more than 10.5 million metric tons in 1976). At home, Japanese husband the seas as farmers husband the land, planting, for example, varieties of seaweed. In rivers and reservoirs throughout Japan freshwater fish are cultivated.

Industria. Although, as has been noted, many Japanese like to think of their culture as one directly descended from rural, agrarian antecedents, many of the so-called traditional Japanese values, it may be argued, emanated from towns. Most Japanese, it is true, are only one or two generations removed from the agrarian village; many Japanese, however, can trace ancestry over a number of generations who were resident in towns and even cities. These were what Gideon Sjoberg has called pre-industrial cities.

In the postwar era, the Japanese have established a number of brand new industrial centers. Most of Japan's cities, however, rest on foundations of traditional urban settlements. There are, for example, those that are descended from classic metropolitan capitals laid out according to Imperial plan (*jōbo*), Kyōto and Nara; from temple towns (*monzen machi*) like Nagano; from stage towns (*shukuba machi*) like Hamamatsu; and, of course, from the celebrated castle towns (*jōka machi*) like Sendai, Kanazawa, Edo, Nagoya, Ōsaka, Himeji, Okayama, Hiroshima, and Kagoshima. Edo (modern Tokyo) was the largest city in the world around 1700. Granted, most of the castles (except for the magnificent "White Heron" of Himeji) were crystal-clear zero aiming points for bombardment during the war and

Shinjuku Metropolitan Subcenter: Shinjuku Station (foreground) handles 1,350,000 passengers daily.

subsequently have had to be reconstructed in reinforced concrete made to look like wood.

Today, of course, the Japanese city is the true center of Japanese culture. The majority of Japanese, as we shall see, live in cities. The dwindling few who may be regarded as rural dwellers have one foot in the city. For everyone, city standards are relayed through ubiquitous mass communication (*masu komi*, as the Japanese call it). City-produced and city-distributed goods and services are now available throughout the country.

At the peak of secondary industrial development in the 1960s, Japan had already created an urban heartland, a narrow coastal band running 600 miles from northeast to southwest. This corridor contained all of Japan's cities with a population of 1 million or more. They included the capital, Tokyo (already with 10 percent of the total population of Japan), and neighboring Yokohama; Nagoya and the Osaka-Kyōto-Kōbe complex; somewhat smaller cities along the Inland Sea; and the industrial concentrations of northern Kyūshū.

The reasons for urban concentration at this manufacturing stage were quite clear: the area was responsible for over 75 percent of all industrial production; it was served by the major ports, an essential factor for the import of raw materials and for the export of finished goods; the corridor had the most efficiently developed transportation network; and its cities housed the skilled labor force. Later in the 1970s, especially after the passage of environmental laws, deconcentration of industry began to make more sense. By that time, however, Japanese cities had entered yet another stage, which seemed to justify even greater concentration. That phenomenon is more fully described in Chapter 7.

To return to the demographers' term, densely inhabited district, by 1960, 43.7 percent of the population lived in DIDs; in 1965, the total reached 48.1 percent; and in 1970, 53.5 percent of all Japanese were in DIDs. Tokyo, viewed in this light, was one vast DID, with a total population (1970) of 18,913,000 (within a 70-kilometer radius from the Tochō, the Tokyo Metropolitan Government headquarters; 18,201,000 within 50 kilometers). Japanese have come to know the area as Keihin, using the Chinese variant pronunciation of elements of the cities' names (Tokyo-Yokohama).

Next in size came Nagoya and its environs (known as the Chūkyō region). In 1970 the DID population of this metropolitan area was 3,569,000 (within a 50-kilometer radius of the city hall). Settlements fanned out from this core and embraced petrochemical production in Yokkaichi to the southwest; automobile plants in Kariya and Toyota to the southeast; ceramics in Seto, Kasugai, and Kajima to the northeast; and textile mills in Ichinomiya and Gifu to the northwest. The total population for the whole region was about 6 million.

Second only to the Tokyo metropolitan region was Ōsaka and its neighbors (known to Japanese as Hanshin [Ōsaka-Kōbe] or sometimes as Keihanshin [Kyōto-Ōsaka-Kōbe]). In 1970 the DID population of the area was 11,468,000 within a 50-kilometer radius from city hall). The whole region facing Ōsaka Bay stretched as far south as Wakayama; west of Ōsaka it included the steel mills and distilling plants of Amagasaki and Nishinomiya; farther west it embraced Japan's largest port, Kōbe; and to the north within commuting range it included the splendid old museum capital and modern bedroom-community of Kyōto. The region had a population of about 12 million.

The metropolitan region farthest southwest, Northern Kyūshū (known to the Japanese as Kita Kyūshū), in 1963 was actually made up of an amalgamation of five smaller cities ranging in population from 100,000 to 300,000 (Yawata, Tobata, Wakamatsu, Kokura, and Moji). In 1970, Northern Kyūshū, center of steel production since the establishment of the government-initiated works at Yawata in 1900, had a population of just over 1 million.

Even this description of population concentration in DIDs may be misleading, for, by the late 1960s, urban settlements in the Pacific corridor reached toward each other in a discontinuous conurbation. By then all important points between Tokyo and Kyūshū had been linked by New Tōkaidō line (Shinkansen) bullet trains. A businessman could leave any point between Tokyo and Ōsaka in the morning, arrive at any other point between the great cities, and return the evening of the same day. Japan's urban phenomenon began to attract the attention of those who had coined the term *megalopolis*, and soon reference was being made to the Tōkaidō megalopolis or to Nihonopolis.[4]

Their Resources

It is a pity that Japan is so rugged and beautiful—at least in places not yet subject to environmental disruption—and is at the same time so poverty-stricken in raw materials needed for the industry built up in the megalopolitan areas. Of course, Japan is not totally without natural resources. In fact, the country enjoys two major blessings: scenery and water.

To some extent even Japan's famous scenery has been defiled. In climbing season, Mt. Fuji is littered with trash over ash. In other famous spots, garish restaurants, inns, and souvenir shops compete for space. Parking lots are jammed with sightseeing buses, engines idling and exuding fumes. There are hordes of dedicated tourists, including bands of schoolchildren in their uniforms. Even so, there are still remote, quiet retreats with great natural beauty. Hokkaidō remains largely unspoiled with sparkling lakes, volcanic cones, isolated beaches, and deep forests. Nara is still impressive, especially at dawn.

Water is Japan's only seemingly limitless natural resource. Abundant rainfall, together with careful management, maintains green forests over two-thirds of the country's area; as a consequence, Japan remains a leading wood-producing nation of the world. Even so, more than half of the voracious domestic demand must be met by imports.

The river bottoms supply limestone, clays, and sand; so production of cement (more than 73 million metric tons a year) is no problem.

Coal, once the rationale for locating cities in northern Kyūshū and southern Hokkaidō, has been reduced to that found in poor, thin veins. Recently, two-thirds of the demand has been supplied by imports. Railways have long since been converted to electric or diesel power. In Japan's industries and homes, coal has been displaced by petroleum and natural gas.

It has become a fact of life that more than 99 percent of the supply of petroleum products must be imported. This means that some 12 percent of Japan's total imports comes from the Middle East, particularly from Saudi Arabia (Japan ranks behind the United States at 18 percent). In recent years Japan, even more than the United States, has become supersensitive to "oil shocks," to the ebb and flow of petroleum to Japan, and to the need to supply technical assistance to the Middle East.

Japan lacks all vital minerals for industry, other than sulphur. Once an exporter of copper, the country must now import 83 percent to meet industrial needs.

In this way, too, the Japanese landscape has proved to be fragile. As industrial growth in the 1960s dominated all governmental policy, so, too, dependence on imports determined Japan's international politics and domestic plans. There were, in the words of the Club of Rome, "limits to growth," and the Japan of the 1970s approached those limits. That subtle shift in mood is dealt with in the following chapters.

NOTES

1. Komatsu Sakyō, *Nihon chimbotsu* [Japan sinks] (New York: Harper & Row, 1976).

2. Kawabata Yasunari, *Yukiguni* [Snow country] (New York: Knopf, 1957).

3. Using the entry "Disasters–Natural" in the *Britannica Book of the Year* as a sample for a five-year span, one can test the incidence of disastrous typhoons and deluges: 1973–none. 1974–April, Honshū: landslide, 17 killed; July, Honshū: typhoon, rains, 156 killed, $400 million damage. 1975–August, northern Honshū: typhoon Phyllis, 68 killed; August, Shikoku: typhoon Rita, 29 killed. 1976–September, southern Honshū: typhoon Fran, 161 killed, 325,000 homeless. 1977–June, Kyūshū: rains, landslides, 11 killed. *Encyclopedia Britannica, 1974-, 1975-, 1976-, 1977-, 1978-, Book of the Year* (Chicago: Encyclopedia Britannica).

4. For one of the first uses of the term, see Jean Gottman, *Megalopolis: The Urbanized Northeastern Seaboard of the United States* (New York: The Twentieth Century Fund, 1961). With a Greek root, the term received further currency through the systematic research at the Athens Center of Ekistics, under the world-renowned planner C. A. Doxiadis. See also C. Nagashima, "Megalopolis in Japan," *Ekistics* 24, no. 140 (July 1967), pp. 6–14.

2

The Japanese Tradition

In January 1979 in the eastern part of Nara, which had been the capital of Japan in the eighth century, a very important archaeological dig was begun. By chance a tomb mound had been found by a farmer, and specialists quickly identified the remains from an engraved tablet as those of Ōno Yasumaro, Japan's first historian. Ōno died in the seventh year of Yōrō by Japanese calculations, or in 723 A.D.

The find was significant from a number of viewpoints. First, the clearly identifiable remains converted into historic fact some of the earliest Japanese legends. It had generally been believed that Japan's earliest written histories, *Records of Ancient Matters* (*Kojiki*, 712) and *Chronicle of Japan* (*Nihonshoki*, 720), were compilations of an oral tradition. Now it was apparent that Ōno Yasumaro had prepared the histories for an early emperor. Second, the archaeological find served to remind Japanese that their documented history began at a rather late date, compared with that of China. Third, a copper plate marking the grave consisted of forty-one *Chinese* ideographs, indicating that in the very beginning of Japan's historiography Japanese were using a borrowed language at least for writing. Indeed, one Japanese professor speculated that Ōno may have been an immigrant Chinese, a theory suggested by his unusual name. Finally, the Nara tomb clearly symbolizes the oldest and most persistent problem in presenting the history of Japan. Shall we emphasize the influence of the long, slow process of domestic culture change on Japanese tradition? Or shall we concentrate on the short, rapid influence of culture contact—the regular and seemingly overwhelming influences from abroad?

ORIGINS

For many years it was assumed that the origin of human habitation in Japan substantially postdated the appearance of the island chain, that is, Japan's physical separation from the continent. The earliest accepted dates were about 4000–3000 B.C., and the first human beings were believed to have come from the continent, perhaps by way of the Korean peninsula, but definitely across water. The culture of these people was already "advanced," since they produced polished stone tools and an artistic clay pottery. It was, in other words, "external."

Archaeological Evidence

In 1949 startling discoveries were made at Iwajuku, just north of Tokyo, in a site that was subjected to scientific dating techniques. The results set back the edge of history of human life on the islands. The finds included rough stone-chipped tools of a certainly mesolithic, possibly paleolithic, era before 8000 B.C. Archaeologists believed they had uncovered evidence of ancient, organic evolution of culture on the islands, in sharp contrast with the assumption that frequent ethnic migrations from the continent produced the ancestors of the Japanese.

Another find, first opened up in 1962 at Lake Nojiri in the mountains of Nagano Prefecture, was even more dramatic. Stone implements of the Pleistocene age (anywhere from 50,000 to 1 million years ago) were found alongside interesting animal remains. The tusk of a Naumann elephant had obviously been carved by humans. And the presence of so large an animal suggested the possibility that a land bridge had provided a crossing from the continent. If this were the case, then the labels "external" and "internal" were meaningless.

To return from prehistoric mists, evidence of a neolithic culture in Japan has been clearly documented in archaeology. More than one hundred skeletons, animal bones, pottery, and shell mounds have revealed a people engaged in making household utensils, dependent on the sea around Japan, and not yet involved in agriculture. This first identifiable Japanese way of life has been called "rope mark" (Jōmon) culture, the name derived from the most remarkable Stone Age pottery in the world, a kind not turned on a wheel but impressed by a rope. Jōmon apparently lasted from about 8000 B.C. to about 300 B.C., when it was displaced by a superior culture.

So sharp was the break between prehistoric (Jōmon) and protohistoric (Yayoi, named after a discovery site in the Kantō Plain) that it has been generally assumed that this transition included massive influence from the continent. At this historical layer, polished stone tools, woven cloth, and pottery turned on a wheel were uncovered, as well as evidence that many Japanese had turned from the sea to the land—from being fishermen to being agriculturalists. Iron implements were found alongside bronze, indicating a rapidly changing technological base. The outstanding contribution of the period, which lasted from about 300 B.C. to 300 A.D., was the growth of wet-rice culture. From that point on, evidence of a Japanese lifestyle can be derived from other sources as well as archaeology.

One does not have to dig beneath the surface to find the remains of the next (semihistoric) stage in Japan's development. Scattered throughout western Japan are tumuli, hill-tombs doubtless used as mausolea, sometimes called dolmen. Some, like one in the Kibi area of Okayama in the Inland Sea region, are small; but one is half again as long as the biggest Egyptian pyramid, 360 yards long, 30 yards high, and built in an unusual keyhole shape. Alongside are found interesting clay figures (*haniwa*) of men, animals, and horses, and also the long sword, the Chinese Han-style mirror, and the curved stone called *magatama*. These last three were to become the Imperial treasures, regalia of an emerging court.

These important finds indicate clearly that by semihistoric times (tomb culture lasted from about 300 to 750 A.D.) Japan was inhabited by a culturally homogeneous folk. Despite their mixed ethnic origins, the residents were unified in culture and in language. It is also apparent that the cultural center of gravity had slowly shifted from extreme western (Kyūshū) to central Japan (the Yamato basin near present-day Nara). One theory has it that sometime between 200 and 500 A.D. Japan was permeated by Korean influence. The huge mounds indicate an organized labor force, with wealth and power concentrated in the hands of a mounted military aristocracy. The first written account, which described these people at a slightly earlier stage, is to be found in Chinese dynastic histories dating from about the third century A.D.

Chinese Accounts, Japanese Legends, and History

Although Chinese accounts prepared at the time of the Wei dynasty (297 A.D.) gave explicit directions on how to get from China through Korea to "Yamatai," they were somehow garbled, so that the destination could have been either in Kyūshū or in the Kansai region (east of present-day Ōsaka). The Chinese wrote that the islands were made up of the land of Wa (the ideograph for dwarf), which was populated by a "hundred" (perhaps meaning many) clans and that these were ruled by an empress. The Chinese account of a matriarchy must not have been far off the mark, in light of the emergence of the cult of the Sun Goddess in Japan.

Meanwhile, within Japan an oral tradition was evolving, ideas to be denounced as "mere legends," but which, just before World War II, were revived to play a key role in extreme nationalism and a disastrous militarism. They have, however, always been recognized as important because of the light they shed on early customs, habits, styles, and attitudes. Although first written down in Chinese (in the *Kojiki* and *Nihonshoki*), they illuminated an indigenous Japanese tradition, which was then embellished with Chinese ideographs and concepts. Obviously, they also represented an important transition from primitive, oral myths about origins to sophisticated, written techniques of governmental control. Few Japanese today have read the manuscripts containing these legends in their original language. Just before the war, Japanese schoolchildren learned the stories from "civics" textbooks, which were required reading.

After an account of the myriad (six generations) of deities, including Izanagi and Izanami, the story concentrated on their child, the Sun Goddess (Amaterasu Ōmikami). She in turn ordered her grandson, Ninigi, to descend from "the plain of high heaven" to "the land of luxuriant rice fields," bestowing on him the Imperial regalia. According to the legend, it was his great-grandson, Emperor Jimmu, who traveled east through the

Inland Sea, conquered aboriginal tribes, and settled in the province of Yamato. In the seventh century A.D. historians calculated his enthronement to be the equivalent of February 11, 660 B.C., which became the date for Foundation Day. In these legends, too, the chief figures of an indigenous cult appeared, later to be given the Chinese ideographs for Shintō.

In the indigenous cult, anything or anyone regarded as "superior" (*kami*) was worshipped. Far more important than ancestral—even abstractly political—deities were the mundane but superior forces faced by men in a simple, agrarian society: the mountains and the streams, the fields and the forests, the big wind and the torrential rain, earthquakes and fire. In this sense, Shintō was, as Sir George Sansom put it, not a system of thought or even a religion but "an expression of national temperament." Langdon Warner called the cult the "nurse of the arts."[1]

Eventually, in the seventh century A.D., more sophisticated ideas swept in from China and helped to formalize Shintō. Later it became a state creed. Even in prewar Japan, however, one could distinguish between an original shrine cult and the evolved state Shintō. Today Shintō still plays a ceremonial role—in festivals that are expressive of village solidarity, in rituals surrounding weddings, and in dedication services used, for example, to launch a supertanker.

Beyond ritual, the original legends now occupy a position similar to that of the Arthurian cycle in British lore. There is one difference: the Japanese legends draw on different and overlapping cycles of stories. One at the core was a series of tales told by tribes in the Yamato district. Another, a more primitive set, was passed along by seafaring peoples of northern Kyūshū. Yet another was a cycle revolving around ancient Izumo (modern Shimane Prefecture), obviously a center of power competitive with Yamato. One set involved Emperor Jimmu and his expedition. Finally, most mysterious of all was a cycle of tales told by folk from the southern seas around Indonesia.

When we combine the evidence of archaeology, hints from the legends, and descriptions from written accounts, we can then begin to divide Japanese history into periods (as in Table 2.1).

TABLE 2.1
Periods of Japanese History

Dates	Period	Event	Characteristics
---PREHISTORY---			
BC?-8000BC	Early prehistoric	paleolithic mesolithic	No skeletons;chipped stone tools; shellfish mounds; no agriculture
BC8000-300BC	Middle prehistoric (Jōmon)	neolithic	Human skeletons; "rope mark" pottery; no agriculture
BC300-300AD	Protohistoric (Yayoi)	continental influence	Polished stone tools,woven cloth, wheel-cast pottery, bronze, iron; wet-rice cultivation
---SEMIHISTORY---			
AD300-750	Semihistoric (Yamato) (Tomb)	Establishment of the Yamato state	Earth-mound dolmen; sword, mirror, magatama; clay haniwa;
(645)	(Hakuhō)	Taika reform	Chinese influence (incl.Buddhism)
---HISTORY---			
AD710-793	(Nara)	Completion of Nara	Chinese influence (incl.Buddhism)
794-1159	(Heian)	Completion of Kyōto	Fujiwara family dominance; dualism (civilian)
1160-1184	(Rokuhara)	Victory of the Taira	Taira clan dominance; dualism (civilian-military)
1185-1333	(Kamakura)	Victory of Minamoto	Minamoto clan (Hōjō family) dominance; dualism (military)

TABLE 2.1 (cont.)
Periods of Japanese History

Dates	Period	Event	Characteristics
1334-1391	(Yoshino)	Kemmu Restoration	Brief restoration of Court dominance
1392-1567	(Muromachi)	Unification, North & South Courts;	Ashikaga clan dominance; dualism (military); feudalism
(1467)	(Sengoku)	beginning of Ōnin War	Civil war; the "upstart lords"
1568-1599	(Azuchi-Momoyama)	Oda Nobunaga enters Kyōto	Unification of Japan begins
(1549-1638)	("Christian Century")	Jesuits and Franciscans in Japan	Christian conversions
(1582)		Toyotomi Hideyoshi succeeds Oda	Unification continues
(1600)		Battle of Sekigahara	Unification completed
1603-1867	(Edo)	Tokugawa Ieyasu becomes shōgun	Tokugawa clan dominance; dualism (military);
(1854)		Arrival of Perry	Impact of the West
1868-1911	(Meiji)	Meiji Restoration	Modernization
1912-1925	(Taishō)	Accession of Yoshihito	Taishō democracy
1926- --	(Shōwa)	Accession of Hirohito	Dualism (military); war and defeat;
(1945-1952)		Occupation of Japan	Dualism (civilian-military) directed change

First is a very broad division into deduced prehistory, derived semihistory, and documented history. Under the last are subdivisions set off to reflect the style and location of political power. Selection of such a scheme of periodicity has two advantages. First, it applies terminology used by the Japanese themselves. Second, it uses specific dates. The chief disadvantage is that such sharp divisions reflect only political history, whereas social and economic changes must have moved at a more glacial pace.

The chart also illustrates our dilemma in choosing between slowly evolving *internal* development and the quickly felt *external* influence. From one point of view, usually that of outsiders, there are certain crucial dates: *645 A.D.*, time of the so-called Great Reform (Taika) and the beginning of overwhelming Chinese influence; *1549–1638*, the "Christian century"; *1853*, the "opening of Japan"; *1868*, the Meiji Restoration and with it the assertion of Western influence; and *1945–52*, the Occupation—again a time of overwhelming American influence. Selection of such dates, however, demonstrates various ethnocentric approaches and reflects an external view of Japanese history.

From another point of view, usually that of the Japanese, the country went through a vital foundation period *before* the advent of Chinese influence in the seventh century. Christian influence practically disappeared *after* the sixteenth century, giving way to the flowering of indigenous Japanese culture during the Edo era. Even under Tokugawa hegemony, slow but significant changes occurred in feudal Japan *before* the arrival of Perry and the Westerners. Alternating currents of peaceful development and wartime energy profoundly affected modern Japan *before* the experiment in directed change under General Douglas MacArthur. And finally, Japan plunged into a stage of high mass consumption and growth *after* the American occupationnaires had gone home.

Once again, these developments illustrate the basic problem of discerning the admixture of a strong indigenous nonabsorbent core of Japanese culture, which is like igneous rock, and the strong external layers of alien culture, which are like sedimentary deposits. Even today, outside observers state that Japan demonstrates the universal principle of "convergence," flowing steadily toward the model of the technologically advanced society. Japanese meanwhile continue to stress the *Yamato damashii*, the original Japanese spirit, the traditional, and the unique.

ANCIENT JAPAN

What the archaeological finds, the Chinese descriptions, and the Japanese legends indicate is that Japan early had a hierarchical society, that is, one arranged according to rank; leaders exercised strict discipline and levied severe punishments, especially for crimes against the group; there were taboos, primitive rituals of a protoreligious character, and a solar cult, which probably predated worship of the Sun Goddess. The society was still relatively primitive, consisting of semiautonomous tribal clans (*uji*) and functional guilds (*be*). There now seems little doubt that Jimmu was an early culture hero, a historic figure who was a contemporary of Julius Caesar. By about the sixth century A.D., a group centered in the Yamato district had established hegemony over much of southern and western Japan.

Culture Contact

Meanwhile, Japan was feeling the effects of contact with the continent by way of Korea. Since about 370 A.D., Japanese had been traveling to a beachhead at the tip of Korea called Mimana. Techniques of metal work, weaving, and tanning were brought into Japan from Korea. Sometime later Chinese ideographs were imported. These complicated little vehicles carried ideas about medicine, astronomy, and the calendar as well as new concepts embodied in Confucianism and Buddhism.

Discovery of an advanced, sophisticated culture in China had an immediate effect on Japan. What followed, according to Edwin Reischauer, was the world's first program of study abroad as Japanese youth went off to the Chinese capital at Ch'ang-an (modern Sian) to study art, science, philosophy, architecture, law, and administration. The Japanese soon revealed a passion for learning, adopting, and adapting foreign ideas to their own use. It was a matter of conscious, organized study and catching up, a path that was to be followed to some extent in the sixteenth and to a larger extent in the nineteenth and twentieth centuries.

Most significant among the imports from China were two quite different systems of thought. They were imported in somewhat the reverse order than they had developed on the continent. One, Buddhism, was a religion that was profoundly to affect Japanese national character. The other, Confucianism, was an ethic that was to provide a pattern on which Japan modeled its society.

In March 1959 Japan issued a deep red 10-yen postage stamp showing a map of Asia with stripes of light radiating from the lower left corner from India across Southeast Asia, China, Korea, and Japan. The commemorative stamp celebrated the Asian Cultural Congress held in Tokyo to mark the twenty-five-hundredth anniversary of the death of Gautama Buddha. It also symbolized fourteen centuries of Buddhist influence in Japan, sometimes violent but more often compassionate and soothing.

In the mid-sixth century, struggles over the new religion involved not only vested interests in the form of sacerdotal privileges, but also the advantages and disadvantages of adopting Chinese ways. The Soga family, Japan's first modernizers, sponsored the alien ideas and techniques. More practically, by about 587 the Soga saw to it through intermarriage that their blood flowed in the veins of the most prominent—what was to become the Imperial—clan. Later, leadership was grasped by a shadowy figure, Prince Shōtoku, who probably served as a regent in the early seventh century. He organized missions to China, began to draft regulations, and launched Japan's first (Chinese-style) central government. His activities culminated in the reforms of the mid-seventh century. Prince Shōtoku built a chain of Buddhist temples linked to the great seminar at Hōryūji.

Even after the decline of the Soga, a generation of reformers continued the borrowing and the innovation with vigor. They successfully blended the indigenous cult, Buddhism, the Confucian ethic, and some Chinese Legalism.

In Japan, a community-centered lifestyle was closely connected with rice culture, in which the Japanese like the Chinese participated. Japanese were prepared for the Confucian emphasis on the group. In their approach to the Imperial family, they came to twist into a somewhat more literal meaning what the Chinese used as a figure of speech. The Japanese emperor's role was to be that of a symbol (whereas the Chinese emperor was an operating administrator). In Confucian doctrine as applied in both countries, administration could be moral or it could be immoral; it could never be amoral. In China, the Confucian classics and examinations based on them provided means for recruiting an elite; in Japan, hierarchy was rooted in pedigree. Thus, basic Confucian beliefs were restated and served to underline native Japanese practices. The Japanese came to believe that:

> the *community* was *more important* than the individual
> the *Emperor* was the font of *benevolent government*
> *ethics, religion,* and *politics* were *one*
> *all men* were created by nature *unequal*

In the year 645, about the time the Roman Empire was disintegrating into anarchy, the reformers began the restructuring of Japanese government along Chinese lines. The objectives, had they been fully reached, would have resulted in nationalization of all land; centralization of administration; registration of all subjects; and taxation by the central government. These plans were later called the Great Reform (Taika).

Although Japanese institutions were not completely remodeled along Chinese lines, the Taika and reforms that followed in the early eighth century did move Japan up one notch on the ladder of integration as a nation-family. Japan thus embarked on its first modernization project, one of several attempts to accommodate superior alien techniques to familiar indigenous conditions. The country was never to be quite the same as it was in ancient Yamato. It was transformed from a collection of primitive tribes into an adopted member of the great Confucian family of nations. The nation-family did not, however, turn its back on its roots. Japanese made a clear distinction between borrowed and native elements. They threw away nothing.

Previously, members of one clan in the Yamato basin had played various roles: those of culture hero, high priest, and middleman between the folk and the gods. Now this clan (it had no family name, for in legend it was *the* Imperial family), with its attendant court, was used to legitimize political power through legend and religious sanction. The Emperor became known as Son of Heaven (Tenshi), and more frequently, Sovereign by Heaven (Tennō); his slogan (which borrowed a Chinese slogan) was "Under Heaven—One Household."

In this earliest form of Japan's central administration (which has been called worship-government), the Emperor's role was symbolic. He was withdrawn, as much as was possible, from day-to-day administration and served to legitimize the political power exercised by other families behind the "screen." Unique to the Japanese pattern of administration was this Imperial institution, which already presented itself ornately wrapped in mystical robes and wearing a mask of legend, like the protagonist in a Nō drama.

Two Cities

The establishment of Nara as the metropolitan capital in 710 clearly symbolized the opening of a new era. Nara (then called Heijō) was a monument to the idea that a respectable nation should have a grand capital city. It witnessed a continuing flood of Chinese influence. Although the Imperial court was to remain there only eighty-four years, this was a formative period and the city lent its name to an era.

Whereas Ch'ang-an was almost completely destroyed, Nara has survived and stands as a tribute to China's great T'ang dynasty (618–907), the exemplar for all of East Asia. The Japanese capital was laid out in gridlike fashion, much like (but a little smaller than) Ch'ang-an, in an area 3 miles square. Nearby Hōryūji was erected (now the oldest wooden building in the world). On a larger scale, Tōdaiji in Nara proper was built to house a 53-foot-tall Buddha, still the largest bronze statue in the world. Also in the capital was built the Shōsōin, a simple but elegant log warehouse containing the collection of artistic, ceremonial, and personal belongings of the Emperor who built Tōdaiji in 752. One art historian has described this heritage as similar to what the West would enjoy if the treasures of Charlemagne had been preserved intact and carefully cataloged.

According to legend, surrounding spirits did not treat old Nara kindly. Concretely, the capital was threatened by increasingly powerful and independent Buddhist monasteries. As a result, a new city, the Capital of Peace and Tranquility (Heian-kyō) was built in 794. It, too, lent its name to an era, the Heian, which lasted for four centuries. Better known as Kyōto, it was the seat of the Imperial court for almost 1100 years. (Even today it remains the traditional capital, where a successor accedes to the throne.) By the year 1000 A.D., Kyōto boasted a population of a half million, exceeded in size possibly only by Muslim Cordoba and Byzantine Constantinople. Some conception of the grandeur of the old city can be obtained today from the handsome Imperial palace (reconstructed in 1854 after a fire). Japanese nationals often wait patiently for a year or more before receiving permission to enter the palace. Citizens of Kyōto, however, can visit the precincts once a year, when authentically dressed wax figures of Heian nobility are placed amidst the silently overpowering architecture.

The Heian era was marked by further Chinese influence, but the flood had been reduced to a trickle by about the ninth century. Meanwhile Heian court life was luxurious, elegant, fashionable, and detached from real life. Literature flourished, as we shall learn, but also indicated a steady decline in the power of the court. On the world scene, the refined culture of Kyōto was scarcely duplicated until the time of the Medici in Italy.

Culture Change

A traditional view of Heian Japan was given by Sir George Sansom:

> Indeed the history of the seventh, eighth, and ninth centuries in Japan might well be written as a description of the building up of institutions after the Chinese model and then their gradual decay as they were displaced or smothered by a luxuriant growth of indigenous devices.[2]

The metaphor almost suggests a Buddhist image, the growth of the lovely lily out of the slime of a pond. However, did Sansom want to emphasize the decay or the luxuriant growth? John Whitney Hall of Yale University has given us another version of this history: the era marked less an experiment doomed to failure, in imitation of T'ang China, than a quiet social revolution that produced new forms of military-aristocratic administration.[3]

For 200 years, between the seventh and ninth centuries, Japan progressed. The capital, a large and impressive metropolis by any measure, thrived. The area under cultivation expanded to the limits of Kyūshū in the south and beyond the Kantō Plain to Sendai in the north. From the mid-ninth century until the middle of the twelfth century there were only minor civil disturbances.

Nonetheless, several developments took the Japanese in a direction quite different from the Chinese. First, the Japanese lacked the imperial, administrative experience developed over several centuries by Chinese even before the T'ang dynasty. Second, a strong sense of heredity, applied at the local Japanese level, persisted and barred adoption of something like China's meritocracy. Third, the Japanese lacked the spirit and the dynamic of an occasional rebellion, which regularly brought new blood into China's elite.

One of the most significant adjustments of the Chinese model was a further fissioning of the Japanese polity, setting to one side the immaculate reigning symbol (the Emperor and the court) and to another the ruling instruments (of practical administration). The process was well illustrated by the predominance of the Fujiwara family from 857 to 1160. This clan married off eligible daughters to the Imperial family. Clan members manipulated affairs from a position they perennially held, the post of regent. Thus appeared the peculiar Japanese brand of dualism, in this instance, civilian in character.

In fact, the Fujiwara simply institutionalized the tradition begun by the Soga and the Taika reformers. The Fujiwara in turn set a precedent followed by the Taira family and, later, by the Minamoto clan in Kamakura. The Ashikaga family was to carry on the tradition in the Muromachi district of Kyōto. And finally, the Tokugawa family raised the tradition to its highest peak, in the form of military dualism.

One of the clearest illustrations of Japanese capacity to

absorb imports and adapt them was the further development of Buddhism in the countryside. This religion had all but disappeared in the country of its birth, India; in China the revival of native ideas had relegated Buddhism to secondary status. All the more amazing, then, that during the Nara and Heian eras it emerged as a strong, thoroughly naturalized unique body of religious thought in Japan.

At first, the intelligent but illiterate Japanese doubtless found it hard to grasp the abstruse doctrines of Buddhism: the dialectics of negation, enlightenment through the mind, the metaphysics of the whole, and law. But the central idea that the world revolves in a cycle of birth, death, and rebirth was not so difficult to understand. Inevitably man faces suffering. He can escape by searching for nirvana, which is not nothingness, but rather the absence of desire and, thus, the absence of suffering. In the doctrine of karma one is conditioned by what has gone before and one conditions what comes after. Thus the present is both child of the past and parent of the future.

At first Buddhism was an esoteric religion of state. As such, however, its religious fervor was expressed in tangible form—the magnificent temples, monasteries, and sculpture—and by real people, scribes, artisans, carpenters, and decorators. The clergy taught Japanese to build local temples, highways, bridges, and irrigation works. Thus Buddhism added to both the intangible and the tangible wealth of Japan. The religion became less and less like the original doctrine, which had been imported as a political instrument, and more and more like a salve, healing life's wounds.

Distinctive Japanese sects of Buddhism began to appear: for example, the Tendai group, with an establishment on Mt. Hiei near Kyōto, and the Shingon sect on Mt. Kōya just south of Nara. Soon there were political disputes. From the ninth to the sixteenth centuries, Buddhist armies repeatedly descended on hapless Kyōto, overawing the court with moral suasion and military menace. The growth of manorial estates and the rise of a new military power to defend them were in large part a reaction to the establishment of temples, and the results proved fateful.

Another clear indication of the emergence of a distinctive

Japanese style lay in the appearance of new social and economic institutions. Out in the provinces, peasants began to drift to estates—really small manors (*shōen*) at this stage—offering their lands in return for protection. A typical manor was a tract of land, often newly brought under cultivation, under the patronage of an influential person or institution (for example, a courtier, a Shintō shrine, or a Buddhist temple); it had a claim to, or enjoyed, fiscal immunity. This complicated system gradually supplanted Chinese-style nationalization and paved the way to a loose form of feudalism.

The key figures in the system turned out to be neither the cultivators at the bottom nor the legal protectors in the court at the top, but local managers. They in turn came to depend increasingly on local bands of warriors, literally called "servants" or *samurai*, in a leader-retainer relationship. It took the ever-widening economic base of the estate to support this growing class of nonproducers. The warriors came to join wider alliances, which were opportunistically formed or dissolved. The elaborate Chinese-style bureaucratic positions and attendant ranks at the center remained, not as instruments of power, but as symbols of ritual and court prestige.

The Fujiwara family reached its peak of power in the late eleventh and early twelfth centuries, but by then it was pouring its considerable resources into the bottomless pit of capital politics. Meanwhile, two dominant provincial clans were laying down far firmer foundations at the local level. Eventually, the court found itself trapped as it was forced to ask first one, and then the other, clan into the capital to preserve order.

One of these clans was the Taira (also known by the Chinese pronunciation of the name, Heike), who built its power base around the Inland Sea and first entered Kyōto. The other was the Minamoto clan (also known as the Genji), who operated from the Kantō in the north and remained aloof after victory. Every Japanese schoolchild knows about the exploits of these military coalitions, if not through the histories,[4] then by way of modern novelized versions that rank as best-sellers, swordplay movies, and television dramas.

For a time, the cloistered Emperor and his Taira supporters emerged victorious and dealt harshly with the rival Minamoto.

The Taira ruled from a palace at Rokuhara in Kyōto (thence the name of an era, 1160–84). By the spring of 1185, the Minamoto had rebounded, gradually gained control of much of Japan, and wisely husbanded their strength around a new stronghold in Kamakura. It was a triumph of military government over civil bureaucracy, the cruder Kantō over cultured Kyōto style. A term that literally means "tent government" (*bakufu*) was applied to the Minamoto headquarters in 1190. In 1192, the leader of the clan, Minamoto Yoritomo, received the title of *shōgun* (originally, *seii taishōgun,* literally "barbarian-subduing generalissimo," who protected the frontiers for the Emperor). Meanwhile, Kyōto had become engulfed in fires, plagues, and famine.

Despite Kyōto's decline, even today something of the delicate, feminine Heian culture remains in the Japanese spirit. It competes with the vigorous, masculine samurai ethos inherited from Kamakura.

FEUDAL JAPAN

For seven centuries after the victory of Minamoto Yoritomo, Japan was to be administered under a military dualism. The Emperor at Kyōto continued to be the de jure sovereign, with all of the attendant court ranks and privileges. The de facto administration was located in a military headquarters, the *bakufu*; power remained in the hands of a military dictator, the shōgun. At the truly local level, certain social and economic arrangements paralleled those we commonly associate with Western feudalism. A discussion of the appropriateness of the term is best postponed until after a summary description of the Japanese variety.

Kamakura Feudalism

At Kamakura the Minamoto clan established a simple, direct warriors' administration. In their semipublic, semiprivate regime they maintained a characteristic lord-vassal relationship with their followers (and thus, some would argue, took the first step toward organized feudalism). Yoritomo did not bestow fiefs, however, and he did not replace the old civil administration.

Nor was the system centralized (as much as the later Tokugawa hegemony would). The Minamoto controlled only about one-third (twenty-two) of the total number (sixty-six) of provinces. Estates were redistributed so the Minamoto-appointed stewards were grouped under the watchful eyes of protectors. The headquarters began to apply simple, customary local law (in contrast with the complicated Chinese-style codes).

The Minamoto left the court and aristocracy in Kyōto intact, but the Imperial estates and nobles' holdings were carefully supervised by warriors loyal to Kamakura. Minamoto Yoritomo thus provided a bridge between two classes: the first, the hereditary aristocrats, remained haughty toward the untutored warriors out on the provincial boundaries of Japanese life; the other, a crude, unlettered band of samurai, was fiercely proud of its martial heritage and quite pragmatic in its approach to life. Increasingly, military prowess rather than birth and genealogy determined the status of these upstart lords. Nevertheless, it curiously remained a definite asset for the local figure to be able to point back to (even a fictional) high station. Moreover, the post of shōgun itself became hereditary. As Minoru Shinoda has pointed out, the Kamakura headquarters felt the need to balance traditional Imperial and feudal institutions. Above all, the crux of the feudal condition, the military tie strengthened by grant of land in fief, did not appear until later.[5]

Some amazing developments in the Kamakura era symbolized the Japanese penchant for diffusion and indirection in government. The Emperor continued to reign in Kyōto, but he had delegated courtly administration to a Fujiwara regent. The Fujiwara on occasion lost control of the court to descendants of a retired Emperor. Meanwhile, administrative power had in theory passed into the hands of the Minamoto shōgun at Kamakura. By 1213 the Minamoto clan had in practice delegated administrative power to the Hōjō family (related to Yoritomo's wife of Taira descent). The Hōjō adopted the formal title of regent to the shōgun.

Undoubtedly the greatest contribution made by the Hōjō regents was the codification of land law. Their legislation replaced the atrophied codes inherited from China and became the predecessor to later military house laws. A military class was thus setting standards for the entire society. Its outlook was of the greatest importance.

Whereas the Heian era was one subsequently identified with high culture, literature, and the arts, the Kamakura period was one in which the way of the warrior (*bushidō*) predominated. The code has generally been compared with chivalry in medieval Europe, but the thrust was really quite different. A slogan of the samurai was, "Death is lighter than a feather, but duty is weightier than a mountain." Rather than submit to shame—arising in most cases from failure in one's duty—the warrior was expected to commit suicide by *seppuku* (or in the more vulgar term, *hara-kiri*, literally "to slit the belly").

Otherwise the samurai found solace in a new, practically Japanese, form of Buddhism. Although Zen (in China called Ch'an) was originally (and has remained) meditative, it took on meaning beyond mere contemplation in military, feudal Japan. With its emphasis on self-reliance and self-discipline, Zen became an enormously popular cult among the warriors loyal to Kamakura. (Its contributions to the world of art will be examined in the next chapter.)

Internal changes contributed to the eventual fall of the Kamakura system. New local leaders, who had once held posts as stewards under the Minamoto-Hōjō hegemony, grew stronger and were the forerunners of territorial magnates later known as domain lords (*daimyō*). The final, fatal blows to the system, however, were delivered from outside Japan.

In 1274 ships built and operated by Koreans, under the command of the great Mongol leader, Kublai Khan, appeared off Kyūshū. The some 25,000 troops were unable to gain a foothold, however, as bad weather put the fleet to rout. Seven years later the Mongols reappeared with the greatest armada the world has seen (until the invasion force mustered by the Allies in World War II). Some 4,000 ships carried an army of 150,000 men to the Kyūshū beachhead. There they fought a desperate battle with samurai for fifty-three uninterrupted days. Then a sudden typhoon practically destroyed the invasion fleet and cut off the Mongol ground force. The Japanese referred to the storm as the divine wind (*kamikaze*, a term adopted again in the battles around Okinawa in 1945). The Kamakura system never recovered from the heroic defensive effort.

In the third decade of the fourteenth century, there was a revival of Imperial rule. The so-called Kemmu Restoration was only a brief interlude, though, and true restoration was postponed for another five centuries. In fact, for a time there were two emperors and two courts, one in the north at Kyōto and one in the south at Yoshino. Warfare continued until 1392, when a new but weak administration under the Ashikaga family was established. It was called the Muromachi shogunate, named after the section of northwest Kyōto where the shōgun then lived.

By the mid-fifteenth century civil war was again ravaging Japan. The violence began with the Ōnin War (1467) and lasted for almost a century. Using Chinese terminology, Japanese have called the last stages of decaying Ashikaga administration the Era of the Warring States (*Sengoku jidai*).

Despite the surface chaos, far-reaching changes were having a deep effect in Japanese society. These had to do with the power structure, methods of landholding, and increasing commercial activity. By the middle of the sixteenth century, the loose control exercised by the Ashikaga had been replaced by decentralized but locally extensive control over land and human resources by independent military lords, the daimyō. Of all the periods of Japanese history, this was perhaps the most feudal.

Indeed, if we compare the Kamakura-Muromachi experience with feudalism in Europe, we find startling similarities:

On the social level, private groups of armed men were united by contracts consisting of aid and service.

On the economic level, these groups were sustained largely on agricultural land and its produce.

On the political level, such groups had come into existence because the previous centralized state had failed to fulfill its functions. The private bodies of men were banded together not only for security but also to perform public functions. The coalescence of public and private, according to Asakawa Kan'ichi and his successor at Yale, John Hall, was a hallmark of feudalism.[6]

Is it, then, wise to use the Western term *feudalism* for medieval Japan? Yes, so long as one always takes into account cultural variables. The term becomes less a pejorative word for a backward system and more a description of a dynamic process of change. Indeed, alterations were leading inexorably to larger and larger units and to their unification.

First of the unifiers was a local daimyō, Oda Nobunaga (1534–82), who crushed most of the warring lords of central Japan. He was succeeded by his brilliant lieutenant, Toyotomi Hideyoshi (1536–98), who was, according to one historian, possibly the greatest world statesman of his century. He brought the turbulent daimyō further to heel, began to set up an efficient national administration, and encouraged commerce. Unfortunately, he mounted disastrous campaigns to invade China via Korea and died before he could be informed that his attempt had ended in failure. The work of unifying Japan was concluded by Tokugawa Ieyasu (1542–1616), who became shōgun in 1603 and laid the foundations for an entirely new kind of feudalism.

Culture Contact

Certainly one of the reasons the upstart lords were able to consolidate wider and wider domains was a distinct, if subtle, change in the state of the arts. This change in turn was at least partially a byproduct of contact with a technologically superior culture once again. This time the contact came from another direction and provided the first Japanese exchange with Europeans.

The first to reach Cipango, as the Portuguese named it, were men who sailed from Lisbon in the mid-sixteenth century. Missionaries followed, among them the Spanish priest Francis Xavier. In addition to Christianity, the aliens brought the smooth bore musket, which to this day in Kabuki drama has been named after the remote island through which it was imported (*tane-ga-shima*). They also brought new architectural designs, which, combined with temple style, resulted in the amazing castles dotted about Japan. The gun in the hands of a commoner forecast conscript armies; castles called for new defensive strategy on the part of the daimyō.

For a time, Western mannerisms and the fad of European dress were encouraged by Oda Nobunaga. Men of Kyōto wore balloonlike trousers, long cloaks, and high-crowned hats. Many Japanese wore crucifixes. Bread (*pan*) and tobacco (*tabako*) entered the Japanese diet and vocabulary. Later the Japanese became disenchanted with the religious intolerance among Dominicans, Jesuits, and Franciscans and feared that local authorities would no longer be able to control converts. The Japanese also built up a fear of the galleons of King Philip II of Spain. By 1614 the Tokugawa shogunate had banned all Westerners, except the Dutch at Nagasaki.

Centralized Feudalism

Ancestors of the administration founded early in the seventeenth century by Tokugawa Ieyasu and based in Edo (modern Tokyo) included the Minamoto shogunate based in Kamakura and the Ashikaga based in Muromachi. Japanese have referred to these predecessor regimes as "decentralized feudalism" (a term that seems to be a redundancy). In similar fashion, Japanese have called the Edo era (1603–1867) "early modern" and the Tokugawa system "centralized feudalism" (seemingly an inherent contradiction).

Here we shall describe the Tokugawa hegemony and estimate some of the lasting effects of the experience. In Chapter 3 attention will be devoted to the cultural heritage of the period, and in Chapter 4 the heritage will be considered in a different light, in a sort of balance sheet of assets and liabilities passed along to modern Japan.

The Baku-han *System*. Perhaps Tokugawa society is described as both essentially "feudal" and "under central control" because many different historical interpretations can be so accommodated. The lords who emerged from the civil strife of the Warring States period in the late sixteenth century and clustered around the three great unifiers were the prototypes of the modern daimyō. They consolidated more and more territory into larger and larger domains.

The Tokugawa clan established their military headquarters, the *bakufu*, in a small fishing village called Edo in the Kantō Plain. The eighth Tokugawa shōgun, Yoshimune, resurrected the title "great ruler" (*taikun*, from which was derived the term "tycoon"). All of Japan was subdivided into Tokugawa-held or

-controlled territory and something over 250 domains (*han*). Thus, the Japanese name for the structure, the *baku-han* system.

The domains were essentially of three types. Key areas were held by related lords, cadet branches of the Tokugawa family itself. Other strategically located domains were under the control of hereditary lords who had allied with the victorious Tokugawa before the critical battle of Sekigahara. Finally there were the outer lords who had joined the alliance after the battle that secured Japan and whom the Tokugawa scarcely trusted. So long as certain principles were adhered to and injunctions heeded, administration of local-domain affairs rested with the daimyō. He was, therefore, in his own territory, a small reproduction of the Tokugawa shōgun.

Thus, a leading family was surrounded by vassals, supported by peasants on the land, and protected by a castle. Military vassalage became increasingly more significant than blood ties. Beyond the family circle, fictive kinship included housemen and retainers. The whole system rested on patron-client ties, which have been likened to the parent-child (*oyabun-kobun*) relationship.

A territorial lord (daimyō) was defined in terms of lands assessed at so many bushels of rice (technically 10,000 *koku* or more; the *koku* was about 5.1 bushels). In other words, the assessed tax yield (*kokudaka*) served as a yardstick of status and power.

Some of the injunctions and security measures of the Tokugawa proved to be important far beyond their design. A system of alternate residence, for example, required domain lords to build elaborate residences in Edo and to keep their wives and children there. Lords then traveled regularly between Edo and their domains. The shogunate thus consciously knitted together the otherwise decentralized system. Regulations guaranteed a lively and colorful flow of traffic from Kyōto and from the domains through post towns and along established routes to Edo.

The Emperor. In one way the Tokugawa family followed in the footsteps of their predecessors, the ancient Soga reformers, the Fujiwara regents, the Minamoto warriors, the Hōjō regents, and the Ashikaga military leaders: they did not usurp the throne. The Emperor remained a symbol of unity, carefully protected by the Tokugawa's Kyōto deputy operating from the Nijō Castle. The Tokugawa version of feudalism never completely smothered the smoldering embers of national identity, symbolized, for example, by the Imperial tradition.

Indeed, the Edo era was marked by an inchoate nationalism, which made the restoration of Imperial rule easier as well as the eventual transformation to a modern nation-state. In the Mito domain, linked with the Tokugawa family itself, the development of "national studies" helped lay the ideological foundation for the late-nineteenth-century transition.

Tokugawa Society. If the political institutions of the Edo era constituted a historical step forward toward the modern condition, the social policy of the Tokugawa regime took a step backward. The Japanese version of Confucian hierarchy included the following rungs on the social ladder (from the top down): samurai-warrior, peasant-cultivator, artisan-craftsman, townsman-merchant. In this fashion, the Japanese completely reversed the Chinese assignment of lowest status to military men.

It should be noted, however, that quite early in the "Great Peace," the samurai-warrior became, in effect, a samurai-administrator. Nor did the other dividing lines remain completely rigid: merchant stock married or was adopted into the samurai circle; lower samurai sometimes occupied a status below peasant-headmen; in the late Edo era, men of ability like doctors often achieved assimilated samurai status.

Almost all historians agree that the samurai were an elite who played a crucial role in the transition from Tokugawa to modern Meiji Japan. To some, the military overlords were an arrogant, nonproducing, oppressive, parasitic class whose values were easily translated in modern times into militarism, imperialism, and aggression. To others, the samurai became civil administrators and scholar-statesmen, in Sakata Yoshio's phrase, "the intellectual and ruling class."

Certainly education, an inherent core of the Confucian ethic, was one of the primary duties of the samurai. He was to master both the military and the literary arts. By the end of the Edo era, a majority of the children of samurai above the lowest ranks were receiving formal education in at least 200 domain academies. Granted, the curricula were largely traditional, that is, Confucian and Neo-Confucian. Nonetheless, these schools became increasingly innovative in quality of education and were widespread throughout the country. Late in the period, mature samurai-scholars traveled widely among the domains as what we would now call consultants. Young samurai began their work in their own domain; some then moved on to Edo, Ōsaka, Kyōto, or Nagasaki to master languages, medicine, and (very late in the era) Dutch studies.

Some historians have remarked that Tokugawa statesmen (under the influence of Confucian doctrine, with its physiocratic bias) thought highly of agriculture in principle but poorly of agriculturalists in practice. Nonetheless, the poor plight of the peasant in the Edo era has doubtless been exaggerated. Modern field studies have demonstrated that agricultural production increased; there was a population exchange between village and city (which has continued to the present); and urban-based commercial activity dynamically affected the countryside.

According to orthodox Confucian theory, commercial profits constituted what economists today would call "unearned increment." In practice, artisans and craftsmen ranked higher than merchants, because the former were of direct service to the samurai class. Actually, by the brilliant Genroku era (1688–1704), it was difficult to separate the contributions of the samurai and others to what the Japanese have called townsmen (*chōnin*) culture. Most samurai and many lords came to be financially beholden to merchants. It is quite clear, however, that during the Edo period the commercial class never seized the levers of power in what we would recognize as a bourgeois revolt.

In any case, the *chōnin* culture of the old castle towns, which in the Edo era became preindustrial cities, did come to dominate the lifestyle not only of the townsmen but also of the samurai. A revived Kyōto continued to be the formal Imperial capital and, equally important, a center for fine handicrafts (as it is today). Ōsaka, "kitchen of Japan," became the great commercial entrepôt for inter-island trade. Edo, with its large population of samurai consumers, artisan producers, and merchant wholesalers, soon outstripped both of the older cities and reached a population of over 1 million in the eighteenth century. It was very likely then, as it is today, the largest city in the world.

Tokugawa Values. Although there were a number of significant changes beneath the surface of Japanese society during the Edo era, the Tokugawa hegemony continued uninterrupted for over two and a half centuries. It was a time of relative peace, not troubles, and the country remained practically isolated from foreign influence. There was ample opportunity to work out a sophisticated indigenous lifestyle. Today, even the Japanese identify native characteristics as stemming from Tokugawa society. Though they are often attributed to the tradition of agrarian village Japan, they were just as much a byproduct of preindustrial, urban Japan.

The Tokugawa values Japanese came to believe are that

- values are achieved in groups (the family, the community, *gemeinschaft, kyōdōtai*)
- these values are endowed with an almost sacred Japanese quality and are best implemented by, or in the name of, symbolic heads of family-style groups
- individual Japanese receive a continuous flow of blessings that establish obligations—in this way individuals demonstrate morality
- social, political, ethical, and religious norms are of value only as they are valuable to the group; there is no universal (only a situational) ethic

These are admittedly traditional (some would say, feudal) values. One question worth considering is did such values have to change before creation of a modern Japan? Put another way, can traditional values and modern society coexist? (This query is discussed in Chapter 4.)

Culture Change

The seeds of change have doubtless been described, at least by implication. These alterations have led observers to apply terms like "postfeudal" or "protomodern" to the Tokugawa system. Four different arenas of change may be singled out: they have to do with education and the level of literacy, intellectual currents and the breaking away from traditional thought, the emergence of a commercial society, and the renewal of outside cultural contact.

Enough has been said about the level of education and knowledge among the samurai elite. There was also a surprising spread of learning among townsmen and, for a male-dominated society, even among women. Merchants in the towns had to be literate, since bookkeeping demanded some education. Among the peasants, at least one head of each five-household group had to be able to read and to interpret regulations. Some estimates have pegged the level of literacy at 40 to 50 percent among males and considerably less for females. In his study of education in Tokugawa times, Ronald Dore concluded that the level of literacy among all classes in Japan was higher at that time than that for Europeans. It is doubtful that any developing nation in modern times has equaled that level.

Many Japanese scholars have emphasized the fact that, among the samurai leadership, training increasingly centered on Neo-Confucian strains of rationalism and pragmatism ("real learning"). One effect was the declaration of the unity of scholarship and politics and the resultant recruitment and training of "men of ability," to be active in politics. Religion re-entered the Japanese scene with the way of the samurai (*bushidō*), a strange mix of Confucian loyalty-obedience and Zen Buddhist contemplation. Loyalty was strictly to the local lord and through him to the Edo shogunate, regardless of whether or not the samurai agreed with orders. Later, this feudal sense of loyalty at the local level was transformed into national loyalty by those who were pledged to lords who in turn supported a new national regime.

In a feudal system dedicated to an economy in kind, the authorities in Edo, the lord-vassals in the domains, and their samurai followers found themselves increasingly beset with problems of money. Horie Yasuzō of Kyōto University has traced a significant evolution: whereas Confucian doctrine continued to lay primary emphasis on agriculture as the "foundation for the economy," agriculture became increasingly commercialized. The local domain economy was independent, so to speak, but its independence was eroded by increasing connections with the Japan-wide economy. Much to the mystification of samurai, merchants perfected a system of payment of rice stipends in advance, in other words, futures. Thus developed the commercial or commodity society.

When foreigners en masse returned to Japan in the nineteenth century, one of their first critical observations was that Tokugawa Japan had remained "backward" because of a policy known as seclusion. The Edo policy, enforced first in the seventeenth century, was never one of isolation, though. Japan always remained in the realm of East Asia. Contact with China continued. Exchange with the West was just strictly limited—the Japanese maintaining only a Dutch door to the outside world at Nagasaki. What came to be known as Dutch studies began as a trickle and, by the end of the Edo era, constituted a small flood that helped to undercut the Tokugawa bastion.

Despite seclusion, the slow, steady (one might even say subversive) permeation of the samurai society by Western ideas, through Dutch studies, was impressive. By the end of the eighteenth century, such learning had been added to the curricula of most domain schools. Dutch studies, which originally focused on medicine, astronomy, and the natural sciences, later led Japanese to mastery of military affairs. Watanabe Masao has concluded that the tradition of Dutch learning paved the way for the Japanese to make rapid strides in assimilating Western science.

There is a danger, of course, in such an analysis of cultural change—the possibility that one will conclude that nothing much of importance happened in the late nineteenth century. It is true that the impact of the West has been exaggerated by outsiders. Nonetheless, the Tokugawa system did have its own grave weaknesses. Godai Tomoatsu, one of the first samurai students to study overseas, likened Japanese to "frogs in a well" because of their ignorance of the outside world. In fact, it was the combination of internal cultural change with external cultural contact that shaped modern Japan.

NOTES

1. Langdon Warner, *The Enduring Art of Japan* (New York: Grove Press, 1952), Chap. 2, "Shinto, Nurse of the Arts."

2. George Sansom, *A History of Japan to 1334* (Stanford: Stanford University Press, 1958), p. 62.

3. John Whitney Hall, *Japan, from Prehistory to Modern Times* (New York: Dell, 1970), Chap. 6, "The Aristocratic Age."

4. The *Heike monogatari* [Tales of the Heike] in a modern retelling appeared as a serialized novel written by the Japanese author of best-sellers Yoshikawa Eiji; the original was translated as *The Heike Story* by F. W. Uramatsu (New York: Knopf, 1956).

5. John Hall described the relationship in *Government and Local Power in Japan* (Princeton: Princeton University Press, 1966), pp. 255 ff.

6. The definition is adapted from K. Asakawa, "Some Aspects of Japanese Feudal Institutions," *Transactions of the Asiatic Society of Japan* 46, pt. 1 (1918), cited by John Whitney Hall, "Feudalism in Japan—A Reassessment," *Comparative Studies in Society and History* 5, no. 1 (October 1962):30.

3

Shibui: A Taste of Japanese Culture

Some art historians and critics have argued that the Japanese artistic tradition dates only from the sixth century, that is, after the introduction of Buddhism to Japan. Thus it has been stated that in painting, sculpture, and architecture, the Japanese found inspiration in traditions already refined in India, China, and Korea. Such was certainly the case in Japan's Buddhist art as well as classical art. The latter imitated Chinese style and was part of the Great Tradition expressive of the tastes of aristocratic classes.

Japan has, however, also enjoyed an older tradition of folk arts and crafts, predominantly secular and expressive of the tastes of ordinary Japanese. These works sprang from the Little Tradition, a lifestyle that has prompted some critics to find the Japanese culture one of the most aesthetically sensitive. Once again in the realm of art, as in history, it is a matter of where the emphasis should be placed: on the admittedly overwhelming influences from abroad, which did affect Japan's artistic tradition, or on the persistent indigenous style, which has apparently survived the effects of alien overlays.

Japanese art is certainly the major, possibly the only, form of the nation's culture that has directly influenced the West. Meissen and other eighteenth-century porcelain makers had Imari pottery as their model; impressionist and postimpressionist painters were profoundly influenced by *ukiyo-e* woodblock prints; architects beginning with Frank Lloyd Wright have expressed a debt to Japanese design. Japanese literature has had an indirect effect, through translation, on Western prose, poetry, and, particularly, theater. Such Japanese film masterpieces as *Gate of Hell* and *Rashōmon* have won worldwide acclaim. Less well known abroad have been films depicting contemporary life, the best of which match in excellence award-winning cinema from Italy and the United States.

Of course, it is not possible in a short review to investigate all the rich veins of Japanese culture. One can, however, appreciate the contribution made by Japanese art, which has always had a great capacity to speak clearly about Japan's cultural values. Indeed, the direct impression to be gained from observation of an art object and the indirect impression to be derived from the written (if translated) word are often far more reliable indexes of Japanese character than the haze of description provided by the historian or the social scientist.

ORIGINS

As indicated in Chapter 2, many of the artifacts representative of Japan's prehistoric and semihistoric periods were found in or near burial sites. They were ritual objects, at first of interest mainly to archaeologists.

Archaeology and Art

Increasingly, archaeological finds were subjected to critical examination by art experts. Pottery vessels from the Jōmon period, for example, revealed a crude technology, but also an extraordinary variety of quite elaborate designs. In fact, Jōmon has been called one of the most interesting and creative of all prehistoric art traditions. So strange—one is tempted to say so modern—were some of the designs of the ceramics that contemporary critics have referred to them as surrealist. Apparently, the Japanese have always had a strong aesthetic instinct.

When they excavated artifacts from the Yayoi period (300 B.C.–300 A.D.), archaeologists uncovered an entirely different ceramic tradition. The pottery was wheel-made for the first time, and utensils obviously emanated from a settled rice culture that enjoyed irregular ties with the continent. The clearest mark of change was the mastery of metals: bronze bells, their surface decorations depicting contemporary life; weapons, including the sword; and metal mirrors, similar to those used in China's Han dynasty.

In similar fashion, archaeological finds from the Tomb (or Yamato) period were indicative of a changing culture from about 300 A.D. The tombs revealed the presence of distinct social units acting on the command of powerful ruling families.

The most remarkable finds from the huge burial mounds were quite small, the hand-fashioned clay cylinder-based sculptures called *haniwa*. These had been placed in a circle around the base and at the top of the mounds. At first simple, these clay figurines of entirely indigenous design later became more detailed. Among the statues were not only the various people of Yamato: noblemen, footsoldiers, priests, and peasants; but also their animals: horses, chickens, deer, monkeys, and birds. Rich in humor and bewildering in variety, the *haniwa* illustrated people of various stations and their dwellings. Miniature farmhouses revealed a style remarkably similar to dwellings of later years. Sometimes the figures were of crude workmanship; but all, like caricatures, were deft and direct in expression. Later artists strove to return to this simple uncluttered style, symbolic of Japan's earliest aesthetic taste.

Besides the tombs, little of prehistoric Japan has remained in architecture. It has been possible to see original structures in reproduction, though, since Shintō shrines have been faithfully built according to the primitive designs and even with old tools. Two examples include the hallowed Imperial sanctuary at Ise and the rival Shintō shrine at Izumo in Shimane Prefecture. One immediately notes the extensive use of wood in its natural state; the simple, almost severe, lines of the walls and roofs, especially the gates (*torii*) and fences; and the way that all of the structures harmonize with the natural forest environment.

Culture Contact

Rich as the indigenous tradition was, Japanese do admit that Japan was immensely enriched by the impact of continental (chiefly Chinese) influence filtered through Korea. At the core of the foreign impact was Buddhism. A converted Imperial court and its Buddhist temples became the patrons of art. Korean and Chinese immigrants taught the Japanese carvers,

The Grand Shrine of Ise: The Inner Shrine (*Naiku*), classic Shintō style.

carpenters, builders, and painters the secrets of their crafts as they all worked together on Buddhist structures and religious sculpture. Art historians have called this first period of Buddhist influence Asuka, after the district in which the capital was located at the time. The Asuka era conventionally is dated from 552—when the first image of Buddha is supposed to have arrived—to 710, when the capital was moved to Nara. Then and

The Hōryūji Temple Complex: Founded in 607, near Nara.

later, Buddhism played much the same role in maturing Japanese art as early Christianity did in the European tradition.

Fortunately much more than archaeological finds remain from the Asuka age, particularly in the realm of architecture. Its most spectacular monument is reputed to be the oldest wooden building in the world, the Hōryūji Seminary, which was constructed near Nara in 607 (damaged by fire, it was reconstructed in 1949). The main units include the gate (*chūmon*), the golden hall (*kondō*), the lecture hall (*kōdō*), and the pagoda (*gojūnotō*). This last five-story structure combines the tradition of the Han tower and that of the even older Indian stupa. The whole project reveals an obvious break from the more simple native style, with the employment of stone foundations, heavy pillars, vermilion paint, white plaster, and broad tiled roofs. The three-storied Yakushiji pagoda, completed in the early Nara period, illustrates the growing confidence and construction skills of Japanese.

ANCIENT JAPAN

As has been noted, under continuing Chinese influence the Japanese in 710 established their first permanent capital at Nara. Since then, Nara has remained a museum-city representing a burst of artistic activity, particularly in the field of eighth-century Buddhist art. Nara symbolized the life of an aristocracy that lived within a narrow radius of the capital. As John Hall described it, "Nara, in its grandeur, was an oasis of cosmopolitan art in an otherwise traditional and rather folkish Japanese plain."[1]

It must be remembered, however, that in the eighth century Nara was not a museum-city, not a settlement created to celebrate the new art. It was a working capital, modeled after the great Chinese metropolis, Ch'ang-an, which has long since passed from the scene.

Continuing Culture Contact

Continental influence on Nara can be seen primarily in the art inspired by Buddhism. To many critics the most remarkable art created then was sculpture, perhaps the finest ever produced by the Japanese. The earliest works were rendered in wood or in bronze; later clay was used. At first the figures were stylized and symbolic rather than representational.

Certainly by the early Nara period Japanese craftsmen had risen above imitation and become skillful artisans in their own right. Witness the polished wood figure of the Miroku (Maitreya), Buddha of the Future. This religious icon, located in the Chūgūji nunnery near Hōryūji, symbolizes religious quietude but also reveals an unmistakable Japanese quality, hauntingly recalling the abstract forms of the *haniwa*. At the other extreme are the guardian kings, fashioned of clay, painted with lacquer, and placed at the temple entrances to ward off evil spirits. These are fierce warriors with muscular frames and contorted facial expressions, in marked contrast with the serene visages of the buddhas and bodhisattvas.

Perhaps the best symbol of eighth-century Nara was the Great Buddha (Daibutsu), a 53-foot-high bronze figure, the biggest statue ever cast in Japan. Dedicated in 752, this sculpture represented a major technical achievement. (Since damaged by fire, it has been replaced by an even more cumbersome figure.) Ten years before, construction of the Great East Temple (Tōdaiji) to house the Buddha had begun. Both temple and statue revealed the growing power of the Imperial family, which sponsored this central headquarters among a network of state-sponsored temples in the provinces.

Of even greater value to the cultural historian is the nearby Shōsōin, an Imperial treasure house dedicated in 760 by the widow of the emperor who built Tōdaiji. Regularly "aired" and inventoried, the collection allows art experts to reconstruct the material culture and wealth of Nara and bears witness to the high development and sophistication of this culture. Nowhere has such a superb collection of eighth-century objects been preserved. No other collection in Japan so clearly reveals the variety of early cultural influences, drawn from Korea, China, India, and even Persia. Included are textiles, gold and silver vessels, mirrors, lacquer boxes, musical instruments, screens, banners, hangings, writing tools, books, maps, saddles, stirrups, and swords, used by both priests and the Imperial court.

After the capital was moved to Kyōto in 794, and until the beginning of the tenth century, the Heian era also showed the strong strains of continental influence. During this period the glories of the T'ang dynasty were imported directly to the new capital. Buddhism remained the major religion of the aristocracy; monasteries, the patrons of fine arts.

Early Heian architecture, however, began to show a distinct penchant for adapting monumental T'ang style to simpler Japanese needs. The best examples were the Fujiwara-sponsored Kasuga Shrine, actually in Nara; and the Heian Jingū (extant in a modern reconstruction) in Kyōto. Once again the woodwork painted vermilion, the complicated and bracketed eaves, and the slightly curved tile roof revealed Chinese influences, while construction methods showed the Japanese carpenters' skill in assimilating alien design. As for Buddhist temples, the Japanese began to build amidst the beauties of nature. For example, in 851 the Tendai sect began construction of Enryakuji in the mountain heights and forested valleys of Mt. Hiei, just north of Kyōto.

After the fall of the great T'ang (906), direct contact with China ceased, and Japanese designers were thrown on their own. Large public buildings like the Byōdōin, built at Uji in 1053 under Fujiwara patronage, continued to show Chinese influence. Yet the placement of the main Phoenix Hall (Hōōdō) was marked by Japanese insight. The building symbolized a huge bird settling on the irregularly shaped pond in the foreground. An even better example of reversion to native instincts was the shrine at Itsukushima, built out over the waters of the Inland Sea at Miyajima. (This setting provided the opening scenes for Japan's first great color movie, *Gate of Hell.*)

The structure that had a lasting effect was not the splendid palace or the towering temple, however, but the typical Japanese dwelling. Style was governed partly by materials available. Stone was rare. In its place, wood, paper, plaster, and thatch were used, following the native tradition of early Shintō structures. Most obvious were the designer's exploitation of contrasts and the carpenter's use of natural materials. The structures had raised wooden floors, removable walls, lightweight partitions, and deep thatched roofs.

Culture Change

After the early twelfth century, Japanese art was on its own. Japanese style began to reassert itself, and nowhere was this better revealed than in language. Our knowledge of archaic Japanese language derives from the first written forms dating from about the eighth century. The *Kojiki* (Records of ancient matters), for example, appeared to be pure Chinese until it was recognized that some of the ideographs made no sense in Chinese. Obviously, they were being used to indicate Japanese personal and place names. When first faced with the problem of writing, the Japanese had two choices: the semantic (Chinese) or the phonetic (Japanese). As one might guess, they began to use both. In other words, the basic Chinese characters suggested the skeleton and body of an idea, which was then clothed in an elaborate Japanese grammatical robe woven of ideographs adapted for phonetic purposes. The latter eventually evolved into a regular system of Japanese phonograms called "borrowed names" (*kana*).

It is not the purpose here to dwell in detail on what Edwin O. Reischauer has called one of the most intricate languages in the world. Suffice it to say that eventually order was created out of chaos: the Chinese ideographs were increasingly used for substantive units (for example, nouns); the *kana* for phonetics and inflections in a regular pattern. A good example of this system is found in the *Manyōshū* (Collection of myriad leaves), which dates from the late Nara period and consists of some 20 books and over 4,500 poems. The style, particularly of the poetry, differed substantially from that of the early (Chinese-style) dynastic histories.

In other words, linguistic confusion was not able to obscure certain deep native themes. Because of the regular meter and rhythm of this early poetry, the *Manyōshū* became a valuable index to archaic Japanese and a symbol of the persistence of Japanese tradition. Moreover, the collection, unlike officially inspired genealogies, was rich in the sentiment of ordinary people.

Among the various techniques employed in the *Manyōshū*, the following may be mentioned: alliteration, to be used in all forms of Japanese poetry thereafter; the pillow-word, used to modify the following word either through sound (in essence, a pun) or by association; and above all, the vivid word-picture. Thus, "grass-for-pillow" was an imaginative word signal for journey. The lyrical poetry displayed an intimacy with nature. Many of the short poems (*tanka*, 31 syllables in lines of 5-7-5-7-7) included a snapshot of a natural scene twisted into a hint of human emotion. Two examples may be cited—

Oh how steadily I love you—
  You who awe me
Like the thunderous waves
  That lash the sea-coast of Ise!

To what shall I liken this life?
  It is like a boat,
Which, unmoored at dawn,
  Drops out of sight
And leaves no trace behind.[2]

In these thoughts, the material was not entirely rhetorical. As viewed also by Shintō, each natural phenomenon retained its individuality, an entity permeated by an awesome and spiritual quality.

The poetry was also imbued with a characteristic Japanese feeling of the vanity and evanescence of life: "life frail as foam," "all is in vain," and "nothing endures"–such phrases doubtless indicate an overlay of Buddhism in the mind of the poet.

The *Manyōshū*, along with the dynastic histories, was a mirror, reflecting society up to the late eighth century. The poems revealed a staid, settled, agrarian way of life in the countryside, but also political consolidation under the court and a measure of progress. Much has been made of the artificiality of the later Heian court and of the oppressive hierarchy of feudal systems even later on. From the *Manyōshū* collection emanated an optimistic spirit, a frankness, a genuineness of feeling, and sheer happiness. The martial spirit was only a minor theme.

Out of this early poetic tradition came Japanese writing in a kind of shorthand–a simplified cursive style called "grass-hand" (*sōsho*). Tradition holds that a priest, Kōbō Daishi (or Kūkai, 774–835), chose forty-seven of the adapted ideographs to create a Japanese syllabary. This in turn led to a fine art, brush calligraphy. In the writing of the ideographs, the Chinese artist was regarded as paramount; in the rendering of script, or *kana*, the Japanese excelled in calligraphy. Basic skills in calligraphy profoundly affected Japanese painting. Thus were blended the various components of an artistic tradition: the abstract calligraphy, the word-pictures of the poems, and, eventually, black-and-white painting. The last was to share the basic canons of calligraphy: balanced tension, use of open space, quality of line, texture, and variation of a basic theme.

It was only one more step to what was called "woman's language" (or "easy *kana*"). In fact, there was nothing easy about the precursors of the modern novel, written by women in the tenth century. Somewhat neglected has been the *Pillow Book*, a shrewd, sometimes sarcastic set of observations on Heian court life prepared by Sei Shōnagon. Far more widely known was the masterpiece of a contemporary and rival in court, a lady since known by her pseudonym, Murasaki Shikibu. Ostensibly the biography of a brilliant sensualist (the shining prince), *The Tale of Genji*[3] is the first Japanese novel. Moreover, it has been called the world's first great work of prose fiction. We know that the author was born about 978. She finished the tale about 1020.

The novel concerns a hero, Prince Genji, who is the son of an emperor by a concubine. He is at once handsome, scholarly, witty, engaging, and sensitive, and yet daring, courageous, and skillful in the military arts. The author spins out the story in a long, episodic, often repetitious style, but also sets for herself the highest aesthetic standards (described in the novel itself). Although written as a romance, the work is full of ideas, complicated human motivations, and psychological insights into personality. In what was to become a characteristic of Japanese style, the episodes suggest pathos in high places and a sense that life is fleeting and all material things impermanent. The use of language is innovative, quite different from previous writing, which slavishly followed Chinese style.

Nor is *The Tale of Genji* without historical significance. Read with hindsight, the novel depicts late Heian court life as luxurious but obviously shallow. Like the *Manyōshū, Genji* was a mirror reflecting contemporary life. This time a foreground of Kyōto refinement is balanced by a background of uncourtliness and provincial vigor.

Never has there been a more fortunate coincidence in combining the written word and illustration than that found in the Genji scroll prepared by an eleventh-century artist. His work marked a reversion in painting, parallel to that in language, to a distinctly native style, since called *Yamato-e* (Japanese-style painting). Even the form of presentation was unique, a horizontally prepared and unrolled scroll (*emakimono*). This art displayed a growing secular concern with everyday life, a reliance on inspiration drawn from indigenous scenes, a stylized quality of representation, brilliant use of color, and a formalized perspective, which looked down and from a slight angle on the scenes as they unfolded.

THE ART OF FEUDAL JAPAN

Just as economic wealth and power in the late twelfth century shifted away from stiflingly confined Kyōto to the provincial vigor of Kamakura, so too Japanese art reflected changing social patterns, local influences, and new tastes and values. The transition was faithfully recorded in the increasingly popular *Yamato-e* style of painting and particularly in the horizontal scrolls. From this period came the *Heiji monogatari* scroll (about 1250), which depicted, in place of languid palace life, the exploits of warrior-samurai—choking smoke, a burning palace, warriors on horseback, the severing of heads, and scurrying aristocrats—all are portrayed with a wealth of narrative detail and vivid realism.

Continuing Culture Contact

During the Kamakura period there was renewed contact with China. The effects of new religious sects were felt in Japanese art, not only at the ancient capital of Kyōto and in the new headquarters at Kamakura, but also throughout the provinces. By this time artists were identified by schools, as the group-centered consciousness of Japanese life surfaced in the arts and crafts.

In architecture, evidence of a sort of classical revival was shown in the rebuilding of Kōfukuji, with its five-storied pagoda, in Nara. Another remarkable example was the Sanjūsangendō (hall of thirty-three bays), in Kyōto. The immense gate of Tōdaiji in Nara built in this period preserved the contemporary multi-story architectural style of Sung China.

Sculpture at Kamakura also demonstrated a renewal of religious spirit, a revival of Amidism (a certain Buddhist tradition), and, at the same time, a new realism. A 49-foot-high bronze statue of Buddha was erected in Kamakura (in 1252) in emulation of the older Daibutsu of Nara.

Nowhere was the new emphasis on realism more clearly evident than in the sculpture of Unkei (1148–1223). He was aided by his six sons and a guild of carvers and carpenters. The team caught the tragedy of human life in marvelously lifelike wooden figures. The Unkei school injected an almost ferocious muscular vigor even into its Buddhist art like the two king-guardians (*niō*) at the south gate of Tōdaiji, reconstructed after the civil wars.

Typical of Chinese influence adapted to Japanese surroundings was the Relic Hall of the Engakuji, near Kamakura. The use of unfinished materials set amid natural surroundings reflected the profound influence of a new teaching, Zen Buddhism, the full impact of which will be described below.

Continuing Culture Change

The great strain of the Mongol invasions in the late thirteenth century eventually brought about the collapse of the Kamakura system. The epic struggle against the invaders was graphically depicted in narrative scrolls prepared in 1293 by Tosa Nagataka, who thus continued the *Yamato-e* tradition. An age of political uncertainty and, finally, endemic civil war followed. Turmoil marked the triumph of provincial forces—particularly the samurai—over the aristocracy and Kamakura nobility. Literature of the times faithfully captures the ethos of the samurai, which essentially consisted of two ideals: bravery in battle and loyalty to the lord. Much more accurate in its details, though, is the semiofficial history of the Kamakura shogunate, *Azuma kagami* (Mirror of the East). But closer to the semifictional war tales of an earlier era is the *Taiheiki* (Chronicle of the great peace), prepared shortly after the civil conflicts of the fourteenth century.[4]

Despite, or possibly because of, this time of troubles, an art not so much of ostentation but of quiet contemplation emerged. Possibly because of the turmoil from the early thirteenth through the fifteenth centuries, Japanese have looked back on the succeeding Tokugawa period to find a culture of peace and on the preceding Heian era to recapture "the classical age" in Japanese art. Nevertheless, the Muromachi period (1392–1567), even with uneasy Ashikaga leadership, provided what were later regarded as characteristically Japanese modes of artistic expression. These included: in painting, a transition from colorful narrative scrolls to quiet, contemplative black-and-white sketches (*sumi-e*); in literature, a change from precious court diaries to somber, classic Nō drama; in domestic arts, a shift of emphasis from aristocratic treasures to ceramics, utensils for the tea ceremony, and the skills of landscape gardening.

Zen Culture

Although the Muromachi era was a period of disorder and significant cultural change on the domestic front, it was also a time of strong continental influence. Nowhere was this more obvious than in the subtle but pervasive influence of a Buddhist sect called Zen in Japan (Ch'an in China). Zen monks became not only the leading scholars and writers, but also designers, artists, collectors, and critics—in short, those who set the aesthetic standards.

In architecture, this was the period when the great Zen temples of Kyōto—Daitokuji, Tōfukuji, and Nanzenji—were established. It was the era too of two masterpieces built by Ashikaga shōgun. The Golden Pavilion (Kinkakuji) was erected in 1397 as a villa at Kitayama, then outside Kyōto. (Completely destroyed by fire, it was reconstructed in 1950.[5]) The Silver Pavilion (Ginkakuji) was built in 1489 as a country retreat at Higashiyama, then north of Kyōto. Both recalled the aristocratic tastes of a classical age and, in their placement in natural surroundings, the deep introspective quality of Zen Buddhism.

Painting was doubtless the greatest art of the Muromachi period, and here, too, the aesthetic principles emanated from the Zen monasteries. Inspiration was derived from the landscape artists of Sung China but steadily evolved into a unique Japanese technique under the guidance of Josetsu and Shūbun (early fifteenth century), culminating with the master, Sesshū (1420–1506). The artists (many were Zen priests) perfected a new monochrome style known as water-and-ink (*suiboku*). Vivid colors were replaced by bold strokes (often perfected in calligraphy), flat washes, shades, line, and balance. Open spaces were used ingeniously. In the quality of stroke and space a direct approach, almost a religious perception, was portrayed.

Such principles were carried over into another great Japanese contribution to the world of art, landscape gardening. Gardens varied from the large and complex like Tenryūji to the cool and quiet like the moss garden at Saihōji (both in Kyōto). The latter cleverly evoked a waterfall and stream, entirely without water. Even the uninitiated have agreed, however, that the abstract rock garden of Ryōanji (constructed about 1500) in Kyōto best carried out the aesthetic spirit of Zen. Here was indeed the *suiboku* style rendered in sand and stone. In a severely limited space (which looks larger to the eye) an abstract sea of carefully waved sand, broken here and there by isolated rock islands, was conceived. The "program" of the garden was minimal, yet its pattern suggested meaning to all.

The impact of the Zen approach, an inner world of elegant but transient beauty, on now-famous Japanese folk art (*mingei*) was enormous. An aesthetic vocabulary was built up: the solitary (*wabi*), the antique mellowed by use (*sabi*), and the astringent (*shibui*). Used to describe the taste of bitter green tea, *shibui* came to be heard frequently in Kyōto and perhaps less so throughout Japan. Astringent best described Zen style: subtle rather than direct effect; economy of means rather than opulence; the power of suggestion and meditation rather than

Ryōanji, Kyōto: Zen-style rock garden (about 1500).

blunt statement. Edwin O. Reischauer called it "the cultivation of the little"; Hugo Munsterberg, "the cult of the subdued"; and art expert Sherman Lee, "tea taste in Japanese art." Indeed, at the very center of aesthetic connoisseurship was the famous tea ceremony (*cha-no-yu*).

A Zen monk, Eisai, had first brought tea from China late in the twelfth century. The serving and consumption of tea in an ordered, slow ceremony were carried to their final formal style by teamaster Sen no Rikyū (1521–91). The greatest impact was, of course, on ceramics. At first, Chinese utensils were used. Later, rice bowls from Korea under the Yi dynasty were popular. Finally, the preference for indigenous and local wares, such as those made at Bizen, Iga, Tamba, Shigaraki, and Seto, won out. During these years, pieces made at Seto approached Chinese quality so closely that the kiln lent its name for the Japanese word for pottery in general (*setomono*). Other utensils used in the ceremony became objets d'art: cast-iron water

A Japanese Meal: Arrangement for the eye as well as for the palate is essential.

kettles, the Bizen-ware tea caddy, the Oribe tile platform, the bamboo tea whisks, lacquer trays, and the delicate wooden scoop for the bitter green powdered tea.

The tea ceremony interacted with the other arts. The architecture of the tea pavilion, with its attendant garden, was designed to be quiet and meditative. In the background in an alcove would be a flower arrangement (*ikebana*) and a landscape modeled after, but not entirely imitative of, the Sung style. The cultivation of tiny trees (*bonsai*) or the arrangement just outside the pavilion of a small garden symbolized the whole universe of nature.

Although Nō drama belongs to the long tradition of Japanese literature, music, and dance, the visual effects of Nō picked up various artistic strains. From the indigenous cult came Shintō legends; from the classical era, the gorgeously embroidered costumes; and from the Zen contemplative tradition, the imaginatively carved masks. These masks represent various characters and in themselves are works of art.

Originally, mysterious and symbolic dances set to music adapted from the continent had been performed for the Nara court. At first Nō plays were concerned with men who were really gods and Shintō divinities. Later secular themes entered the repertory and involved ghosts of famous warriors, doomed to reenact their last battles in afterlife, elegant ladies in women-plays, and devils in drama concerned with the supernatural. *Hagoromo* (The robe of feathers), for example, contained many of these elements and used as its backdrop the beautiful Miho pine-clad seashore (just below Shimizu). "Crazy words" (*kyōgen*) interludes provided the comic relief. Nō was molded into what it remained essentially for 600 years by two great masters, Kanze Kanami (1333–84) and his son, Seami (or Zeami, 1363–1443), who founded the Kanze school of performers. Nō worked a powerful influence later on the grand Kabuki theater, which in turn represents Japan's greatest contribution to the world stage.

Japan's art did not remain for all time simple and understated, as expressed in Zen. During the era of the great unifiers, Oda Nobunaga, Toyotomi Hideyoshi, and Tokugawa Ieyasu, style returned to the grand, the opulent, and the monumental.

The great castles built by Nobunaga at Azuchi and by Hideyoshi at Momoyama became not only the centers of political gravity, but also the focal points for patronage of the arts, lending their names to a cultural era, the Azuchi-Momoyama (1568–99). The castles had unusual architecture, combining knowledge of defense imported from the West with Japanese temple style. The one built at Ōsaka (destroyed during World War II and since reconstructed) was a symbol of the wealth and power of the unifiers. Some 30,000 workers were employed to construct the outworks and tower. Most of the castles, except two prominent ones—the famous White Heron at Himeji, west of Kōbe, and Nijō in Kyōto—were victims of modern bombardment. Nijō was built in the early years of the seventeenth century for Tokugawa Ieyasu as a residence for his stays in the old capital.

The interiors of the palaces and residences were richly endowed by the Momoyama decorators. The Kanō school, founded by Masanobu and Motonobu during the latter part of the Muromachi period, set the standards in multiple-panel screens (*byōbu*) and wall paintings. Similarly, weaving, dyeing, and embroidery were used to produce bold and colorful patterns. Momoyama textiles are probably the finest the Japanese have ever produced.

Despite this burst of opulence during the late sixteenth century, the Japanese never forgot the Zen heritage. Especially in the ensuing Tokugawa period, aside from flashes of brilliance, Japanese art withdrew to subdued expression and to an astringent quality described as *shibui*, the soul of Zen.

EDO STYLE

There is nostalgia in Japan for the Edo era. When the young directors backstage at NHK (Nippon Hōsō Kyōkai, "Japan broadcasting corporation") wish to project a traditional background for one of their soap operas, they faithfully reconstruct a scene from the Edo era (1603–1867). The narrow alleys, the faithfully reproduced architecture of the houses, the gorgeous costumes of the protagonists—all these are drawn from Japan under the Tokugawa hegemony. It is true that much of what is generally regarded as the uniquely Japanese contribution

The White Heron Castle, Himeji: Completed in 1609.

to world culture did emerge during the relative disorder of the Muromachi. But its character had evolved from an earlier feudal era, the Kamakura, and both owed a large debt to an earlier classical period, the Heian. Yet the strands of all three ages came together in the long and peaceful Edo era.

As far as art was concerned, the relative isolation of Japan for two centuries had the effect of turning the country in on itself. Edo became the most completely Japanese era in the cultural history of the nation. There appeared, of course, the great public buildings in Chinese style, monuments symbolic of Tokugawa power. Classical schools, however, declined in originality and strength. At the same time, popular art and folk crafts flowered as never before. Nor was good taste confined to the metropoli—ancient Kyōto, brash Ōsaka, and colorful Edo—the period of peace and prosperity saw a widespread diffusion of arts and letters. Each of dozens of castle towns became a center for arts and crafts; each of a number of daimyō, a patron for artists and craftsmen. In the towns, subsidy was available from samurai and wealthy merchants. Of all the periods of art, Edo is the best represented in Western museums.

Tokugawa Treasures

There were two tributaries to the mainstream of Edo culture. The lifestyle of the samurai class (which included the Tokugawa, related families, and the various daimyō) tended to carry forward without much change the aristocratic emphasis inherited from the Muromachi and Azuchi-Momoyama eras. In sharp contrast to these upper-class arts were the marvelous inventions of the townsmen and the folk crafts of the agrarian villages.

In public architecture, too, representations ranged from the elaborately ornate to the elegantly simple. The Momoyama tradition of decoration was best reproduced in the mausoleum dedicated to the founder of the Tokugawa, Ieyasu, and located at Nikkō (1617). The various structures at Nikkō were to many Japanese "splendid" (*kekkō*), to others, gaudy in the extreme, even fussy. For example, the Gate of Sunlight (Yōmeimon) has, despite its embellishment, been regarded as a masterpiece of Japanese architecture.

The elaborate mode of Momoyama painting went in several different directions. The Kanō school, for example, divided and evolved into the decorative art of Kōrin (1658–1715). The *Yamato-e* tradition of Japanese painting also produced new schools, the forerunners of those that would produce the woodblock prints of the next century.

Built about the same time as the Nikkō mausoleum but at the other extreme were the small, residential rather than public, detached palaces of Shūgakuin and Katsura outside of Kyōto. The latter particularly has received worldwide acclaim. The principles of design renowned architects have cherished in Katsura are extreme simplicity, economy in materials, functionalism in form, and beauty in design. Floors were covered with squares made of thick dyed rush (*tatami*). Once again, the colors of nature were preferred over paint. An old twisted tree trunk, rather than finished lumber, ran alongside the alcove (*tokonoma*) and held up the latticed ceiling. Just outside, worn stones served as steps, pebbles as a bed for cool flowing water, deep eaves as protection against changes in weather.

Katsura, of course, must be considered a public work of architecture. But often overlooked is the fact that the ordinary farmhouse had a similar simple unity. Now rare in either original or reconstructed form, the classic Japanese farmhouse is a prime contribution to the world of architecture. The key features include the use of plain wood, rush matting, and the alcove, already described; also the sliding weather partitions (*amado*), thick sliding panels (*fusuma*), light rice-paper partitions (*shōji*), and the separate bath (*ofuro*) and facilities (*benjo*). Many of these features have been picked up and reproduced in modern houses throughout the world; if not, they appear in almost every interior decorating magazine as models of the best in modern design.

Mention should also be made of the host of fittings and accoutrements that also lay between the samurai and commoner traditions. Many have withstood the impact of the West and modernization and remain today as heirlooms from Japan's rich past. There were nests of boxes (called *inrō*); miniature carvings (*netsuke*) that served as toggles; sword guards (*tsuba*) of iron inlaid with gold and silver; folded paper figures (*origami*);

and, of course, utensils for the tea ceremony and flower arranging.

Chōnin *Culture*

Japanese like to think back to a traditional rustic lifestyle, which they often identify with the agrarian village rooted in rice culture. Nevertheless, much of the traditional heritage came, not from the countryside where most Japanese indeed lived, but from the network of castle towns built up under Tokugawa hegemony. In these towns lived most of the samurai, but the tone of the settlements was sounded by townsmen (*chōnin*). *Chōnin* culture was shared by samurai and nonsamurai alike.

During the Edo era, there were actually at least three urban traditions. Kyōto retained an aristocratic outlook, but the nobility had little functional significance. Thus Kyōto became a center for elegant crafts. Ōsaka came to represent the mercantile outlook, even though in Neo-Confucian theory merchants had low status. Edo, originally settled by the warrior class, came to represent a synthesized mass culture.

Popular culture emerged from an urban environment dominated by the entertainment district, the pleasure quarter, and the way of the courtesan. The mood was captured by racy novels, popular drama, and garish woodblock prints. For a long time after, Japanese regarded all these phenomena as common, even vulgar, since they dealt with an ephemeral world in sharp contrast to the universe of Confucian learning and Buddhist meditation.

The most brilliant flowering of *chōnin* culture appeared in the Genroku era (1688–1704), the style of which was essentially Japanese in origin and little affected by outside influence. A key to understanding the culture lay in a Japanese term, *ukiyo*. Originally, as Donald Keene instructs us, the word meant simply "the sad world"; by means of a pun, it came to mean "the floating world."

First to capture this atmosphere was Ihara Saikaku (1642–93), the first important novelist in five centuries since the Lady Murasaki. Indeed, some of his work was deliberately modeled on the classic Genji tale. Saikaku was at once poetic in the classic style, flavorful in the aesthetic style, and colloquial in Genroku style. On the surface, his work was highly secular, dealing with the latest fads, fashions, and foibles of his society. At the depths, his writing reflected the traditional Japanese view of the evanescence of everyday life. He worked with three types of stories: tales of love, stories about merchants, and samurai legends. Of these, the first were perhaps the most successful and the last, the most popular. His masterpiece, *Five Women Who Loved Love*,[6] was filled with an intimate knowledge of Genroku society.

Saikaku the realist has been contrasted with Japan's Shakespeare, Chikamatsu Monzaemon (1653–1725) the romanticist. To appreciate Chikamatsu we must recall how urban culture had produced new dramatic forms with far greater popular appeal than that of the aristocratic Nō. The seventeenth and eighteenth centuries witnessed development of a puppet-theater, in which the action was carried by amazingly realistic doll-figures about half life-size. Dialogue and commentary by chorus, something like the Greek version, was intoned from a platform on the side by reciters (*jōruri*). Originally a kind of storytelling in the street, *jōruri* was elevated by Chikamatsu to become *bunraku* puppet-theater, which then worked a powerful influence on the more popular Kabuki dance-drama.

Chikamatsu preferred, in fact, to write for the puppets, because he was suspicious of Kabuki actors who often added their own variations to his plays and used them as vehicles to promote their own success. Often, parts of the plays were adaptations of classical Nō drama, but the language was entirely colloquial. Chikamatsu wrote two kinds of plays: domestic tragedies, like modern soap operas, and historical pieces, which were fictionalized versions of famous events and personages.[7] Although the former were superior as literature, the latter were more beloved by audiences. In the historical dramas, the playwright, like Shakespeare, demonstrated clearly that persons of status also felt ordinary human emotions and suffered tragedy. In the domestic pieces, characters displayed noble human feelings (*ninjō*) in conflict with duty (*giri*). And thus were the lifestyles of samurai and commoners fused.

After Chikamatsu, Kabuki was performed by live actors

Bunraku Puppet Theater: The late Yoshida Bungoro, manipulator.

(always men), with huge and revolving stages, runways through the audiences, elaborate but stylized scenery, and brilliant costumes. Often the jerky halting movements of the ancestor-puppets were faithfully reproduced on the Kabuki stage. Contents of the drama never quite matched the skills demonstrated by Chikamatsu, but the Kabuki as theater became more and more splendid, what Joshua Logan has called among the best in the world. Doubtless the most popular play in grand Kabuki has been the *Treasury of Loyal Retainers.*[8]

This floating life, this novel urban style, this popular drama, all were captured in one of the most remarkable and famous Japanese contributions to the world of art: the woodblock print depicting the floating world (*ukiyo-e*). Tapping an ancestry of aesthetic expression in the *Yamato-e* style of Japanese painting and the black-and-white impressionism of Zen art, the new genre was deeply folkish in inspiration. It was used to illustrate novels, to advertise dramatic productions, and to commemorate famous places of natural beauty along well-traveled routes. When in the nineteenth century these prints reached the West, their impact was great on a number of artists: Dégas, Manet, Monet, and Whistler among the impressionists; Toulouse-Lautrec, Van Gogh, and Gauguin among the post-impressionists. The *ukiyo-e* woodblock print has enjoyed more popularity in the West than any other form of Japanese art.

The first to turn the energy in Japanese painting to woodblocks was Hishikawa Moronobu (died about 1694), who realized that prints could enjoy wider circulation than individually painted scrolls. He and Torii Kiyonobu (1664–1729) specialized in portraits of Kabuki actors. At first the prints were in monochrome, but later color was added. Then the work became a collaboration among the publisher, who commissioned and financed the enterprise; the artist, who prepared the overall design; the skilled engraver, who transferred the design to block; and the printer, who painstakingly fitted each block of different color to the paper and turned out the finished print.

Harunobu (1724–70) was primarily responsible for developing the color print; he concentrated on the human figure, either the courtesan or the Kabuki actor. Utamaro (1754–1806) was most famous for his "picture girls," well-known courtesans and geisha. Meanwhile, entire families were devoting themselves to subjects drawn from Kabuki. Possibly theatrical prints were carried to their heights by Sharaku (eighteenth and nineteenth centuries), whose portraits of actors often also constituted biting caricatures of public figures. Of all these artists, Sharaku constitutes the enigma, for he worked only a brief ten months (1794–95) and disappeared again into obscurity.

By the end of the eighteenth century, *ukiyo-e* printmakers had turned from figures to landscapes. The artists pictured everyday life and well-known scenes. Increasingly under the subtle influence of Western prints, they began to use perspective in their designs. Two men were not only famous during their own lives but are celebrated for their designs to this day: Hokusai (1760–1849) and Hiroshige (1797–1858). Hokusai is said to have produced some 35,000 original prints; Hiroshige, more than 5,000 original prints. (Commonly, artisans later pulled duplicate prints from the blocks originally prepared by the artists.) Hokusai has become best known for his thirty-six views of Mt. Fuji. Hiroshige is remembered for his delightfully graphic sketches of the fifty-three stages on the old Tōkaidō road.

Even those who on the surface seemed to reject the superficiality of the floating world were nonetheless profoundly affected by it. Bashō Matsuo (1644–94), for example, seemed to work apart from the Genroku bustle, like a Zen hermit of an earlier age. His striking poetry symbolized the fact that the older (*tanka*) verse forms had fallen out of favor, replaced by an even briefer and more indirect style of expression (the *haiku*, a 3-line, 17-syllable poem with a structure of 5-7-5). In the hands of Bashō, the shorter *haiku* poem probably reached its zenith. By convention, the lines were associated with seasons of the year. They also painted in sparse words a picture of nature while evoking a deep human emotion. In one sense, the detachment of Bashō has been exaggerated–his poetry, like that of Saikaku, plumbed the Edo style.

During the Tokugawa period, Japan was admittedly a storehouse of Chinese art. In some cases, the original had disappeared on the continent. Was the Japanese artistic impulse, then, mere imitation? The answer is no, since in any Japanese collection of Edo art the very finest items have unmistakable Japanese qualities. With an acknowledged debt to continental–as well as indigenous–origins, the *Yamato-e* painting, the Bizen pot, the carved Nō mask, and the woodblock print nonetheless stand out as unique contributions to the world of art. At the very least, Japan's art and literature document a long tradition, a tradition with which Japanese faced the impact of the West and the process of modernization.

There has been some speculation whether, after the uniquely Japanese quality of Edo style, the art of Japan has been able to withstand the typhoon of Western influence. An answer to that question must be postponed until Chapter 4, after an examination of the process of modernization as a whole has been made.

NOTES

1. John Whitney Hall, "The Visual Arts and Japanese Culture," in John W. Hall and Richard K. Beardsley, *Twelve Doors to Japan* (New York:

McGraw Hill, 1965), p. 273.

2. *The* Manyōshū; *One Thousand Poems Selected and Translated from the Japanese* (Tokyo: Iwanami Shoten, 1940; distr. in U.S. by the University of Chicago Press, 1941), vol. 4, p. 600; vol. 3, p. 351.

3. From the *Genji monogatari* [Tale of Genji], we are fortunate in having two translations, both fine works of literature in themselves. The long-standing, classic rendition was accomplished by Arthur Waley, trans., *The Tale of Genji* (Boston: Houghton Mifflin, 1925-33), 6 vols. Now we have, as well, the version by Edward G. Seidensticker, trans., *The Tale of Genji* (New York: Knopf, 1976), 2 vols.

4. There are masterly translations of both works: Minoru Shinoda, *The Founding of the Kamakura Shogunate* (with selected translations of the *Azuma Kagami*) (New York: Columbia University Press, 1960); *The Taiheiki: A Chronicle of Medieval Japan,* trans. with introduction and notes by Helen Craig McCullough (New York: Columbia University Press, 1959).

5. In our day, we have a complicated psychological novel about the burning of the Kinkakuji by a deranged youth, a work written by a controversial author, Mishima Yukio: *Kinkakuji* [The temple of the golden pavilion] (New York: Knopf, 1958), trans. by Ivan Morris.

6. *Kōshoku gonin onna* (1686), trans. by William Theodore DeBary (Rutland, Vermont: Tuttle, 1965). Often, as explained in the preface, a writer or artist was known by his given (pen or artistic) name: thus, Saikaku.

7. Again we are fortunate in having faithful translations: *Chikamatsu Monzaemon: Major Plays*, trans. by Donald Keene (New York: Columbia University Press, 1961).

8. *Chūshingura* (1748) was a play about the forty-seven *rōnin* (masterless samurai). The plot has become a favorite literary and dramatic theme of modern Japan as well. In capsule, about 1701 a minor daimyō drew a sword against an antagonist within the headquarters of the shōgun. For this offense he was ordered to commit suicide. His retainers thus became *rōnin*. Biding their time under the eyes of the shogunal police, they lived dissolute lives in order to allay suspicion. Then, finally, they broke into the house of their lord's enemy, took his head, and thereafter, on order of the authorities, commited *seppuku*. Even today their graves, in a quiet temple courtyard in Tokyo, are visited by tourists.

4

Kindaika: Modernization

In the postwar Japan of 1968, members of conservative groups, which dominated Japanese politics, were preparing to celebrate 100 years of modern society and a century of cultural exchange with the West. Those who opposed the conservative majority tried to ignore the anniversary. Not entirely successfully, they denounced the appearance of "absolutism" in the Meiji Japan of a century before and decried the "inevitable results": militarism, fascism, aggression, imperialism, war, and a disastrous defeat.

For about a century many Japanese have been fascinated with the term "modernization" (*kindaika*) and intrigued by the process. Ordinary Japanese have used the term to cover a generalization. Scholars and critics have tried to sharpen the usage, implicitly to describe a complicated process and usually without complete success. Many Japanese and some foreign observers, too, have argued that the modernization process has been proceeding over the last *two* centuries. Other Japanese and other foreign observers have replied that, whatever has happened since the 1860s, the net result has *not* been a modern Japan. It must also be noted that whatever the process and the results, only a minority of the Japanese have taken a look at the various modern masks and then deliberately decided to lay them aside in favor of a purely traditional appearance.

In pursuit of the modern muse, thoughtful Japanese and informed outsiders have reflected upon the ancestry of nineteenth- and twentieth-century Japanese society. Post-1868 Japan, most have agreed, has been a descendant of Tokugawa feudalism. Many observers have also used the word *feudalism* to cover a generalization. Some have used the term in a pejorative sense. Others have tried to confine the usage to a neutral and comparative description of a complicated historical phenomenon.

THE TOKUGAWA PERIOD

The Tokugawa era that preceded the transition begun in 1868 has had, in the words of John Hall, a "bad press."[1] A second generation of foreigners in Japan (those who became the foreign employees of the new Meiji government) were particularly harsh in their denunciation of "isolated, feudal Japan" under the Tokugawa family. William Elliot Griffis, probably the most widely read of the old Japan hands, spoke of Tokugawa society as "a chamber of horrors." Men like Griffis simply could not wait until Japan became a Western, Christian outpost in Asia.

In their first forays into comparative history, some Japanese scholars used the newly coined term for feudalism (*hōken*) in an objective, historical context, rather than in a pejorative sense. They followed in the footsteps of European historians like Frederic William Maitland. In the 1920s, other Japanese began to adopt a Marxist definition of the term and thereby revealed a growing ambivalence. On the one hand, they regarded feudalism as a stage in development on the way to a bourgeois, modern age. For them, feudalism in Japan had been a welcome—even an inevitable—development in the evolution dictated by the laws of history. On the other hand, they denounced the persistence of "feudal characteristics" in what should have been a middle-class Meiji revolution. Marxist coloration has been found in much twentieth-century Japanese thinking (including non-Marxist analysis) and accounts for the generally negative view in which feudalism has been held.

In contemporary Japan, popular attitudes toward Tokugawa feudalism have also been somewhat ambivalent. The average Japanese, voracious reader and avid television viewer, has displayed a distinct nostalgia for the swashbuckling samurai, the resourceful merchants, and the attendant ladies of the Edo era vividly pictured in best-seller historical novels and in TV daytime drama. This is in part a yearning for times past, similar to the American fascination with a frontier long closed. There is a vague feeling that Japan is not what it was. And in Japan, as in the United States, the cynic responds that the old imagined society never resembled the re-creation of it.

Serious scholarship, in which both Japanese and foreign observers have engaged, has produced a sharp division of attitude toward pre-nineteenth century feudal Japan. Nor is the debate strictly of academic interest, for the assumptions have profoundly affected contemporary policy considerations. Without plunging into the controversy in detail, one can usefully note what the various views have in common.

Preconditions

In most of the descriptions of the transition from Tokugawa to Meiji Japan, it has been assumed that a traditional system, which was fully developed during the Edo era, served to color the society in the later period. These traditional norms were analyzed in Chapter 2 and may be summarized here. Values were achieved and reinforced in family-style groups, within a patriarchal hierarchical structure. Individuals received blessings and, in return, assumed social obligations. There were no universal norms; rather there was a situational ethic. For some observers, such values made up feudal residues that blocked any hope for a truly modern society; for others, they provided the firm foundation for modern society, Japanese-style.

Feudal Residues. In the first view, Tokugawa feudalism provided the background out of which Meiji and the later Japan emerged. Feudal society had been dominated by a narrow privileged ruling class, with an oppressed peasantry living on the threshold of starvation. Famine had been endemic. In place of political movements had been intrigues, plots, treachery, assassinations, and arbitrary justice. Moreover, under Tokugawa hegemony, particularly in the late stages marked by contradictions, feudalism had lived on beyond its natural life and left "hideous wounds upon the minds and spirits of both rulers and ruled."[2]

Much of the Japanese writing on this theme (as well as

some foreign scholarship that picked it up and translated it abroad) attempted to explain a paradox. True, Tokugawa contradictions had indeed led to the overthrow of the feudal regime. The result was *not*, however, a full-fledged bourgeois revolt. Instead, according to this line of thought, the long-suffering Japanese had been burdened with Meiji militarist absolutism. And thus the laws of history must have been amended in the Japanese case. The feudal residues guaranteed an abortive modernization and eventual disaster. This interpretation of history appeared most prominently in the 1930s and 1940s in a vain rearguard action against the steady advance of militarism in Japan.[3] After a respite, an echo of the same interpretation reappeared in postwar Japan. The feudal residues have been further reinforced, the argument has continued, by the alliance between Japan and the U.S. military-industrial complex. Thus, the inevitable revolution into modernity has been postponed.

The Revisionist View. In the other view, Tokugawa feudalism also provided the background from which modern Japan emerged. Those who have expressed the revisionist view of history, however, have attributed to the Edo era an entirely different set of qualities. Less committed to a specific evolutionary theory, they have argued that traditional norms and practices were not necessarily displaced by modern institutions. Indeed, the Japanese case has dramatically illustrated the capacity for the two to coexist. The Japanese scholars and the foreign observers who have expressed this revisionist view have arbitrarily been dubbed the modernizationists.[4]

In modernization theory, traditional Japanese emphases on group loyalty, group coherence, group decisionmaking by consensus, and obligations to the group (as compared with an emphasis on individual rights) made possible the smooth and swift transition from Tokugawa to Meiji Japan. Thus, the Edo era had been more accurately a postfeudal or a national feudal society.

John Hall, Marius Jansen, and other Western scholars have tried to refute the dogma that held that the Tokugawa system constituted a "refeudalization" in order to rebut the view that Japan in the Edo era "stagnated in isolation." Empirical evidence amassed by postwar Japanese researchers and by outsiders has shown that the country, although it was indeed relatively isolated, experienced a considerable amount of growth. Chapter 2 summarized conclusions drawn from such empirical findings.

In brief recapitulation, under the Tokugawa system truly feudal forms came to be replaced by a highly developed (if, until Meiji, classbound) bureaucracy staffed by samurai. While lip service was paid to the principle that administration remained in the hands of a military (feudal) elite, the samurai increasingly underwent a significant transformation into a civil bureaucracy.

Thus the delicate check-and-balance system built up by the Tokugawa marched straight into modern Meiji Japan. A new central government in the hands of an oligarchy of former samurai displaced the feudal military headquarters (*bakufu*). Modern prefectures replaced the old domains. Members of a new civil service stepped into the slots that had been assigned to feudal bureaucrats. Thus by the mid-nineteenth century, during the Edo era, the prototype of the modern Meiji government of the late nineteenth century had already been established.

The modernizationists have admitted that Tokugawa authorities preserved a feudal outlook, almost to the very end. They have insisted, however, that Edo society at large developed well beyond the boundaries of a feudal system. The castle towns laid down the foundations for Japan's modern urban structure. There was rapid economic growth (without foreign trade) in a commercial society. Literacy levels were very high.

Tokugawa thinkers even contributed to a theory of social organicism. The shōgun-to-daimyō relationship was one of the whole to the parts. Administrators stood at the top not for the sake of personal or family interests, but for the benefit of the country. One may doubt the true motivation, of course, but at least the rationale for power seemed almost modern. Policy was made in the name of the national interest and for public welfare. Despite the continuing formal division into domains, an inchoate sense of nationalism never entirely disappeared. Respect for the Imperial tradition was sustained so that Japan had, in the late nineteenth century, a clear alternative form of rule. After the Meiji Restoration, Confucianism provided the matrix of loyalty to the Emperor and to the state.

In these various ways, according to the modernizationists, Tokugawa Japan was in fact a protomodern society. Feudal values, although they were definitely not the product of cultural contact with Europe, made it possible for Japan to accommodate to the West and allowed the nation to begin the process of modernization quickly. This thesis has been described as a grand design drawn by Edwin O. Reischauer, the father-figure of the modernizationists; it has also been denounced as the "Reischauer line."

It should be noted that both the modernizationists and their critics recognize the existence of a link between the Tokugawa period and what followed. From one vantage, feudalism of the Edo era was a dynamic hinge on the door opening to modernity. From the other, Japan's was an abortive modernization that never escaped the effects of feudalism.

Both views imply that the second coming of the West (most dramatically symbolized by Commodore Matthew C. Perry's black ships) was the important occasion for, but not the basic cause of, the transition. The Western impact was a catalyst that precipitated modern elements out of a traditional solution. As a catalyst it was historically significant.

Impact of the West

Many Westerners came to be interested in the maturation of Japan in the nineteenth century. They became intrigued by things Japanese displayed in the world's fairs. They also read descriptions of exotic Japan written by the early foreign employees, the "Japan helpers." Meanwhile, Japanese came to be fascinated by outsiders' views of Japan. As a result, the role of the West has been exaggerated (by Westerners and on occasion by Japanese) to such an extent that often nineteenth-century change was discussed in terms of the "Westernization" of Japan. Fortunately, this culture-bound term has been cast out of the literature, giving way to the more neutral "impact of the West."

Having abandoned Westernization as an inaccurate description, however, one encounters different kinds of difficulties with its replacement. It, too, is a generalization. But the critical questions are: Impact on whom and under what circumstances? Does the impact consist of certain people, of specific goods, and of identifiable ideas? Again, it must be recognized that many Japanese thought that what they were engaged in was something like the Westernization of Japan.

In any case, goods, people, and ideas reaching Japan in the 1850s and 1860s were not the first to come from the West. The Japanese had experienced what has been called the "Christian century" (1549–1638) before Tokugawa seclusion. After the Franciscans and Jesuits were expelled or crucified, Dutch traders remained in Nagasaki. Dutch studies subtly influenced Tokugawa thought. After Perry but before the flood of foreign influence, Dutch missions advised the Japanese on naval affairs (in 1854–59). The British came to Nagasaki in 1858. The French, however, did the most for the fading shogunate. They established the Yokosuka naval complex in 1865.

Although it has been the convention to say that the United States opened Japan, between 1853 and 1868 U.S. advisers were few. Samuel R. Brown and Dr. J. C. Hepburn in Yokohama and Guido Verbeck in Nagasaki were missionary educators. Since the teaching of Christianity was still banned, they worked as teachers of English and as students of Japanese. Then there was William Elliot Griffis of Rutgers College, who made the long foray to Japan while the Tokugawa still administered the country. He observed and described the collapse of the feudal domain in Fukui and the establishment of the new prefecture. He also taught science in Tokyo at an institution that later became Tokyo Imperial University. Griffis's most important role, however, was to be the unofficial historian of the early foreign employees.

THE MEIJI MODERNIZERS

When the Tokugawa banners were folded away and the flag of the new regime unfurled, as usual it was in the name of the Emperor that the transition was effected. In theory it was a restoration of power to the Meiji Emperor and, therefore, it has been called the Meiji Restoration. In practice, the drama was stage-managed by remarkably young samurai from the outer domains, men who formed an oligarchy. Japanese scholars have drawn a distinction between the early stages (1868–69) of *restoration* and the later (1870–90) of *renovation*. In the latter period, the fad for foreign goods, the prominent role played by foreign advisers, and the wide currency of translated foreign ideas were important enough to lead observers (including Japanese) to conclude that the country was indeed undergoing Westernization.

More Western Impact

After the restoration, the new government followed in the footsteps of the shogunate in seeking knowledge throughout the world. The search was now enshrined in policy, however, in a famous Imperial promise, usually referred to as the Charter Oath (April 1868). Specifically, the fourth and fifth articles pledged a breaking off of "evil customs of the past" and a search for knowledge "to strengthen the national polity."

If the outcome did not constitute the Westernization of Japan, the Meiji experiment certainly did represent one of the first instances of development with foreign aid. The least desirable form such aid could take as far as the modernizers were concerned was the borrowing of capital from abroad. However, the Meiji leaders did, like their predecessors (the Tokugawa authorities), advocate collecting information through translation (technical assistance, so to speak, through books), but there were obvious limitations in this method. They also sent young Japanese overseas to study and to become, as Robert Schwantes phrased it, nineteenth-century "counterparts." Trained Japanese were intended to replace, and soon did supplant, employed foreigners and alien advisers.

In all of these processes of absorption of foreign techniques, the Japanese made all the critical decisions. They adapted the Western models of development to their own needs. They mobilized domestic resources and paid most of the costs. Above all, as many of the prominent foreign employees soon discovered, the Meiji modernizers adhered firmly to the policy of *Japanese* control and management of the transition.

In an historical context, then, it is fair to say that in the nineteenth century Japan was no more a second-class Western state than it was a minor Chinese state between the seventh and ninth centuries, a Christian outpost as a result of missionary activity in the sixteenth century, or an American society in the late 1940s.

Nonetheless, Japanese have not forgotten the contributions of the foreign employees. They have been impressed by the statistics compiled by Hazel Jones, who estimates that the advisers provided the Meiji government with more than 9,500 man-years of service. The peak years of foreign advice were 1877 and 1888. After the 1890s the number of foreign employees declined sharply as the Japanese took firm control of further growth.

The Modern Society

The various steps taken by the modernizers, aided by foreign advisers, may be quickly reviewed. In 1868 the new regime maneuvered the former feudal lords into returning their land registers to the Emperor. In many cases the daimyō became the Emperor's new governors in 1871 when the modern prefectures were carved out of the former domains. In 1872 came the fundamental law of education (followed in 1890 by the more formal Imperial Rescript on Education). Thereafter each son and daughter was socialized into becoming a subject of the Emperor. In 1873 the Imperial Rescript on Conscription gave each male, whether of samurai descent or not, the privilege of laying down his life for the modern state. Also in 1873 each person gained the modern privilege of being taxed directly by the central government.

Meanwhile, the central administration was streamlined, on the surface modeled after European-style cabinets, court complexes, and civil and criminal legal systems. In fact, all the institutions were firmly in the hands of an oligarchy, which, in typical Japanese fashion, eventually made up a body of elder statesmen (*genrō*). The capstone was the promulgation, after meticulous preparation (and little discussion), of a new constitution in 1889.

In the economic realm, banks were established, railways built, lighthouses erected, and port facilities improved. Government-sponsored strategic industries were nurtured and privately financed small-scale businesses encouraged. The Japanese began (and continue to perform, with one major interruption in the 1940s) the modern miracle.

Meiji Japan thus provided the historical data on which to speculate about the whole process of development, although it was not until later that systematic analysis was labeled "modernization" in a technical sense. Most often outsiders, familiar with the Western model, referred to Japan's emergence as "late development." Now, a century later, it has become apparent that the Japanese transition occurred quite early in the game, as compared with presently developing areas in Southeast Asia, Africa, Latin America, and the Middle East. Whether Japan's success at modernization provides a model for other societies is a moot issue. Conditions in today's world and in developing nations are quite different from those in the nineteenth century and in Japan. Nonetheless, the Japan experience has contributed to modernization theory.

Viewed historically, Meiji Japan faced what has been called a crisis of security in the form of perceived pressure from the Western powers. Nonetheless, the new regime enjoyed sufficient stability to withstand external and internal threats and to allow for planning and action. A strong sense of nationalism was widely shared, even during the Tokugawa period, at least by members of the ruling elite. The capacity of traditional attitudes to coexist with, and contribute to, modern institutions has been noted. The best illustration was the use made, for better or worse, of the venerable Imperial tradition.

Restoration and the subsequent renovation were rationalized in the name of the Emperor. This was not an instance of "divine right" in the European sense. Rather, to borrow the felicitous phrase of a constitution drafted much later on, it was a matter of the Emperor serving as the symbol of the state and of the unity of the people.

Politics. The politics of Meiji Japan, like the politics of any modern society, witnessed the enormous expansion of the sphere of governmental action. Individual Japanese became involved, some for the very first time, in the political process, just as human beings in modern societies elsewhere became subjects, citizens, comrades, or cadres. Heretofore many Japanese had been socialized in relatively self-sufficient, extralegal agrarian villages. Many had been touched only indirectly by government. Most Japanese had been members of the great mass of East Asian peasants (like the Chinese, who were to be described by Sun Yat-sen several generations after the Meiji transition as "a loose sheet of sand").

The modern state is marked by a high degree of integration, and politics tends to become what the social scientists call a "system." The system usually leads to the egalitarian involvement of the masses. They in turn may be administered under the iron law of oligarchy, or they may move toward participatory democracy. The case of Meiji Japan offers a strong argument to the effect that if swift and efficient modernization is desired, then firm direction should be provided by an oligarchy. During at least the first decades of the transition, the Meiji modernizers were not interrupted in their tasks by rapidly rising expectations on the part of the disciplined and obedient Japanese.

Edwin Reischauer has cited the fact that the men of Meiji set a course under which Japan would, in a generation or two, alter its society from one in which position was primarily determined by heredity to one in which status depended largely on the education and achievements of the individual. Again, tradition and modernity were mixed: the result was not a society in which all were to be considered equal, but a meritocracy in which sophisticated screening processes were used to select the elite.

Other features of the Meiji system have contributed to our understanding of the modern state. Government evolved a system of allocating and terminating roles of political leadership that on balance took into account achievement rather than ascriptive status. Thus emerged the celebrated Japanese civil service. Recruitment for this service was (and remains) largely the function of the great public institutions of higher education, most particularly Tokyo Imperial University (now the University of Tokyo). Max Weber would have quickly identified in the civil service a certain functional differentiation that reflected the growing division of labor and specificity of roles in a modern society. Henceforth public administration was marked by an increasingly secular, impersonal, and—it was claimed in

Japan as elsewhere—rational system of decisionmaking.

Psychology. The psychology of modern man is marked by a difference in attitude. In contrast to his ancestor, who was born, grew up, and died without ever expecting to see anything but a traditional society, leaders of the modern state (and gradually most individuals, too) come to regard change as desirable, necessary, and even inevitable. This has something to do with the scientific revolution. Doubtless man's increasing control over the forces of nature prepares him for the systematic, purposeful application of his energies to a more rational control of his social environment.

Changes in the thrust of Japanese slogans clearly illustrate the shifts in attitude on the part of transition leaders. Faced with the sea-coming aliens, spokesmen first called for "reverence to the Emperor, expulsion of the barbarians." Instrumental politics then articulated "unity of the military and the Court." The planners moved on to specific steps "to strengthen the army, to enrich the country." Human goals, even ideals, were expressed in "civilization and enlightenment" (*bummei kaika*).

Even in the late Tokugawa era, certainly by the Meiji period, horizons were steadily expanded. Eyes lifted from the tiny villages to the already established towns, from the towns to the industrial cities, and from the port cities to the world. Men (more quickly than women) acquired geographic and psychic mobility.

Economy. The economy of the modern society moves toward diversification. The term is more precise than "industrialization" because, particularly with those called "late developers," the economy leapfrogs through the familiar industrial revolution into more advanced stages of technology. First agriculture and then industrial know-how provide the surplus for further development; diversification guarantees a sustained increase per capita in gross national product (GNP). Everyman *thinks* he is better off.

Although the Meiji modernizers were often impatient with what they regarded as slow economic progress, between 1885 and the end of the century the GNP doubled; the rate of increase rose from 1.2 percent per annum in 1885 to 4.1 percent in 1898; per capita GNP increased from about 65 yen in 1885 to 115 yen in 1898.[5]

Society. A society that is called modern tends to be much more complex than its traditional forebear. Borrowing the metaphor of nineteenth-century natural science, it has moved from a simple single-cell organism through differentiation into a complex multicell organism. Beyond the figure of speech are some interesting historical issues.

Most descriptions of the modern condition include the degree of urbanization as a measure of cultural change. In contrast, most members of relatively nonmodernized societies (for instance, in traditional East Asia dominated by rice culture) live in a rural rather than an urban environment. It is natural, then, to think of the two ways of life as occupying opposite ends of the spectrum. A society is either traditional or modern, which is to say that it is rural or urban.

In the case of Japan, the statement is generally true, especially if one remembers that the majority of the population still lived in the villages during the Edo era. And yet, as has been observed, many of the traditional values of premodern Japan were formulated by the minority of Japanese who lived in the lively cities. The problem has been partially solved by using the worldwide framework designed by Gideon Sjoberg, who has identified the preindustrial city. Well after the Meiji period, Japanese urban settlements reached beyond the industrial function (see Chapter 7). If the city has indeed been the mode of modern man, then it cannot be identified simply with industry.

There has also been a question as to whether the urban settlement constitutes the cause of change, the effect, or both. In the late Tokugawa and early Meiji transition, the artificial treaty port may have caused at least a temporary Westernization of surrounding Japanese life. After the Meiji Restoration and during the renovation stage, directed political reform resulted in a grand expansion of a new bureaucratic system whereby city-based administrative organs were integrative agencies working on the entire nation. This is why Ernest Weismann, in his United Nations study of the Japanese city, reported that modernization was effected under the leadership of government. The reasons for the appearance of the modern city in Japan were therefore quite different from those that accounted for the rise of Western urban settlements.[6] The situation was not unique: literature on the development of cities in other parts of the world has illustrated the critical role of the political apparatus as the key independent variable.

Finally, urbanization, the growth of a commercial society, and the political style of the Meiji modernization have all illustrated a difficulty in generalizing from experience in Western Europe or in the United States. It has since become quite clear that in Japan the government usually made the critical choices and played the leading role in entrepreneurship. As one Japanese observer put it, the "political businessmen" were "samurai-in-spirit" and "merchants-in-talent." This is why some Japanese historians have searched in vain in the Meiji period for middle-class entrepreneurs whom they would expect to lead Japan out of feudalism into a society managed by the bourgeoisie.

In the Japanese transition, the oligarchy made political choices. Of course, their decisions were affected, but not determined, by economic factors. The process of making decisions illustrated the autonomy of choice, the very core of policy-making in a modern society.

THE DILEMMAS OF GROWTH

In the above analysis, one may immediately detect several problems in the use of the term *modernization*. Inevitably, the concept implies a built-in bias related to time. Primitive and traditional societies are often viewed as "backward." The modern society is usually regarded as looking "forward." Modernization is not only change; it appears to constitute progress. The appearance is what Charles Frankel has referred to as "changes in the concept of social time."

Although most Japanese have thought that by modernizing they were progressing, in fact it is impossible to find an empirical link between the two processes. As the economist points out with statistical evidence, it is true that in modern times the GNP per capita in Japan has increased. Moreover, Japanese have come to boast of a longevity equal to that of citizens of the most developed nations. It is also true, however, that contemporary Japanese (like their American brethren) have discovered that satisfaction of material wants and a long life only bring them to the more subtle problem of affluence. Japanese live longer perhaps only to survive in "the lonely crowd." Modernization made possible electric lights and streetcars on the Ginza. But it brought Zero aircraft and bombs to Pearl Harbor and B29s over Japan itself. In any objective evaluation, modernization holds both promise and peril.

Taishō Transition

Meiji was an imperial era name (*nengō*)[7] for the period beginning in 1868. By allusion to Chinese classics Meiji meant "enlightened government." It also was the posthumous name for the Emperor who died in 1912. His successor was known as the Taishō Emperor. This classical term referred to "great rectification, adjustment."

This contrast is not meant to imply that the year 1912 marked a clean break between the Meiji (1868–1912) and the Taishō (1912–25) eras. Nonetheless, the periodization does provide an interesting milestone. In his masterpiece, *Kokoro* (The heart, 1914), the novelist Natsume Sōseki brings his main character to suicide on hearing of the death of Emperor Meiji and of the sympathetic suicides of the national hero, General Nogi, and his wife. In fiction at least, it was the end of an era.

Change from the steady diet of faith in progress had, of course, begun even in the late Meiji period. Culture, heretofore identified solely with the nation-family and the state, came to have a life of its own. Industrialization had continued apace, with concomitant shifts in class lines. By 1907 universal education (for six years) was achieved; higher education (mostly for males) expanded rapidly. New, white-collar, middle-class Japanese came to resemble those found in urban Western countries. They stood between the elite leaders of the Meiji period and the mass citizenry of Taishō. Intellectuals, spawned by the new middle class, in turn began to express doubts about consumerism, mass culture, and the new secularism. Contemporary literature clearly revealed a tension between new values and the older statist claims of Imperial Japan. The historian Harry D. Harootunian has hinted that Taishō may have marked the height of individualism as we know it in the West. Writers of the time denounced "individualistic dissipation," "preoccupation with carnal desire," and "the general celebration of luxury."[8]

Nor did political institutions move precisely along the path laid out by the Meiji modernizers. In 1890 they had established, in response to forces released from the pandora's box, a bicameral Diet (legislature). A lower House of Representatives was to be elected by male voters who were upper-level taxpayers (less than 1 percent of the population). An upper House of Peers (modeled on England's House of Lords) represented a select peerage. Despite these restrictions, this Japanese legislature turned out to be the first successful parliamentary experiment outside the West.

During the first decade of the government's experience with the Diet, control of even limited representative government proved far more difficult than had been anticipated. The legislature vigorously opposed the founding fathers until the latter adopted an officially backed party system of their own. In the decade after the turn of the century, the old oligarchs retired in favor of their bureaucratic followers. Until 1912–13, protégés of the elder statesmen alternated in holding the position of prime minister. By 1918, in response to press and public pressure for "normal constitutional government," the bureaucrats had retreated before cabinets dominated by political parties.

Meanwhile, the number of voters was steadily expanding as tax requirements were lowered in 1900 and again in 1919. By 1920, the original limited electorate (1890: 450,872) had grown sevenfold (1924: 3,288,368). Finally, in 1925 the vote was given to all adult males, and by the next election the electorate had quadrupled (1928: 12,405,056). Cabinets were being chosen from one of two parties with similar ideological stances. Indeed, Japan between Taishō and the early Shōwa period (1926–present) seemed to combine modernization and democracy. This span of time has been referred to as Taishō democracy.

Critics and Crisis

Beneath the giddy changes that produced a jazz age in Tokyo—the appearance of outspoken modern boys (*mobo*), flappers (*moga*) with Clara Bow haircuts, and a wave of liberal, even radical, ideas—there were intractable problems. Diet control over cabinets was only a superficial convenience, for men like the last *genrō*, Saionji Kimmochi, exercised the Imperial prerogative by screening the leadership of Japan. A gap between traditional-rural and modern-urban sectors of society was matched by a dual structure in the economy. There was a difference in productivity as well as in wages between new industry with advanced technology and what Freda Utley called "Japan's feet of clay" in agriculture. Growth, encouraged in Japan by the absence of competition on the part of European powers (who were engaged in World War I), gave way to stagnation, which was born of resumed competition and matured in deep depression.

Soon the force of tradition, so useful in the early modernization process, was channeled into reaction. Purists began to link behavior in the Diet, corruption in the corporations, the selfishness of individualism, and a liberal lifestyle. Often these were blamed on Western influence. Such trends were reflected in the culture of "Taishō adjustment."

In the literature of late Meiji and early Taishō, some poetry flirted very tentatively with Western form, but most of it continued to be written in classical Japanese. Perhaps understandably, the theater never really broke with colorful Kabuki in favor of the introspective dialogues of Western drama. Modern literature, to the majority of the Japanese, has meant the novel or short story. And in subtle style Japanese writers have served as the social critics—the skeptical observers of modernization and its effects.

At first, however, novelists embraced modernity and even imitated Western style. The primary effect was seen in the abandonment of classical Japanese and the adoption of colloquial language. Soon Japanese writers found their own idioms for new views. For example, *Ukigumo* (The drifting cloud, 1889)[9] by Futabatei Shimei was probably Japan's first modern novel (according to Donald Keene), because it adopted everyday language and depicted the dilemma of a young man, a product of strict samurai training, facing the values of a new and strange society.

Many of the modern Japanese novelists gradually unfolded a pattern of development. The first step was to experience strong influence from the West. The second was to borrow writing methods from abroad and use them in novels. The third was to turn their backs on Western influence, to peer back into traditional sources, and to develop individual Japanese styles. Three examples have been offered by Donald Keene.[10]

Mori Ōgai (1862–1922) studied medicine in Germany in the late 1880s, and his early stories carry a romantic German tenor. After his return home, his writing began to picture life in Meiji Japan.[11] He, too, was apparently deeply moved by the Emperor Meiji's death and the Nogi suicides and in his later writing confined himself to true tales about samurai.

Although his novels are quite different, the experiences of Natsume Sōseki (1867–1916) were similar to those of Mori. His early writing clearly reveals the influence of his residence in England in the early 1900s. Later back home, he became obsessed with the disastrous effects of individualism (what he called "egoism"). His best-known work (already cited) is *Kokoro,*[12] in which a man is tortured by the memory of his betrayal of a friend.

The third representative writer is one who lived through the late Meiji and early Taishō periods and the war and on into another period of puzzling change after defeat. Tanizaki Junichirō (1886–1965) early on also moved from unashamed admiration for the West to a position of doubt. In his novel *Tade kuu mushi* (Some prefer nettles, 1928),[13] he skillfully spun certain contrasts between backgrounds and, with psychological insight, wove conflicts among the main characters. Thus Tokyo is a city of horns and headlights, movies and modern youth, beauty parlors and hot baths. Ōsaka, with its *bunraku* puppet theater, represents Japan's past. In this tale the young mistress of the hero's father-in-law, a doll-like, dream-like figure, represents tradition; the Eurasian prostitute, a lingering interest in the West; the hero's stylish young wife, the inevitably modern. The latter's father sums it all up in a phrase: "Misako's education has been half old and half new, and all this modernness of hers is a pretty thin veneer."

Japanese art, as might be expected, responded to the epochal changes in a bewildering variety of ways. In the late sixteenth century, artists working in a genre painting style produced outlandish scenes, screens showing the arrival of alien ships, and portraits of tall foreigners with huge noses. This was called "southern barbarian" (*namban*) art (which has since achieved museum quality rarity). There was some Western influence on the Edo woodblock prints. Although the quality of the so-called Yokohama prints declined during the early Meiji era, their subjects have proved to be of great historic interest. They picture the European style of the Yokohama treaty port, the Napoleonic costumes of the first Diet, and the artifacts of the modern technology, such as the telegraph pole, the railroad, and Victorian-era architecture. The majority of artists, however, continued to work in Japanese style. Meanwhile an American, Ernest Fenellosa, and his disciple, Okakura Kazukō, were responsible for impressing on Japanese consciousness the greatness of the Japanese artistic tradition.

In some areas, for example in architecture, modernization did equal Westernization. The Ginza area, today Tokyo's most famous shopping district, was developed artificially and quite consciously to be a Western showplace for Japan. The marvelous old red brick structures (of which only one or two survive) represented one of the deliberate attempts to convince the Western powers of Japan's emergence as a modern state and of the need to relinquish the unequal treaties inherited by the Meiji regime. Similarly, in public sculpture Western-trained artists erected imposing statues of the cultural heroes of the Meiji transformation.

Meanwhile, in a strange shift caused by cultural contact, Japanese decorative arts became extremely popular in the West, and native pieces were eagerly collected by foreigners. In the provinces at least, fine folk art continued to express Japan's traditions through the Meiji period. By the early Shōwa era, Japanese artists (particularly those working in woodblock style) were beginning to adapt Western techniques to their needs. Their creations were traditional and ultramodern at the same time.

Japanese Pottery: The late master potter Hamada Shōji.

MILITARISM AND MODERNIZATION

Until 1945 Japan could be accurately described as another of those thoroughly modern nations in which military considerations gradually served as dynamic shapers of policy and even culture, rather than instruments in the hands of civilian policymakers concerned with defense. To some, as has been noted, this was an inheritance from feudalism. To others, the phenomenon was a much more complicated aspect of the modern condition.

Origins

Some of the elements of Tokugawa feudalism (for example, the samurai dominance of early Meiji government) inherited by Japanese in the modern era did encourage militarism. The Japanese quickly moved toward mass conscription, however, and a conscript army certainly cannot be described as feudal. It was more in tune with modern mobilization for war.

One of the factors that permitted the rise of militarism in Japan was a fatal flaw in the modern Meiji Constitution, which allowed army and navy leaders direct access to the Imperial symbol. In addition to this provision was the practice of appointing only officers on active duty to the cabinet as service ministers (men who were therefore under armed forces orders). The privileged position of the military, however, did not forestall the rise of Taishō democracy or, for a time at least, civilian control of the military. Nonetheless, social critics like Katō Shūichi have argued that there was a connection linking rapid Meiji modernization, Taishō liberalism (with very shallow roots), and aggressive Shōwa militarism.

At first Japan's wars in the modern period were fought in remote areas, with only a modicum of discomfort at home. Japan's domestic reforms and successful war against China (1894–95) led England, as well as the other powers, to relinquish extraterritorial rights in 1899. Victory over Russia (1904–05) set Japan on the then modern road of empire, to the control of Taiwan adding the acquisition of southern Manchuria, the lower half of Sakhalin, and, eventually, Korea. After World War I, Japan joined the Allied victors and in the process sought concessions from China, seized German concessions in Shantung, and took control of former German islands in the Pacific. The latter were colonies thinly disguised as mandates. No wonder that many Japanese came to believe that war solved internal problems and paid direct dividends.

In the late 1920s and in the 1930s, the Imperial army clearly revealed the commingling of traditional and modern forces and, at the same time, the torque of change. On the one hand, the army was the legitimate heir to the samurai code; its officers and sergeants were highly paternalistic to the conscripts. On the other hand, leadership was increasingly drawn from the underprivileged peasant classes (not from samurai families); ordinary soldiers, too, came from the countryside. Japan provides one more illustration of the historical role of the armed forces—often among the most important agencies for modernization and among the most significant groups for socialization. As Lucian Pye has suggested, the soldier has been to some extent a modernized man.

Young military officers were among the most strident critics of Taishō democracy, of what they considered corrupting influences at home, and of what they regarded as Western ideas. One of their solutions was to propose a "Shōwa restoration" of power to the Emperor, whom they would then manipulate for their own purposes. The young militarists of the early Shōwa period were not altogether reactionary, however; they were often puzzlingly radical and even revolutionary. Drawn from depressed rural areas and returned as veterans to poverty-stricken villages, peasant conscripts of the Imperial army in the 1930s and early 1940s stood against landlords, against capitalists and their "bourgeois" political parties, and against Communists.

Mobilization: Successes and Failures

After 1937 Japan was in almost uninterrupted conflict for almost eight years. Before and during the great Pacific conflict, every single Japanese was to feel the effects of modern war.

The chief differences of opinion within Japan among civilian politicians, financial leaders, generals, admirals, and Imperial advisers were over the issue of how far Japan should become involved on the Asian mainland. There was no disagreement over the assumption that Japan was destined to become the leader of East Asia. Differences were related to methods, not basic aims.

China's unification and growing resistance to Japan's assumed role of policemen dedicated to the extermination of Communism in Asia appeared to many Japanese to be aided by the Western powers, which had special privileges in conflict with those of Japan. It was claimed that Japan's very survival was being threatened by encirclement on the part of the United States, Great Britain, and the Soviet Union.

Various shifts in government, from the first Konoye cabinet (1937) to the selection of General Tōjō (1941), were indicative of the struggle over methods, not over basic aims, between extremists and moderates. Army extremists became convinced that direct action was necessary to solve "the China problem," regardless of consequences. Moderates, who were drawn from the Imperial navy, the diplomatic corps, and business circles, hoped that Japan's objectives in East Asia could be achieved without friction with the Western powers. By June 1941, naval circles, alarmed over oil shortages and a U.S. embargo, joined those in favor of direct action and advocated moving into Southeast Asia even at the risk of war. As Japan's aims became more clearly identified with those of the Axis powers, moderates retreated and acquiesced to the plans of those who advocated forceful action. Although the Japanese did not make a single identifiable decision to go to war, they narrowed the options to such an extent that all policy issues had to be settled in a military manner.

Perhaps the closest historical parallel (although there are marked differences) was the (at first almost unconscious) involvement of the United States in Vietnam in the 1960s. Somehow the need to police Southeast Asia came to be perceived as a U.S. "national interest" (just as the new order in East Asia had been the "Imperial will" for Japan in the 1940s). Slowly and inexorably, all other options were eroded so that Americans came to handle all policy matters in Vietnam in military fashion (just as Japanese had allowed militarism to rise in the 1940s). After 1965 Japanese were quick to point out that Americans were repeating some of the earlier Japanese mistakes (including a bankrupt military campaign on the continent of Asia).

To return to the case of Japan in the 1940s, the plunge into world war held a paradox. Various Japanese leaders did develop plans for industrial mobilization and even a blueprint for a monolithic state dedicated to total war. Sketches included designs for the grandiose Imperial Rule Assistance Association, which was to become a transcendent national party. The old political parties were subjected to "voluntary dissolution," but the association was never a success. In similar fashion, plans were drawn for a new authoritarian political structure (the *shintaisei*). Characteristic Japanese indirection in politics and diffusion of power in government, however, led to a surprising failure to mobilize completely and eventually contributed to defeat. There was no corporate state (as in Fascist Italy), no dictator with popular support (as in Nazi Germany), and, indeed, no formal change in the old Meiji political structure. The experience has cast doubt on the wisdom of applying to Japan's wartime society the modern term *fascism*, although Japanese opponents to the rise of the militarists freely used the word. Even in the postwar period, those who opposed what they saw as a revival of militarism applied the pejorative word *fascist* to their opponents.

Another interesting contradiction—thus far hidden in the multifold effects of modern militarism and the impact of war—was the experience of women, the largest social group in the country. Thomas H. R. Havens has informed us that during the war years the state continued to encourage male precedence, to sanctify motherhood, and to applaud supportive home-front activities by women's groups. Large numbers of unmarried women were mustered late in the disaster, but the government to the very end avoided fully mobilizing them in the war effort. Yet modern war further eroded the patriarchal ideology in a manner difficult to describe.[14] Due attention has been paid to the Occupation reforms, which laid out a new path for Japanese women after the war. These and the modern miracle of further economic development, which so affected the entire family as a unit, have been emphasized (and will be summarized below). The modernizing effect of the war on women has thus far been neglected.

Certainly women of the postwar period took the lead in the pacifist, antimilitarist stance of the Japanese. They were joined by the surviving veterans of the war, youth, and intellectuals and reinforced by the writings of social critics and novelists. Ōoka Shōhei (born 1909), for example, produced the most vivid denunciation of militarism and war in his *Nobi* (Fires on the plain, 1952).[15] Writing from a home for the mentally ill on the outskirts of Tokyo, the author's chief character, former Private Tamura, reflects on the horrors of the Philippine campaign. Then he adds:

> The reports in the newspapers, which reach me morning and evening even in this secluded spot, seem to be trying to force me into the thing that I want least of all, namely, another war. Wars may be advantageous to the small group of gentlemen who direct them, and I therefore leave these people aside; what baffles me is all the other men and women who now once again seem so anxious to be deluded by these gentlemen. Perhaps they will not understand until they have gone through experiences like those I had in the Philippine mountains; then their eyes will be opened.

Toward the end of the Pacific war and after the defeat of Japan, the Allied victors (led by the United States) explicitly proclaimed and implicitly revealed through Occupation policies that "irresponsible militarism," in the words of the Potsdam Proclamation, had misled the Japanese people, brought disaster to their nation, and delivered woe to the world. The defeated Japanese, then thoroughly disillusioned with the leadership of the early Shōwa era, agreed. Therein lies the origin of modern antimilitarist sentiment in Japan.

One irony in postwar demilitarization policy was the fact that distaste for German and Japanese military adventures had led Americans to make militarism a vital factor in U.S. life during World War II. After a brief respite, Americans plunged into the cold war, fought in Korea, and became involved in the disastrous Vietnam War. Viewed historically, militarism—rather like the phenomena of feudalism and modernization—defies generalization and requires precise definition.

NOTES

1. John Whitney Hall, "The New Look of Tokugawa History," in J. W. Hall and Marius B. Jansen, eds., *Studies in the Institutional History of Early Modern Japan* (Princeton: Princeton University Press, 1968), p. 55.

2. The words are chosen from the writing of an influential Canadian historian, E. Herbert Norman, in a previously unpublished manuscript,

"Feudal Background of Japanese Politics." The analysis in detail is to be found in Norman's seminal work, *Japan's Emergence as a Modern State; Political and Economic Problems of the Meiji Period* (New York: Institute of Pacific Relations, 1940). Pantheon Asian Library has reprinted this work in a paperback edition, which includes a long introduction by the editor, the unpublished essay, "Feudal Background" (1944), and other materials. See John W. Dower, ed., *Origins of the Modern Japanese State: Selected Writings of E. H. Norman* (New York: Pantheon Books, 1975). Some who have revived Norman have claimed that the modernizationists have deliberately suppressed Norman's pioneering work.

3. John Dower states that Norman, writing in the 1940s, tried to identify the feudal origins of, and to denounce, Japanese militarism. Dower, *Origins*, p. 86. Writing in the context of later scholarship, critics of Norman and opponents of the Norman revivalists have suspected that, for the revivalists, the Canadian's interpretations of feudalism served (in the 1960s) a contemporary social need; that is, they drew a parallel between Japanese militarism of the 1940s and U.S. policy in the 1960s, as illustrated in the Vietnam disaster.

4. The modernization literature related to Japan is remarkably rich. Witness the series of six volumes, *Studies in the Modernization of Japan*, published by the Conference on Modern Japan of the Association for Asian Studies: Marius B. Jansen, ed., *Changing Japanese Attitudes Toward Modernization* (1965); R. P. Dore, ed., *Aspects of Social Change in Modern Japan* (1968); Robert E. Ward, ed., *Political Development in Modern Japan* (1968); William W. Lockwood, ed., *The State and Economic Enterprise in Japan* (1965); Donald Shively, ed., *Tradition and Modernization in Japanese Culture* (1971); and James William Morley, ed., *Dilemmas of Growth in Prewar Japan* (1971) (all volumes, Princeton: Princeton University Press). Lest the reader think I am hiding behind scholarship, I am affiliated with the "modernization" school.

5. The yen figures are for internal comparison. They are figured roughly on 1934–36—that is, prewar—prices (¥ 1 = $0.33).

6. Kagaku Gijutsu-chō Shigenkyoku (Science and technology agency, resources bureau), *Kokuren ohosadan oboegaki* [Report on a U.N. mission] (Tokyo, 1963).

7. In June 1979 Diet legislation formally reinstituted the Imperial era name system. Opponents argued that the bill had turned the clock back, served to deify the Emperor, and violated the new constitution, which declared that sovereignty rests with the people. *Japan Times Weekly* (International Edition) 19, no. 24 (June 16, 1979).

8. H. D. Harootunian, "Introduction: A Sense of an Ending and the Problem of Taishō," in Bernard S. Silberman and H. D. Harootunian, eds.,

Japan in Crisis: Essays on Taishō Democracy (Princeton: Princeton University Press, 1974), especially p. 20. This volume should be read with the modernization series listed in n.4 above. Also see E. O. Reischauer, "What Went Wrong," in Morley, ed., *Dilemmas of Growth.*

9. *Ukigumo*, trans. by Marleigh G. Ryan as *Japan's First Modern Novel* (New York: Columbia University Press, 1967).

10. In this section I have leaned heavily on the succinct and witty survey prepared by my colleague and coauthor, Donald Keene, entitled "Literature," in Arthur E. Tiedemann, ed., *An Introduction to Japanese Civilization* (New York: Columbia University Press, 1974), vol. 12, pp. 376–421.

11. *Gan* [The wild geese, 1913], trans. by Kingo Ochiai and Sanford Goldstein (Tokyo: Tuttle, 1959).

12. *Kokoro*, trans. by Edwin McClellan (Chicago: Regnery, 1957).

13. *Tade kuu mushi*, trans. by Edward G. Seidensticker (New York: Knopf, 1955). The quotation later in this paragraph is from p. 189.

14. Thomas H. R. Havens, "Women and War in Japan, 1937–45," *American Historical Review* 80, no. 4 (October 1975):913–34.

15. *Nobi* [Fires on the plain], trans. by Ivan Morris (New York: Knopf, 1969; Penguin Books, 1969). Quotation is from the paperback edition, p. 232.

5

Postwar Politics

Since the mid-nineteenth century, change in Japan has involved choice. After the early 1930s, Japanese chose a path of development that led to militarism, aggression, war, and defeat. Japanese revisionist historians have since argued that Japan had little or no choice. Their country was forced out into the Western nation-state system ("opened" was the euphemism); Japan was steadily hemmed in by Western imperialism, so the nation responded in kind; in 1941 a metronome was set to ticking that forced the country into what sober Japanese hoped would be a limited war. The result was total disaster.

And yet, surprisingly, defeat, the downfall of militarism in Japan, and the nature and timing of the surrender also allowed choice. In other words, there were significant conditions in the so-called unconditional surrender. There was, to put it inelegantly, a shotgun wedding between the chief avenging victor and the vanquished, who had sinned. The result was a marriage that was to last for at least three decades, in sickness and in health, for better or for worse.

Once again some have argued that there was no choice in 1945; little or no choice during the Occupation (1945–52); and narrow choices, if any at all, in the majority peace treaty, the security arrangement with the United States, and Japanese foreign policy that followed the end of the alien administration.

Whether choice existed or not, the defeat, the manner in which Japan surrendered, the nature of the Occupation, and characteristics of the eventual peace arrangements set the tone for the immediate postwar politics in Japan. Modernizationists have fitted postwar developments, allowing for the militarist aberrations of the 1940s, into the century-long pattern of change. Critics have offered a rebuttal to the effect that feudal residues have remained in Japanese society and that a true revolution into modernity has once again been aborted as a result of decisionmaking at the top.

MORE MODERNIZATION

A great deal of the literature on Japan's defeat has held, with the remarkable vision available to hindsight, that the island nation lost because it entered a protracted struggle that it could not win. The fact remains that, for millions on either side, the conflict was in doubt until almost the very end. Furthermore, such ex post facto reasoning has tended to overlook the political occasion for surrender in favor of a somewhat futile attempt to weigh the causes of defeat.

The Politics of Surrender

It is understandable that Americans, with a growing guilt complex, would continue to emphasize the first atomic bombs as punctuation marks that closed the conflict. Use of the new and awesome weapon was only one among a number of factors, however, in the timing of the surrender. It was probably not the chief reason why underground peace movements in Tokyo were able eventually to maneuver toward the decision for peace.

First, appalling though the effects were, especially for the future of all mankind, the immediate psychological impact was remarkably localized to Hiroshima and Nagasaki. The bombs affected Japan's shaken leadership more than they did ordinary civilians, for it was only after the war that the cloud of secrecy enshrouding the bombings disappeared. This is not to say, of course, that the long-range political effects of the use of atomic weapons were insignificant. On Monday, August 6, 1979, some 30,000 persons attended the thirty-fourth anniversary memorial service held in Hiroshima for the more than 200,000 Japanese killed in the attack. Two representatives of victims' families struck the Bell of Peace, and speakers urged the government to take the lead in a movement to eliminate nuclear weapons.

In 1945, however, Japanese had given every indication that they could and would continue to resist. The will to defend Japan had continued after the equally devastating, if less efficient, fire raids on some ninety Japanese cities (with twenty more than half destroyed). Stubborn defenders in the living hell of Iwo and catastrophic casualties in the so-called iron typhoon of Okinawa demonstrated to invaders that Japanese would defend the main islands to the death, with bamboo spears if necessary.

Japan's leadership and the man in the street were much more deeply affected by Russia's entry into the Pacific war on August 8, 1945, just six days before the actual surrender. In this last-minute violation of a neutrality pact, the Soviet Union had signaled to Japanese what a joint occupation would be like. The Japanese were almost desperate to seek a formula by which they could surrender to the United States.

The key factors determining the occasion for surrender—short of total annihilation—involved political decisions on both sides. The bankrupt formula of unconditional surrender, cavalierly enunciated by Franklin D. Roosevelt at Casablanca (1942), had to be modified at Potsdam (1945). The Allied proclamation at Potsdam hinted at the conditions, so to speak, in unconditional surrender. In good negotiating style, the terms were deliberately left vague. Until that stage, the peace party in Japan had no leverage; die-hard militarists could incite the people to greater sacrifices because of unconditional surrender. Beyond that point, those who sought peace could use the oldest political symbol known to Japan. On August 15, 1945, the Emperor's voice, recorded for broadcast for the first time, read an Imperial rescript accepting the Potsdam Proclamation. Speaking for the Japanese people, Emperor Hirohito decided "to endure the unendurable." The political significance of all these developments, without trying to rank them in order, may be quickly summarized:

- Japan, like the other Axis powers, was militarily occupied, but the country was not divided into zones as was Germany.
- Japan was occupied in theory by the Allied powers,

but in fact was controlled by Americans.

- Japan was not placed under the direct military government of alien forces, as was Italy.
- Japan maintained a government intact and was soon administering the Occupation under, of course, strict supervision.[1]

The Occupation: Directed Change

Almost as soon as the Allied, overwhelmingly U.S., Occupation got under way, another significant political effect of the developments that led to surrender became apparent. Perhaps because they were Americans, the occupationnaires launched a program of what Robert Ward has called "planned political change."[2]

The Occupation was of historical significance, then, because it constituted more modernization. Like the tightly controlled experiment carried out in the nineteenth century by Meiji modernizers, the effort was applied from the top down on obedient and disciplined Japanese subjects. Like the leaders of Meiji, who were drawn from a military (samurai) class, the majority of the men of the Occupation were drawn from a military command, Allied soldiers who had fought their way out of Corregidor to Australia and thence across the southwest Pacific to the Philippines and eventually to Japan.

Unlike the Meiji modernizers, the directors of the Occupation were dedicated democrats. Although the elements need not be linked in an objective definition, to the occupationnaires modernization meant "democratization" (whatever the latter might have meant). Although militarism had often been part and parcel of modernization in Japan, at first the Americans found it impossible to visualize democracy without demilitarization of the Japanese. It was one of the small ironies of history that directed change, planned development, democratization, and demilitarization were implemented in occupied Japan by professional military men. Unlike the Meiji modernizers, the Taishō democrats, and the early Shōwa militarists, the U.S. occupationnaires were, of course, aliens.

The men attached to the Supreme Commander for the

Allied Powers (SCAP) liked to refer to the process of change as "induced revolution." This process was monitored (sometimes criticized as going too far, at other times encouraged to go further) by means of belated Allied policy guidance drafted by an international body in Washington (the Far Eastern Commission) and, on the spot, by a small watchdog group (the Allied Council for Japan, in Tokyo).

Initial policy guidelines set forth goals of demilitarization, collection of reparations, and the restitution of all overseas territories. The Japanese government was to remove all obstacles to the "revival of democratic tendencies among the Japanese people." The reference, which surprised many hard-line critics of Japan, was, of course, to the promising development of Taishō democracy prior to the rise of the military. One other provision seemed to offer an intriguing dilemma: Occupation forces would be withdrawn when Allied objectives were reached and when a responsible government was established "in accordance with the freely expressed will of the Japanese people." During the Occupation the Japanese, on the one hand, were under the strict control of a military headquarters and, on the other, were to eventually determine the form of their political institutions by their own expressed wishes.

In any case, the first steps in directed change were punitive. They included a three-stage purge of wartime leaders (almost 9,000 Diet members, local government officers, and financial and industrial leaders) as well as indictments upheld between 1946 and 1948 of twenty-five major war criminals (seven were hanged).

The occupationnaires then turned to positive political planning. Once again, as at the time of surrender, the stance designed for Emperor Hirohito was crucial. A majority of the Japanese elite had decided not to resist (but to delay) revision of Japan's earlier organic law, the Meiji Constitution (1889). Indeed, they had very shrewdly arranged for the Shōwa Emperor to write his own preamble to a new constitution. In the Imperial Rescript of January 1, 1946, he clearly explained that his status as a symbol did not depend on myths about his divinity. Rather, his importance lay in representing the state and the unity of the people. The very manner of the presentation may have confirmed in the minds of many Japanese the very special invulnerability of the throne to simply verbal or strictly legal definition. Moreover the rescript was another step that probably helped avoid removal of the Emperor as a war criminal. Other moves preparatory to constitution making had to do with the Emperor's subjects.

By October 1945, a virtual bill of rights had been adopted following SCAP fiat. Political prisoners were ordered released, and drastic modifications were made in police organization. Restrictions on political and religious liberty were forbidden. The men of SCAP made quite clear that they wanted state and religious sects (the prime examples, Shintō shrines) separated.

Because the occupationnaires were Americans, they thought of social engineering primarily in legal terms. In their view, modernization meant democratization; and democracy was assured by constitutionalism. Just as the Meiji Constitution was the capstone of the structure built by the nineteenth-century modernizers, so the MacArthur Constitution (1947) was the cornerstone in the foundation laid down by the twentieth-century modernizers.

By February 1946, Supreme Commander Douglas MacArthur and his advisers had become impatient with the Japanese penchant for delaying revision of the Meiji Constitution. On February 4 behind closed doors, General Courtney Whitney, chief of the Government Section of SCAP, briefed his assembled personnel. They were, in effect, to become a constitutional convention for Japan! Full discussion was to be allowed within the section in preparing the so-called Whitney draft, except for three points, which General MacArthur explicitly required. First, the Emperor's powers were to be exercised constitutionally and then only according to the basic will of the people. Second, Japan was to renounce war forever. Third, the Japanese would abolish "all vestiges of feudalism." The general added a cryptic word of advice: "Pattern budget after British system."

In brief summary, thereafter the Japanese leaders writhed, delayed, discussed, and (for reasons that will be detailed) eventually gave in. The Whitney draft with modifications became a SCAP version of an organic law; the SCAP draft with minor changes became a cabinet version; the government draft finally became the new Constitution of Japan. It was promulgated by the Emperor on November 3, 1946, the anniversary of the birth of his ancestor, the Meiji Emperor. It went into effect on May 3, 1947 (which to the present has been celebrated as Constitution Day). Product of persuasion, some cajolery, and more than a hint of threat, the new constitution articulated at the time more an American outlook than a Japanese viewpoint.

Because the so-called MacArthur Constitution has remained intact, unamended, and in effect to date, its characteristics will be described by implication in the section on the contemporary governance of Japan. For the moment, we may single out five features of the cabinet draft (none of which was fundamentally altered by subsequent formal or informal revision).

First, the draft redefined the Emperor's powers. The sovereign was to become "the symbol of the State and of the unity of the people." His position derived "from the will of the people with whom resides sovereign power" (Chap. I, Art. 1).

Second, the Diet was to become "the highest organ of state power" (Chap. IV, Art. 41). Executive power was to be vested in the Cabinet (Chap. V, Art. 65), which would be collectively responsible to the Diet. In one of the few Japanese contributions to the structure, the draft provided for an upper House of Councillors (replacing the old House of Peers) as well as a lower House of Representatives (Chap. IV, Art. 42).

Third, the draft offered (after firm U.S. prodding) an extensive bill of rights (Chap. III). They were not subject to law as were rights under the Meiji Constitution. This was the section that most clearly reflected American thinking. Rights included the familiar life, liberty, and the pursuit of happiness and provided for equality before the law. In addition, they went beyond U.S. constitutional definitions by guaranteeing academic freedom, the right to select residence, collective bargaining, and full employment. Indeed, as one wag described them at the time, the rights were so extensive that it is doubtful they would have passed the U.S. Senate.

Fourth, the Japanese government agreed to press for a complete renovation of the judicial system. The "whole judicial power" was to be vested in a supreme court and attendant inferior benches (Chap. VI, Art. 76). Again, the American hallmark was left on the judicial process by a provision that the supreme court was to determine the constitutionality of any law, order, regulation, or official act (Chap. VI, Art. 81). The Japanese, not by tradition committed to defining social norms by adversary law, have since warily skirted this thoroughly American procedure of judicial review.

Fifth, and doubtless most significant, was the provision that has lent the organic law another of its names, the Peace Constitution. The idealistic ideas about security thrust upon the Japanese originally included abolition of war as a sovereign right; Japan's renunciation of war as a means for settling disputes "and even for preserving its own security"; and refusal to authorize any army, navy, or air forces or to confer "rights of belligerency" upon any Japanese force.[3] Fortunately (from the point of view of later SCAP officials whose views of security were to differ from the first draft) and unfortunately (from the point of view of Japanese opposed to any rearmament), the final operational section of the constitution was reworded, reportedly by Japanese lawyers, to leave an ambiguity about security.

In the version eventually accepted by the Japanese, a wordy preamble of the constitution prepared the way by stating, "We the Japanese people, desire peace for all time." Leaving aside the imported Jeffersonian overtones, the statement accurately reflected Japanese sentiment at the time (and in the 1980s probably still articulates the desire of the majority). Considerably less realistic, in light of later developments, was the implied faith in the new United Nations, with the Japanese people "trusting in the justice and faith of the peace-loving peoples of the world."

The final operational provision (Chap. II, Art. 9) reiterated sincere Japanese aspiration "to an international peace based on justice and order." Using the old and ill-defined formula from the Kellogg-Briand Pact (1927), Japan forever renounced war "as a sovereign right of the nation and the threat or use of force as a means of settling international disputes. *In order to accomplish the aim of the preceding paragraph*, land, sea, and air forces, as well as other war potential, will never be maintained. The right of belligerency of the state will not be recognized" (italics added). Thus, in the celebrated Article 9, the stage was set for some lively postwar politics.

Strict constructionists have since argued that Japanese armed forces, by whatever name, and even the presence of U.S. forces in Japan, have been unconstitutional. Conservative realists have countered that, by the peace provision, Japan did indeed forswear the use of armed forces as instruments of national policy *on offense*; the nation did not and could not, however, waive the inherent right of *self-defense*. In either case, the Peace Constitution of Japan has set a very interesting precedent for the vanquished, for the victors, and for the world.

Other Occupation Reforms

In general, SCAP headquarters vigorously followed the path of reform of Japanese institutions for about one-half the Occupation period, that is, until 1948. SCAP directed countless changes during this phase, but three major economic programs may be singled out.

The men of SCAP, in the best U.S. trustbusting tradition, identified the giant *zaibatsu* (literally, "finance cliques") and ordered them dissolved. As a result, the huge combines—firms like Mitsui, Mitsubishi, and Sumitomo—were broken up. Eventually this antitrust drive stalled because the United States became more interested in reconstruction than in reform after 1948. The *zaibatsu* as a *method* of doing business (in contrast with *zaibatsu* as specific prewar firms) was familiar and useful to the Japanese, and they revived the form.

A second directed change had to do with labor. Occupationnaires encouraged creation of the Labor Ministry (1947), which sponsored legislation designed to nurture modern labor-management relations. Under SCAP encouragement, trade union membership, which at the surrender totaled only 5,300, rose to a total of almost 7 million by 1949. The sudden rise of labor as a postwar political force proved to be an embarrassment to SCAP, which on January 31, 1947, had to step in and forbid a general strike that would have disrupted further directed change.

The third significant area invaded by the men of SCAP was the agrarian countryside—the directed change, a breathtaking land reform. In brief, the program, which was administered by the Japanese, allowed 3 million cultivators to acquire 5 million acres of land. In the short run, redistribution of land by parcelization probably reduced agricultural production. In the long run, land reform greatly strengthened the rural economy, increased production, and provided a stable foundation on which to build post-Occupation government.

All the formal statistical data on land reform was not as impressive as informal direct observation of the effects on rural Japan in the 1950s. The little hamlets looked the same, except for the fact that technology was steadily upgrading production. Lives revolved around the same crop cycle. Age and status were still used to choose village leadership. However, one link in the chain of tradition had been broken. In many fine old houses, the collection of documents signifying descent from lower samurai or magistrate status through village chief to modern elective post was still intact. The distinctive signature in cursive script of a prominent Meiji or Taishō political boss still dominated the largest room of the house. His political stakes, driven into the Japanese soil, had once marked out a circle of political influence subtly mixed with the pattern of landholding. The documents and sometimes even the political memento were for sale, though, because the land surrounding the fine house now belonged to the neighbors.[4]

The Occupation: In Retrospect

The balance sheet of assets and liabilities during the Occupation can only be filled in after an analysis of development since the end of this truly unique experiment. We shall hazard a few comments here on this stage of modernization and on directed change.

Anyone interested in the social sciences should find of interest the classic dilemma that the occupationnaires faced when they held almost absolute control of Japan. Should they let history take its course, allowing the Japanese, after a disastrous defeat, to slowly find their own way to reorganize society? Or should the men of SCAP erect a scaffolding for renovated institutions and expect that everyday habits would eventually develop to fill in the frame, something like the Japanese manner of constructing a building from the top down?

Because the Americans were impatient modernizers and because they so firmly believed in the desirability of change, they chose the latter method. Shortly thereafter in the United States, there was a parallel between the experiment in Japan and a quietly revolutionary step taken at home. In *Brown* vs. *Board of Education* (1954) the Supreme Court clearly enunciated the principle of unconstitutionality in segregation. The Court hoped that social habits would eventually fill in the framework of law.

Many Americans and some Japanese believe that the true modernization of Japan got under way only with the defeat and the Occupation. Those with a longer historical perspective have adopted the description of that momentous period chosen by Kazuo Kawai, who referred to the 1945–52 era as "Japan's American interlude."

The phrase was not designed to denigrate the U.S. effort: rather, it quite appropriately served to emphasize what had gone on before and to highlight what happened after the Occupation. If one has faith in growth, the experiment was a success story. If, on the contrary, one has grave doubts about some of the results of growth and marches to the beat of a different drum in the development parade, the Occupation accounted in part for what was wrong with Japan in the late 1950s and 1960s.

THE POLITICS OF PEACE

When one considers the tremendous changes that have occurred in Japan over the past century, the relative stability of formal political institutions is astounding. When the peace treaty finally took effect on April 28, 1952, observers were gloomy in their estimates of the staying power of largely alien, imposed institutions. The MacArthur Constitution had been practically thrust on the Japanese; furthermore, in parts its language sounded strange to their ears. All the more surprising, the organic law has yet to be formally amended (and informed Japan watchers see little or no chance for revision in the immediate future). There were a number of reasons for the unexpected stability.

The Reverse Course Stalls

As we have seen, the Occupation operated with relative efficiency, finished its work rather swiftly, and left a reservoir of goodwill. Prime Minister Yoshida Shigeru later wrote, "Judged by results, it can be frankly admitted that Allied (of course, predominantly American) occupation policy was a success." After 1948, the Americans turned (some would say, because of the cold war) from reform to reconstruction. In the latter half of the Occupation, the aims of SCAP came closer and closer to the desires of a majority of the Japanese.

Moreover, the framework imposed by the occupationnaires was never so inflexible as to rule out adjustment. For example, like its counterpart, the Constitution of the United States, the Japanese organic law allowed informal revision in practice. Thus (despite Art. 9) a covert and then a limited rearmament for defense was not only permitted but was also encouraged by the Americans, particularly after the outbreak of the Korean conflict. In practice, Japanese increasingly cast aside unworkable principles of federalism (encompassed in Chap. VIII), which had been imported by SCAP. Informal change saw the reestablishment of centralized control of fiscal policy, education, and, to some extent, police standards.

Finally, beginning in the early 1950s, socioeconomic changes within Japan picked up speed at a geometric rate, making an accepted organic law out of what appeared to be a highly idealistic constitution and turning alien institutions into viable organizations. Some of the credit can be attributed to the afterglow of the Occupation; the major impetus, however, was thenceforth in the hands of the new Japanese modernizers. They in turn were identifiable descendants of the men of Meiji.

Establishment Gambles

It should come as no surprise to learn that because of the nature of the surrender, the evolution of the Occupation, and the results of developments after 1950, political institutions in Japan have been dominated (at least until the 1980s) by conservatives. Once again, the Japanese plunged into change—into further modernization, if you will—paradoxically in order to conserve their unique lifestyle. They thus followed in the footsteps of Meiji leaders, who were the first to engage in conservative modernization. Since 1952, conservatives (often called the Establishment) have deliberately engaged in two gambles.

First, post-treaty conservative governments (enduring the unendurable, to paraphrase previous surrender terms) purchased the return of the exercise of sovereignty and their security by placing Japan under a U.S. defensive umbrella. There were advantages and disadvantages to the decision. For at least two decades Japanese enjoyed a security greater than the one they had when they poured out their wealth to maintain the Imperial army and navy. Japan has spent less on defense from its per capita GNP than any comparable power in the world. As long as Americans continued to make this commitment to defend Japan—and as long as the commitment was credible to all parties concerned—this system offered protection.

On the other hand, security arrangements with the United States necessitated a continuing U.S. presence (in the form of military bases). Like most people in such circumstances, the Japanese never have become enamored of involuntary tourists. Even after the military presence was limited in Okinawa and restricted (to air and naval units) on the main islands, for a proud people the security was at the cost of dependence. Japan's security policy was literally set at Pearl Harbor.

When Americans acted in an unpredictable and even irresponsible manner (and on occasion they did, in the opinion of the Japanese), the protected Japanese were concerned. For example, the late stages of the Korean conflict, which threatened to become a major war against China, and the Vietnam engagement, which also could have become a thrust against China, worried the Japanese. Finally, if and when the United States wavered or if its commitment no longer seemed credible, then odds on the gamble of the U.S. defensive umbrella would lengthen. One day Japanese were bound to ask, if the United States were at the same time threatened by a major power, would Americans still spring to the defense of Japan?

The second gamble taken by the conservative governments was parlayed out of the first. After 1952, having seen to security, Japan's leaders pledged to achieve an unprecedented growth rate, which would double the GNP in a decade. The results were beyond the wildest dreams of even the most sanguine conservative politician, for Japan at one point doubled its GNP in only seven years.

Growth as a Religion

From about the time of the peace treaty (1952) until the stormy days of renewal of the U.S. security arrangement (1960), and even until about the 1973 "oil shock," much noise was made by opposition politicians and conservative leaders about foreign affairs and security. Every cabinet after 1960 and into the 1970s, however, paid primary attention on a day-by-day basis to questions of growth, full employment, the balance of payments, and exports.

Japan thus entered upon a second stage "takeoff"; urbanization accelerated at an exponential rate; a new white-collar, middle class of wage earners (the celebrated *sarari man*) emerged; and Japanese plunged into what at times seemed to be an obsession with durable consumer goods. Citizens watched GNP statistics like they followed baseball scores or the results of *sumō* wrestling matches. Japan was in second or third place; the country had arrived in the heavyweight class. To shift the image, growth became the only religion besides ritual in which Japanese had faith.

Measured in the economist's rather precise terms of increasing per-capita GNP, growth constitutes one of the cleanest, least complicated definitions of modernization. It is a neutral definition and has the advantage of being measurable. The effects of what Lawrence Olson has called "economism" in 1960s Japan run well beyond the economic, however. GNP per capita is only an average: it does not take into account the tangible and hidden costs of growth; it says little or nothing about the distribution of the fruits of growth; and, in terms of net national welfare, it ignores any goal other than the acquisition of goods and services.

In any case, growth has left its stamp on Japan's post-1952 politics. For two decades, it provided the platform on which conservative leaders mounted perennial political victories. Opposition politicians were voices crying in the wilderness.

THE GOVERNANCE OF JAPAN

In the period of growth of the 1960s (as in the 1860s) the Japanese were able to carry with them a large measure of traditional behavior to protect themselves against the shocks of change. The real tests of stability and instability were to come later. Meanwhile, conservative leaders supported by a majority of the public built as efficient a machine to encourage further growth as the world has ever seen.

The Conservative Establishment

Despite the often revolutionary nature of the directed change sponsored by SCAP, the overall effect of the Occupation was conservative, as was that of the New Deal (a ghost of which lived on in Japan long after its demise in the United States). Large numbers of Japanese acquired a stake in stability, even in the new democracy.

Post-1952 politics in Japan came to be dominated by groups that deliberately conserved Japanese values while they were engaged in further modernization. They included the majority Liberal Democratic Party (LDP—Jiyūminshutō), supportive business organizations, and the closely allied elite of the civil service bureaucracy. Some observers borrowed British terminology to describe this intricate structure as the Establishment. One Japanese political scientist called it a "pluralistic hegemony." Those who tried to compete with Japanese businessmen came to use a pejorative term, "Japan, Inc."[5]

There are, however, several reasons why any conspiracy thesis misses the mark in trying to describe conservative hegemony. First, the opposition (made up of the so-called progressive parties) has always held just enough power to act as monitor and to guard against any reactionary course. Second, conservative forces were never organized in any monolithic fashion. Various parts of the Establishment, particularly the several factions of the LDP, have engaged in intense competition and have served to aggregate various interests in the society. In this sense, they have played the roles of political parties. Finally, in the 1970s the absolute majority enjoyed by the LDP gave way to coalition by compromise.

National Indoor Gymnasium, Tokyo: Designed by Tange Kenzo for 1964 Olympiad.

A somewhat unflattering view might see the majority of the Japanese in the 1960s armed with relative security provided by someone else; enjoying increasing levels of prosperity discounted by inflation; and content to drift in the mainstream of what they thought was progress. Throughout the decade, the LDP rolled up impressive (if in each election slightly decreasing) majorities (see Table 5.1). As Akuto Hiroshi has pointed out, since the merger of conservative parties in 1955, party preferences have changed very little. The LDP started by enjoying just below 50 percent of respondents, dipped sharply in 1960 (the year of the riots attendant upon renewal of the U.S. security treaty), rose to above 50 percent in 1964, and then hovered around 45 percent through the election of 1976 (see Figure 5.1). Akuto expressed his belief "that supporters of the Liberal Democratic Party have a 'mainstream' life style and are simple-minded, good at taking a broad view of things and, relatively speaking, realistic."[6]

The LDP. Post-1952 conservative political parties had as their ancestors embryonic political organizations established as early as 1874. By 1900 the oligarch Itō Hirobumi had seen the necessity of seeking party support and founded the Constitutional Political Friends Association (Rikken Seiyūkai). In 1918 this party provided the platform for the first full-fledged party cabinet under Prime Minister Hara Takashi. From 1924 until 1932 parties followed a pattern of alternate rule, power being shared between the Constitutional People's Party (Rikken Minseitō) and the Political Friends (Seiyūkai). By the 1940s even conservative groups had dissolved themselves in favor of transcendental or military-led cabinets.

Immediately after the surrender, a number of new parties made their appearance either as new entities or as resurrected forms of the old conservative parties. The 1946 election constituted an important milestone in that it enfranchised all adults, both male and female. As a result of this election, the president of the Liberal Party (Jiyūtō), Yoshida Shigeru, was selected to be prime minister and began perfecting the politics of Occupation patronage. There was a brief interruption of conservative rule with Japan's first (and only) socialist government (1947), followed by a coalition cabinet (1948). Yoshida then returned

TABLE 5.1
Votes and Seats in Lower House (Elections 1967-79)

Party	Year	Popular Vote	Percent	Seats	Percent
Liberal	1967	22,447,834	48.8	277	57.0
Democrats	1969	22,381,566	47.6	288*	59.2
(LDP)	1972	24,563,078	46.8	271*	55.2
	1976	23,653,624	41.8	249*	48.7
	1979	24,084,127	44.6	248*	48.5
Socialists	1967	12,826,099	27.9	140	28.8
(JSP)	1969	10,074,099	21.4	90	18.5
	1972	11,478,600	21.9	118	24.0
	1976	11,713,005	20.7	123	24.1
	1979	10,643,448	19.1	107	20.9
Democratic	1967	3,404,462	7.4	30	6.2
Socialists	1969	3,636,590	7.8	31	6.4
(DSP)	1972	3,659,922	7.0	19	3.9
	1976	3,554,075	6.3	29	5.7
	1979	3,663,691	6.8	35	6.8
Communists	1967	2,190,563	4.8	5	1.0
(JSP)	1969	3,199,031	6.8	14	2.9
	1972	5,496,697	10.5	38	7.7
	1976	5,878,192	10.4	17	3.3
	1979	5,625,526	10.4	39	7.6
Kōmeitō	1967	2,472,371	5.4	25	5.1
	1969	5,124,666	10.9	47	9.7
	1972	4,436,631	8.5	29	5.9
	1976	6,117,300	10.9	55	10.0
	1979	5,282,682	9.8	57	11.2
Minor	1967	101,244	0.2	0	0.0
Parties	1969	81,373	0.2	0	0.0
	1972	143,019	0.3	2	0.4
	1976	2,363,984	4.2	17	3.3
	1979	2,069,571	3.8	6	1.1
Independents	1967	2,533,988	5.5	9	1.9
	1969	2,492,559	5.3	16*	3.3
	1972	2,645,530	5.0	14*	2.9
	1976	3,227,462	5.7	21*	4.1
	1979	2,641,063	4.9	19*	3.7
Totals	1967	45,996,561	100.0	486	100.0
	1969	46,989,884	100.0	486	100.0
	1972	52,423,477	100.0	491	100.0
	1976	56,612,755	100.0	511	100.0
	1979	54,010,108	100.0	511	100.0

*Addition of 12, 9, 7, and 10 independents to LDP resulted in 300, 280, 256, and 258 seats (1969, 1972, 1976, and 1979 respectively).

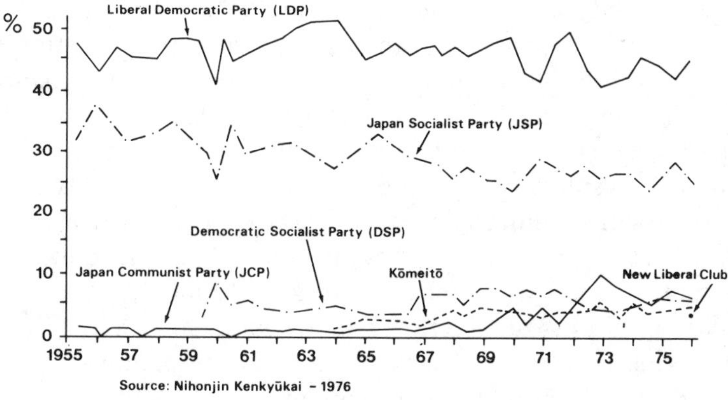

Figure 5.1: Trend in Party Preference (1955–76)

to form his second (October 1948) and third (1949) cabinets. During this period, he laid down firm foundations for continuing conservative rule by preparing protégés like Ikeda Hayato and Satō Eisaku (who later became prime ministers). Yoshida's fourth (1952–53) and fifth (1953–54) cabinets saw consummation of the peace treaty.

Following the treaty there was a brief reaction to Occupation reforms, under the leadership of the formerly purged Hatoyama Ichirō. His second (1955) and third (1955–56) cabinets were marked by the reappearance of other purged politicians such as Miki Bukichi, Ishibashi Tanzan, Kishi Nobusuke, and Kōno Ichirō. Hatoyama's most important contribution, however, was the merger of the Liberal and Democratic (Minshutō) parties in November 1955. Thus was formed the Liberal Democratic Party (LDP; Jiyūminshutō), which one witticism described as neither liberal nor democratic, nor even a party.

The LDP gave the prime minister's mantle to Kishi Nobusuke twice (1956–58 and 1958–60). He lost it in 1960 during the riots protesting the renewal of the U.S. security treaty. His retirement then opened the way for what has been called the Yoshida School, premiers who implemented the U.S.-Japanese security arrangement in subdued style and emphasized economic growth. Ikeda Hayato was particularly famous for his low-key approach. He was succeeded by Satō Eisaku, who held the post of prime minister for a record seven years and eight months (1964–72).

A second glance at election results (again, see Table 5.1) will reveal the reason for another unflattering interpretation of LDP strength during this long period of conservative dominance. It is quite clear that the percentage of LDP seats in the Diet was regularly higher than the LDP percentage of the popular vote. This was a result of gerrymandering, whereby LDP bastions in the conservative countryside were overrepresented as compared with opposition parties' bases in the cities (that is, it took more voters in urban areas to return a progressive member than was required in rural areas to return a LDP Diet member).

Having been successful in every postwar election save one, the LDP could have and (as the opposition charged) often did exercise a dictatorship of the majority. According to one description, up through the 1960s Japan had not a two-party but a one-and-a-half-party system. Nonetheless, even in the heady days of growth and successive LDP victories, the party was constitutionally, politically, and morally accountable to the public; through elections the LDP was indirectly monitored by the citizens; the majority was subject to minority pressure in the Diet; and always the LDP cabinets were audited by the media.

Despite the checks and balances, the LDP enjoyed hegemony until the 1970s. There were several reasons for the party's success. First, the top LDP chieftains, high-level bureaucrats, and powerful business leaders built a closely knit network. Business provided the bulk of LDP funds through the Federation of Economic Organizations (Keidanren). Bureaucrats cooperated until they reached the retirement age of fifty-five, when they entered upon a second career in business, in the public corporations, or even in the Diet under LDP sponsorship.

A second reason for LDP success is also often listed as one of the weaknesses of the party. The LDP has been a conglomeration of readily identifiable factions (*habatsu*) whose interminable maneuvers have frequently been criticized even by LDP leaders themselves. Thus, although the prime minister is technically elected by the Diet, it has been apparent from alert newspaper commentary that the selection has actually been made by factional groups within the perennial majority party. Even more obvious has been the need to balance these forces in order to form a cabinet. And yet the factions have represented a marriage of convenience between the traditional and the modern. A patron-client relationship—something like the traditional parent-child (*oyabun-kobun*) relationship—fills a traditional need and has at the same time come to serve a new function. Patrons within the Establishment serve their clients in constituencies, and thus reflect various interests.

This brings us to a third, related reason for LDP success. The party engaged in what Watanuki Jōji has called "organizational clientelism," the provision of public benefits to constituencies through personal sponsoring associations (*kōenkai*) that back LDP candidates. Indeed, the party was very responsive in meeting personal, regional, and occupational demands.

Finally, the LDP made it a rule to tolerate extremely prolonged Diet sessions (one notable exception caused the 1960 riots); so on the surface it appeared to be the most tolerant majority party in the world. In fact, discussion was often limited to procedural matters, with little or no time for substance, with the result that policy was decided within the LDP. Even so, LDP members have had opportunities to express a wide range of views within the majority. Some (the doves) supported and engaged in travel to the People's Republic of China before recognition; some (the hawks) held onto ties with Taiwan. Some made contact with the Democratic People's Republic of (North) Korea; others enjoyed close business ties with the Republic of (South) Korea.

The patron-client structure also has supplied one of the LDP's most serious problems. It has been said that in the 1960s the minimum expenditure per month by a Diet member in a nonelection period was 3 million yen (then about U.S. $10,000). LDP factions spent five times more than the total spent by all four opposition parties. This did not take into account the "hidden" money.

Indeed, so serious were the earlier "black mist" scandals and so alarming the money politics of Prime Minister Tanaka Kakuei that they contributed to the decline of LDP support. The statistics on "party support" as compared with those on "party preference" demonstrate a subtle difference and reveal a critical party problem (see Figure 5.2). Through the late 1960s and into the 1970s the number of disenchanted was growing. They were voters who would name the LDP when asked for party preference but who would not feel obliged to go to the polls voluntarily in party support. For Japanese politics at large, it was significant that apparently many voters were leaving the LDP to support no party.

Yet another criticism of the LDP has been that the party has been marked by bureaucratic leadership. Certainly many of the cabinets—for example, those of Ikeda Hayato, Satō Eisaku, Tanaka Kakuei, Fukuda Takeo, and Ōhira Masayoshi—have been indelibly marked by failings of bureaucrats: passivity, inability to search out new approaches, and conservative equilibrium (among factions). It has also been charged that the LDP has converted the entire administrative state into a bureaucracy dedicated to keeping the LDP in power.

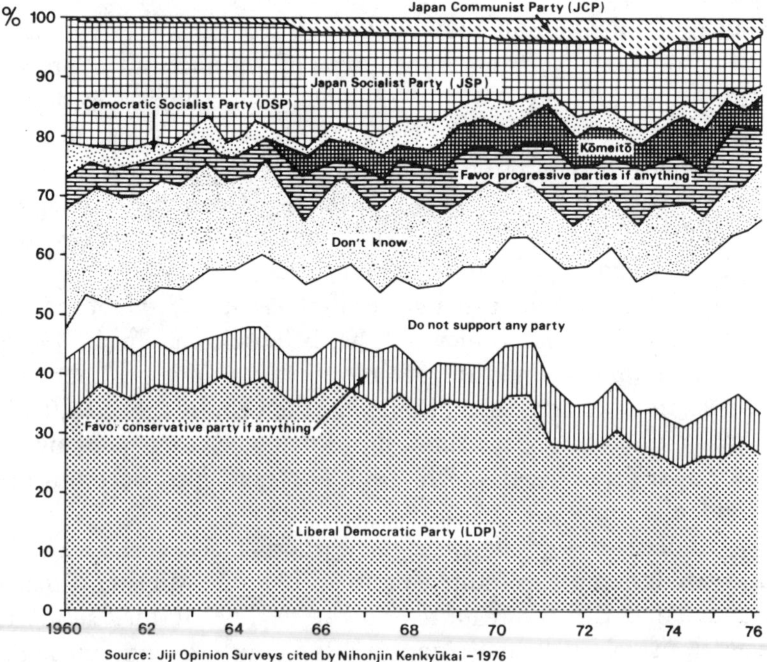

Figure 5.2: Trend in Party Support (1960–76)

The Bureaucracy. It is safe to say that the bureaucracy has been as little changed by war, defeat, Occupation reform, and post-treaty change as any sector of Japanese government. In the long process of change since the nineteenth century the "ministers of modernization" were the first to emerge. Second, the demands of modern war and mobilization strengthened the strategic position of the bureaucrats. Third, even under the Occupation, directed change demanded clean lines of authority from SCAP to the Japanese government. Finally, the Establishment effectively used the power of government to launch the society into an orbit of advanced economic development. In modern times, each and every step has served what may be called the administrative state.

These are also the reasons why the cabinet has been more important in its role as head of the civil service than as a leadership drawn from the Diet. In recent times the cabinet has consisted of twelve ministries: Finance (inner citadel of the bureaucracy), the Ministry of International Trade and Industry (MITI), Foreign Affairs, Education, Health and Welfare, Agriculture and Forestry, Transportation, Postal Services, Labor, Construction, and Local Government. Equal to all these ministries combined in the exercise of power has been the Office of the Prime Minister (something like the U.S. Executive Office of the President). The specific roles of several of these ministries, particularly of Finance and of MITI, will be discussed in Chapter 6.

Business and Politics. Perhaps the most popular criticism of the LDP denounces the organization as "only a party of business." That the LDP has had close ties with big business and, indeed, has received much of its funding from large corporations, there can be no doubt.

Once again, however, this oversimplification obscures the fact that business circles, like the Establishment, represent plural interests. Business organizations differ sharply in their approaches to problems. They range from the staid Federation of Economic Organizations (Keidanren, something like the National Association of Manufacturers in the United States) to the more liberal Japan Committee for Economic Development (Keizai Dōyūkai, deliberately translated to mirror the Committee for Economic Development). Far more conservative is the Federation of Employers' Organizations (Nikkeiren).

It must always be remembered that big business was not the sole clientele of the LDP. A persistent stronghold of traditional values and political support for conservative parties, the old urban middle class figured as well. The LDP has also enjoyed support from what increasingly must be called the sector of agribusiness. Through their agricultural cooperative associations, farmers have held a tight rein on local conservative candidates. The fact is that through the 1960s the LDP garnered support from every sector of the society.

Establishment Policies and Policymaking

In the period when Japanese attention was riveted on growth, the LDP very effectively tapped majority desires in its policies. Thus, although further industrialization and urbanization were expected to alter traditional values, the emerging middle class remained essentially conservative.

LDP campaign pamphlets emphasized, for example, the need for "A Bright Japan, An Abundant Life." In 1960 the party's so-called Philosophers' Group aired a policy statement that, in typical political party style, tried to strike a happy medium between neo-conservatism and neo-nationalism on the one hand and the necessity for "revised capitalism"—provision of full employment and rectification of imbalances of wealth—on the other. The LDP repudiated prewar racism, adhered to parliamentarism, rejected the dogmas of Marxism, and promised to eliminate undemocratic activities. In short, the LDP emphasized "that the entire [Japanese] people should be turned into the middle class and owners of capital."

The foreign policy platforms of the LDP revealed one paradox. Although successive conservative governments supported continuation of the Tokyo-Washington security axis, the LDP also favored an eventual revision of the American-inspired constitution. Party leaders wanted to remove constitutional barriers (in Art. 9) to a further buildup of defense forces, and to an eventual withdrawal of U.S. forces from bases in Japan. No conservative leader ever dared advocate the acquisition of nuclear arms, even for defense.

Although the LDP regularly supported close political and

economic (as well as security) ties with the United States, the party bowed to the force of nationalism and favored the return of Okinawa to Japanese control. (Reversion of administrative control over the Ryūkyū chain to Japan was the price the United States paid in 1970 in order to obtain renewal of the U.S.-Japanese security arrangement.)

Under the new constitution (Chap. IV, Art. 41), the Diet was supposed to become the highest organ of state power and the sole lawmaking body of the state. The ultimate weapon of the Diet was its control over all appropriations and expenditures, over taxation and revenue, and over monitoring the budget. In theory, then, the legislature was expected to enjoy constitutional supremacy over the executive.

In fact, planning of the legislative program in postwar Japan (as has been the case in all so-called administrative states) has increasingly been a function of the cabinet. The cabinet, actually a coalition of LDP faction leaders, has in turn relied almost totally on the bureaucracy. Drafting of legislative bills has almost always begun in administrative departments. Individual members' bills have been scarce in Japan.

After careful scrutiny by a legislative bureau of the cabinet, a draft bill has then been submitted to rigorous study by various vice-ministers, permanent members of the higher civil service. At this cabinet level, too, there has been an increasing use of public commissions to study, modify, and even to implement legislative objectives. Once approved, the bill has been introduced in the legislature, where, particularly in the committees, the government has been questioned and opposition testimony aired. Until the mid-1970s, however, the LDP controlled all committees, so it was entirely up to the majority party whether or not a bill would be amended. On very serious issues, the opposition had only one alternative course: to boycott the Diet and committee sessions, particularly those dealing with the annual budget.

Empirical research on public policymaking, even in the 1960s when the LDP was dominant, has clearly revealed that the process was nonetheless heterogeneous. To repeat, the Establishment was a pluralistic hegemony. In some cases (as in the United States) conservative policymaking was closed (even to business circles) and out of public view. For example, Prime Minister Tanaka's visit to Peking in 1972 and the decision to normalize relations with the People's Republic of China were carried out despite substantial opposition within the LDP, among a minority of the bureaucracy, and in some segments of big business.

In other cases, a large number of individuals and pressure groups in the public at large were critical to the outcome of policymaking. To cite two issues—the pollution problem in the early 1970s grew to dominate a session of the legislature (the Pollution Diet of 1970), despite the reluctance of the LDP and business to face the dilemma; and the perennial procedure for setting of rice price support has involved a complicated network of segments of the LDP and of the various ministries.

In some other instances, such as the issues involving investment liberalization and university enrollment expansion, the presumably all powerful Establishment remained inactive until forced to respond to pressure applied by foreign governments or by broad sectors of the domestic society. At other times (to cite again Tokyo's decision to normalize relations with Peking), the government was capable of major innovation.[7]

The Emperor

Where does the Emperor fit into this conservative scheme of government? By tradition, the Emperor has usually been a ceremonial symbol rather than an operating executive. The new constitution assigned no power to him and made the Imperial institution subject to the authority of the cabinet.

Nonetheless, the opposition to the Establishment has argued, not without reason, that the Imperial symbol has been used to bolster LDP rule. Even progressive parties have been very reluctant to tamper with what is also essentially a symbol of stability amid rapid change. Every spring Emperor Hirohito has celebrated a birthday (he was seventy-eight on April 29, 1979), with several tens of thousands subjects visiting the Imperial Palace compound to offer congratulations.

Political stress lines have been located slightly off center from the Imperial institution. For example, in April 1979,

Prime Minister Ōhira paid a visit to the Yasukuni Shrine, the Imperial Shintō edifice founded in 1869 by the Meiji Emperor to pay homage to those who had died for the state. The prime minister insisted that his visit was "a private affair." There were objections, however, that were constitutional (stressing separation of state and religion); moral (a few days earlier fourteen Class-A war criminals, including General Tōjō Hideki, had been enshrined there); and personal (Ōhira claimed to be a Christian). In somewhat similar fashion, opposition parties, the press, and segments of the public opposed legislation that formally reinstituted Imperial reign eras.

The Progressive Opposition

Although growth was the religion in the decade of the 1960s and conservative politicians the high priests of ritual GNP, it should also come as no surprise that growth created problems. Inflation (which discounted growth), environmental disruption, a severe housing shortage, and the rise of traffic accidents—all of these offered the opposition forces salient issues on which, by and large, they failed to capitalize at least until the 1970s.

Successful conservatives and the frustrated opposition were coming up against an increased political apathy spreading among the new urban middle class. It was a studied indifference the result of high levels of literacy, expanded technology, scientism, and pragmatism. This new middle class also suffered from being in the center of a polarized struggle between the Establishment and those in opposition, who chose to call themselves the "progressives." On the one hand, the Establishment and a large majority of the middle class were distrustful of Marxism and anyone whom they regarded as a Marxist. The LDP stressed authority and order, often at the expense of minority rights. On the other hand, some of the thinking and much of the rhetoric of the organized opposition have been framed in Marxist categories. The progressives proved to be quite inept, often inappropriately carrying irrelevant nineteenth-century dogma into the political fray.

Dissenting Interests. Trade unions have provided the bulk of support for the progressives, specifically for the socialist parties. A criticism of labor (and of its support for socialist parties) has been that unions represent only a fraction of the total population (indeed, only about 30 percent of all employed personnel).

As the labor movement has split, so have the socialists. The General Council of Trade Unions (Sōhyō) embraces about 4.5 million members (about 12 percent of the employed labor force) and has lined up behind the socialist left wing (the "mainstream"). The All-Japan Congress of Trade Unions (Dōmei Kaigi) has a membership of something over 2 million (or 6 percent of the labor force) and has supported right-wing socialists. Other labor voices have been heard from employees of public corporations, like railway workers; there has also been the smaller but vocal dissent articulated by the Japan Teachers Union (Nikkyōso).

Labor has often been joined, and socialists supported, by the *interi* (the intellectuals, meaning almost anyone who has gone to college). Although some intellectuals have lent counsel to conservative governments as advisers, there has been a wide gulf between most of the *interi* and the Establishment. Older intellectuals have been profoundly affected by the rhetoric, if not the thought, of Marxism. There has also been an opinion gap between intellectuals and the middle class, although the latter pay exaggerated respect to television commentators and social critics drawn from the *interi*.

Although opposition forces have never fully capitalized on the tensions generated by rapid growth, they have gained support from those who have not enjoyed a proportionate share of the rising GNP: some technical and professional personnel, some white-collar workers (including low-level bureaucrats), small merchants, some youth, and many women. The latter have been particularly concerned with the effects of inflation on household accounts. Other dissenters have joined opposition parties in criticizing "black mist" corruption within the LDP, in uncovering scandals related to aircraft purchases (in the 1970s), in opposing covert rearmament, and in defending the Peace Constitution. The urban proletariat, called by one observer the "industrial peasants," on occasion have shown a penchant for real radicalism.

The Socialists. The major and most effective opposition to the LDP has been provided by various kinds of socialist parties. The Japan Socialist Party (JSP, Nihon Shakaitō) was established in November 1945. "Japan" was used to distinguish these socialists from brethren abroad. The term "social democratic," a frequent translation, was meant to link Japanese socialists to similarly named groups abroad. In fact, the JSP inherited diverse elements—Christian reformism, proletarian radicalism, evolutionary and scientific socialism—from prewar social democracy. In June 1947, Katayama Tetsu became prime minister and formed the first socialist party government in Japan's history. Unfortunately, this experiment in responsible opposition failed in the face of severe economic recession and a series of scandals. Since then the JSP, never tempered by the probability of achieving power nor moderated by the responsibility of governance, has perceived politics as a struggle and has looked at political issues in doctrinaire terms.

Right- and left-wing socialists first parted company over the issue of the majority peace treaty in 1952. The threat of the merger of the conservative parties and a complicated compromise brought the two wings back together in October 1955. Although the JSP could count on relatively large blocks of voters at election time, the party had only a small regular membership (of about 60,000) and represented only one large pressure group (labor).

JSP platforms, as contrasted with those of the LDP, have been more wordy, more theoretical, and more intensely concentrated on issues of foreign policy and security. On the domestic front, the dominant left faction defines the JSP as a class-mass party. Although the aim of the party ought to continue to be socialist revolution, under existing conditions this revolution should be effected only by peaceful means. The objectives of the JSP have been to increase the income of the "working public," to reform the economic system in order to limit the profits of large enterprises, to nurture backward industries (agriculture, fisheries, and forestry), and to perfect a social security system.

The foreign policy platform of the JSP, like that of the LDP, has revealed an interesting paradox. Whereas the party fought against any revision of the U.S.-imposed Peace Constitution, it also advocated termination of the U.S.-Japan security treaty. In its place a collective security arrangement among Japan, the Soviet Union, the People's Republic of China, and the United States was urged. Asia was to become a nuclear-free area. Early on, the JSP advocated recognition of the People's Republic as the official government of China.

In 1959 a long-simmering rebellion against domination of the JSP by left-wing factions and against the party's preoccupation with class struggle led Nishio Suehiro to bolt from the JSP with forty members of his faction. In 1960 rebels established the Democratic Socialist Party (DSP). Steadily improving economic conditions offered a promise that the DSP would grow, as had moderate social democrats in Western Europe and the Labour Party in Britain. By the 1972 election, however, support for the DSP had declined to a point where the party commanded only 7 percent of the popular vote (the JSP, 22 percent).

The Communists. In the case of the Japan Communist Party (JCP, Nihon Kyōsantō), as in the JSP, "Japan" was used to distinguish the Communists from other such parties abroad. Often the JCP proved to be far less radical than the JSP. Severely hampered by splits among the pro-Soviet, the pro-Chinese, and neutral wings, the JCP nevertheless became one of the most pragmatic of the progressive parties at the local level. In the 1972 election, it grew to become the third-ranking opposition party (10.5 percent of the popular vote and thirty-eight lower house seats). Moreover, all along, the JCP could boast of a larger rank-and-file membership than that of all the other progressive parties combined.

The Kōmeitō. Far more strident than the Communists—and for a time their bitter enemies—were the voices representing one of the new religions (see Chapter 8). They in turn produced another opposition party. The social programs of the so-called Value Creation Society (Sōka Gakkai), founded in 1946, appealed to *rōnin* students, the sick, the dispossessed, and some women, particularly those who resented the discrimination inherent in a male society. Sōka Gakkai soon grew in membership to 15 million. Its political arm was the Kōmeitō (Clean government party), but later under pressure there was a formal division between the religious and the political organizations.

The Kōmeitō entered the lists slowly and deliberately, and in 1967 finally put up candidates in the election for the lower house. By 1969 it commanded 10 percent of the total popular vote and had increased the number of its seats to forty-seven in the House of Representatives. By 1972, however, its share of the popular vote had fallen sharply (to 8.5 percent), so it held only twenty-nine seats in the lower house. The Kōmeitō has in effect represented both tradition (in its emphasis on discipline, its familial face-to-face cells, its appeal to nationalism, and its exclusivist religious beliefs) and modern style (in its efficient organization, its great material wealth, and its establishment of an overseas network).

Forces opposed to the LDP did not leave a clear stamp on Japan's politics until the decade of the 1970s. By then, Japan had entered a new period, the era of the postindustrial society, and Japanese faced new issues. Even in the growth cycle of the 1960s, however, charts showing support for all parties (see Figure 5.2) clearly reveal an apolitical trend, as the individual became less confident of the effectiveness of any government, party, or leader. "Japanese people became decreasingly political."[8]

Those Japanese who supported no party rose from about 10 percent in 1960 to more than 30 percent by 1975. Elections were obviously in a state of flux as the floating middle-class vote moved from established parties into this or that coalition. Another way of describing this development is to state that affluence practically eliminated the possibility of revolution, so sharp ideological differences played a more and more minor role. Somewhat paradoxically, but easily understandable in terms of traditional style, the image of a party and of a candidate became more vital than ideology in Japanese thinking.

NOTES

1. Some explanatory comments need to be added. First, there were no zones *except* for three areas: (1) part of the Ogasawara (Bonin) chain

held outright (returned by the United States on November 15, 1967); (2) most of the Ryūkyū chain (including Okinawa) was held under direct U.S. Army administration (Okinawa reverted to Japanese administration on May 15, 1972); and (3) what the Japanese call the "northern territories" (the southern Kurile chain claimed by the Japanese), which have remained under the Soviet Union's control. Second, until 1948, about 5,000 British Commonwealth Occupation Forces (BCOF) were based in southern Honshū and in Shikoku. Third, the Eighth Army and each of the various corps had a military government section, but as far as SCAP headquarters in Tokyo was concerned, military government was simply one staff activity at tactical level. Finally, supervision was provided by the Supreme Commander for the Allied Powers (SCAP), a post occupied by U.S. General of the Army Douglas MacArthur (until April 11, 1951, when President Harry Truman replaced MacArthur with General Matthew B. Ridgway).

2. Robert E. Ward, "Reflections on the Allied Occupation and Planned Political Change in Japan," in Robert E. Ward, ed., *Political Development in Modern Japan* (Princeton: Princeton University Press, 1968).

3. There can be little doubt that these earlier extreme ideas originated with General MacArthur. They were taken from his notes, February 3, 1946, in *Political Reorientation of Japan, September 1945 to September 1948*, Report of Government Section, Supreme Commander for the Allied Powers (Washington: U.S. Government Printing Office, 1949), vol. 1, p. 102.

4. I made these observations of rural Japan in the 1950s; see Part 2, "The Government and Politics of Japan," in Paul M. A. Linebarger (ed.), Djang Chu, and Ardath W. Burks, *Far Eastern Governments and Politics* (Princeton: D. Van Nostrand Company, rev. ed. 1956), especially p. 539.

5. The label "Japan, Inc.," apparently originated from a cover story of *Time*, May 10, 1971.

6. Akuto made an interesting connection between political preference (support of the LDP) and consumer behavior. The supporters of the LDP usually choose top brands, he reported, for they will simply think that the best-known products must have high quality to enjoy top status and that it is realistic and safe to choose them. See Akuto Hiroshi, "Changing Political Culture in Japan," in *Text of the Seminar on "Changing Values in Modern Japan,"* organized by Nihonjin Kenkyūkai in association with Japan Society (Tokyo: Nihonjin Kenkyūkai, n.d. [ca. 1977]), p. 92.

7. Such empirical research has been incorporated in T. J. Pempel,

ed., *Policymaking in Contemporary Japan* (Ithaca: Cornell University Press, 1977); see conclusion (Chap. 9).

8. Remarks by Professor Akuto Hiroshi, seminar with members of the Nihonjin Kenkyūkai, Japan House, New York, March 14, 1977 (see citation to text, n.6 above).

6

The Postwar Economy

At times it seems that only the skilled economist, the mathematically trained econometrician, or the knowledgeable businessman can understand the intricate Japanese economy and its complicated relationships with the outer world. Laymen can attempt, however, to grasp the manner in which the basic culture of Japan has directly affected Japanese economic behavior. They can understand, in reverse, how economic development has profoundly affected the lifestyle of the Japanese.

THE BACKGROUND

The modern economy, including particularly the industrial structure of a nation, is conditioned by the variety of people's wants expressed in the market (demand); by the level of development (specifically the technological capacity) and the relative accessibility of raw materials (supply); and finally, by the underlying value system, the social structure, and individual behavior. These last factors constitute what is called the culture or national character.

Social Foundations

In the postwar—and even more in the post-treaty—period, Japan has been controlled in the political realm by those whom we have called the Establishment. Both in politics and in the economy, according to some foreigners, "Japan, Inc.," has offered restraint of trade and unfair competition. The Japanese economist Kitamura Hiroshi has used more moderate terms—

in French, *dirigisme*, and in English, sponsored or controlled capitalism.[1] Others have argued that the Japanese economy has constituted an unrestrained free enterprise system. The first task is to try to reconcile these apparent contradictions.

A review of the evolution of Japanese tradition has clearly revealed the persistence of one value that the process of modernization has not eroded. In Japan there has always been a highly developed sense of loyalty and dedication to some kind of close-knit group (the family, the clan, the domain, or the firm). In the nineteenth century, modern technology and a kind of capitalism were transplanted to Japan, but a certain degree of collectivism remained in the highly homogeneous society. One can detect indelible marks of group loyalty on, for example, the management of individual enterprises.

Japan's unique modern system began to take shape in the mid-1930s. For a Japanese high school graduate (at age eighteen to nineteen) or college graduate (at age twenty-two to twenty-three), the most important consideration in choosing a position has been the balance sheet of benefits to be gained at the time of retirement (at age fifty-five to sixty). Before the 1970s the Japanese employee seldom changed employers; the employer seldom discharged employees before their retirement. The worker always knew that the pay scale depended, at least in the first half of his career, on seniority (only later would merit and achievement produce differential rewards).

During a period of rapid growth (for example, in the 1960s), businesses grew steadily and took on more employees each year. Thus the younger came to outnumber the older employees; so the labor force was in the form of a pyramid. The elders could be paid well if the younger workers would accept lower wages for a time; the latter could look forward to accelerating pay raises and promotions, providing business remained on the upswing. During a short slump it did not pay to discharge employees who had made a lifetime commitment to the firm. It did make sense to sell below cost in a recession, particularly if the transaction involved exports; so unemployment figures were not a good indication of the status of the economy. Of course, during a slump there might be an increase in the number of unemployed employees, called sunshine boys if they were elders of not high merit, men who were marking time until retirement. In times of prolonged recession (and perhaps when the economy entered a later stage, as we shall observe), the pyramid of workers had a tendency to convert into a diamond. The ratio of highly paid, slightly older employees increased in proportion to newly recruited workers.

Such practices have imparted very special characteristics to Japanese economic behavior. First, there is the frequently observed strong corporate loyalty: employees have come to believe that they share the same fate as their employers. Second, there is the very low level of unemployment, even during recession. These are the more traditional collectivist features.

On the other hand, government decisions in the economic sphere were (and still are) arrived at through a long and complicated process of consultation, compromise, and consensus between bureaucrats and party faction leaders, between the bureaucracy and business, and among all groups in the Establishment. Despite appearances, there has been a surprising degree of decentralization in the decision-making process. This is a mixed (traditional and modern) feature of the system.

There has also been a lively, even fierce, competition among the units of the oligopolistic economic structure. This is the modern, capitalist feature of the economy. Here is yet another illustration of the coexistence of traditional values and modern techniques in Japan. After a brief review of the history of the development of this unique system,[2] it will be possible to assay some of its accomplishments, its shortcomings, and (in Chapter 7) its most recent transformation.

Modern Development

Japan's economy has often been included among those called late developers, and it has usually been regarded as one of the most rapid developers. As a matter of fact, the emergence of the modern Japanese economy was relatively early as compared with other nations in the developing world, its growth was relatively slow when measured against the desires of members of the economically underdeveloped world of our day.

One of the clues to Japan's later growth was the fact that in the beginning of the modern era (1868–90), Japan did not sit by and await the establishment of large, complete, technologically complex industries imported from the West. Rather, the Japanese first fully exploited traditional crafts—for example, silk production. As a result, the annual output of the economy doubled before imported technology was put to use.

The first Japanese industries to modernize were in the field of textiles (particularly cotton). Even in the last twenty years of the nineteenth century, however, the Japanese were content to reestablish and upgrade traditional light industries (paper, sugar refining, food processing), and to establish new production on a sound footing (cement, glass, beer). Already by the late 1880s, the agricultural, traditional, and light industries had provided the necessary surplus for further expansion. Aside from those industries directly tied to strategic defense, the choices of sectors within which to expand were made on the basis of sound business prospects rather than on ideas of national prestige.

By the turn of the century, Japan was ready to embark on what Watanabe Tsunehiko has characterized as an "imitative process" of development. It was a matter of obtaining what in our day would be known as technological assistance from abroad.

The era of World War I was marked by Japan's first "takeoff," as analysts of development label it. The country's military contribution to the Allied victory was minimal; so Japan was left to concentrate on industrial growth at home and on the expansion of overseas markets. Huge export surpluses meant that the nation no longer had to rely on agriculture and traditional crafts to produce the surpluses necessary for further investment.

This period (1910–20) nonetheless saw modern industry grafted onto a labor-rich semideveloped (if not still underdeveloped) economy. This was not a phenomenon confined to Japan, but its effects were striking there simply because of the size of the contrasting sectors. On the one hand were the traditional labor-intensive pursuits (agriculture was a good example) operating on a small scale and local base. On the other were the modern, Western-style projects requiring large amounts of capital equipment and therefore investment.

In the 1920s, the widening gap between the two sectors, together with worldwide depression, contributed to political tension in Japan. The modern sector continued to expand as weaker firms were weeded out and the celebrated *zaibatsu* (finance cliques) reached their peak of power. By the early 1920s the output of workers in the modernized sector was at least four times higher and wages were at least three times higher than comparable figures for workers in the traditional sector. Continued growth hid the serious social and economic problems in the more traditional parts of society. This double standard or "dual structure," as economists identified it, was destined to play an important role in the postwar economy.

In the late 1930s and early 1940s mobilization for war and engagement in conflict served to widen the gap in the dual structure. Exploitation of colonies and military ventures on the mainland also added to the number of corporations in the modern sector. New firms competed with the older *zaibatsu* in Manchuria and in the outer empire. In one decade (1930–40), the output of modern industries doubled, and even production contributed by agriculture increased by about 25 percent. Since most of the surplus was plowed back into heavy industry and military expenditures, the standard of living of ordinary Japanese did not go up proportionately. Most important of all, the first chapter in the story of Japan's modern development ended in total war. By the time the nation's leaders brought themselves "to endure the unendurable" and surrender, fully half of Japan's industrial capacity had been destroyed.

Occupation policies had a long-lasting effect on Japan's economy. In the beginning (just after the defeat of Japan), the results of SCAP's actions were quite mixed. On the positive side, massive economic assistance, particularly the provision of food, staved off complete collapse and chaos. Initial encouragement of, and then later limitations on, activities of the labor movement had both positive and negative effects. In terms of immediate agricultural production, the impact of land reform was probably negative; but in the long run, this quiet revolution laid down a firm foundation in the countryside for solid growth. Many of the older corporations, stripped of the *zaibatsu* form and operating procedure, found it difficult to carry on.

The economic policies of the Occupation were, of course, initially imposed on the Japanese. They proved to be effective, however, only insofar as they were in accord with Japanese aspirations. After a mixed beginning, Occupation directives tended to reinforce Japanese hopes for a better life. Such visions had first been widely shared in the period of Taishō democracy in the 1920s. In any case, by 1948 the ideas held by the occupationnaires began to change as economic stabilization and industrial reconstruction became the high priorities. By the time of the Korean conflict (1950), the Japanese economy was reasonably stabilized and running smoothly, if still at low levels of output. The preparatory stage was timely, for Japan's industry was then in a position to profit from large-scale procurement orders placed by the United States for military use in Korea. By 1953 Japanese output per capita had been resurrected and was close to the level of the mid-1930s.

THE ERA OF GROWTH

Historians may come to characterize the middle decades of the twentieth century as an era of rather unexpected economic development. After all, for a century critics had accurately identified inherent weaknesses in capitalist economies, pointing to contradictions in their uneven development, and had made dire predictions about the future of the capitalist world. Although it could empirically be demonstrated that economic factors were not the sole, or even the major, ones that caused conflict or even imperialism, it is nonetheless true that war was a terrible waste of economic resources. Two world wars had indeed threatened to wreck free economies.

One difficulty with the gloomy forecasts was that so-called pure capitalist systems, if they ever existed at all, lasted for only brief periods of time. Reforms came as much from the conservative center and right as from the reformist left; as a result, in the 1950s there was a remarkable resurgence of what were called free enterprise economies. In fact, these were already mixed capitalist economies for the most part, with varying degrees of public control melded with private sectors (as in the U.S. economy). Until the 1970s and the stage to which the Club of Rome referred as the "limits of growth," such economies registered outstanding performances and thus reinforced foundations for further expansion. The difficult problem of equitable distribution of the proceeds of production may have remained, but by and large there was enough diffusion of the fruits of growth to make for a sharp reduction in the ideological component of politics and to permit the majority to believe that revolution was not probable.

In this pattern of postwar development, Japan's economy is unique both in its record of aggregate growth and in its relatively low expenditure on social overhead. The Japanese economy is also an exception in that, in the process of growth, the share of national income accruing to labor tended to decline during the two decades (1950–70).

The Post-Treaty Miracle

It will be recalled that, in one of the Establishment's deliberate gambles, leaders promised that national income would double in a decade. In bald figures, the results were almost unbelievable. Japan's gross national product in current prices actually increased 1.9 times in a five-year period (1955–60), jumped another 2.1 times in the next five-year period (1960–65), and increased another 2.5 times in the succeeding five-year period (1965–70). Put in a slightly different fashion, the *annual* rate of growth in GNP in real terms (nominal terms do not take account of inflation) averaged 8.8 percent in the first five-year period, accelerated to 10.1 percent in the second, and reached an incredible 12.1 percent in the third, ending with 1970. (Three percent is considered an excellent rate in a country like the United States.) Between 1962 and 1971 the output of Japan rose to give the nation the world's third largest GNP after the United States and the Soviet Union (see Table 6.1).

A somewhat more meaningful comparison can now be made in terms of income per capita. The figure came to a little over $200 in the early 1950s. By 1972, only two decades later, the level was at $2,300 (allowing for an exchange rate adjustment made in 1971). GNP figures were in gross amounts, and even national income per capita was only an average. Neither spoke to the equally basic issue of equitable distribution; high

TABLE 6.1
Selected Economic Indicators: An International Comparison

Economic Indicators	Japan	USA	UK	West Germany	France	Italy
1971 GNP ($ billions)	256.6	1050.4	146.7	235.5	176.7	108.2
1971 National income per capita	1991.0	4133.0	2026.0	3056.0	2646.0	1635.0
1972 Steel production (metric tons)	96.9	120.7	25.3	43.7	23.9	19.7
1972 Exports ($ billions)	28.6	49.1	24.3	46.2	26.0	18.5
1969 Passenger cars (per 1000 pop.)	67.0	526.0	250.0	244.0	270.0	185.0
1970 TV sets (per 1000 pop.)	215.0	412.0	293.0	272.0	201.0	181.0
1966 Social Security	52.3	258.9	229.1	332.7	321.2	177.9

Sources: Bank of Japan; EPA; adapted from Kitamura, Choices for the Japanese Economy.

GNP levels said very little about the quality of life. Such problems were to be seriously raised in the 1970s.

Factors in this astounding performance can easily be identified with hindsight. In one sense, development proceeded according to conscious plans. The Economic Planning Agency (Keizai Kikaku Chō; the EPA's forerunner during the Occupation was the Economic Stabilization Board) made the breathtaking projections. The strategy was to expand the modern industrial sector fast enough to draw more personnel into high-productivity, high-wage employment from the primary agricultural sector and thus to dissolve once and for all the dual structure.

In another sense, no plan was able to keep up with growth. Except in years when there were fiscally induced recessions (1958, 1962, 1965, 1971), growth rates consistently outstripped projections. The result was a kind of rolling plan, meaning that projections were revised after each year according to annual production results.

Hugh Patrick has expressed the belief that the powerful Ministry of Finance provided certain problems in planning.[3] While the high-ranking bureaucrats in the ministry were certainly bright, as graduates of the public law faculty of the University of Tokyo they were legalistic in their outlook—they worshipped balanced or surplus budgets. They lacked the background in economics usually expected of planners. Nevertheless, Finance bureaucrats saw themselves as the leaders who made the final decisions about what was good for the nation. They were certain that their people made the best prime ministers; and they regularly had the support of the incumbent prime minister, who often as not had been graduated from their ranks. Although the press regularly grumbled about the close ties between the planners and big business, a majority of the public consistently approved the path chosen.

A second factor in the success story (if growth is considered success) has to do with the Japanese public and its capacity to save. This capacity was translated into the possibility of a high rate of investment, that is to say, Japanese at large were willing to forgo consumption in favor of plowing back surpluses into capital goods and even more growth. Statistics showing international comparisons of GNP and savings (in Table 6.2) readily revealed the extraordinary Japanese rate of savings. Japan's high growth rate was a product of the rate of investment, the high quality of the labor force, the acumen in business organization, and the diffusion of technology.

The third factor in Japan's rapid growth has to do with technology. Beginning in the nineteenth century, Japanese accumulated know-how and experience. Their nation was then effectively cut off from world technological development during World War II. Having paid the formidable costs of waging war, the Japanese by historical accident were able to move in laterally during the postwar era and make use of the latest

TABLE 6.2
Gross Savings: An International Comparison, 1961-70 Average (Percent)

Country	Ratio: gross savings to GNP	Share of GNP household savings	Ratio: personal savings to disposable income
Japan	37.5%	12.6%	18.6%
W.Germany	27.4	9.8	14.7
France	25.7	8.7	12.5
Italy	23.6	11.6	15.4
UK	18.7	3.8	5.6
USA	15.4	4.4	6.4

Note: Order of countries in accordance with gross savings - GNP ratios; derived from Bank of Japan

Source: Kitamura, *Choices*

technological improvements in order to rebuild their industry. Because a large proportion of the nation's industrial plant was destroyed or scrapped during and after the war, by the 1960s the great bulk of Japan's equipment was brand new (ten years old or less). Japanese also made breakthroughs of their own—for example, in the use of transistors. The postwar era marked the beginning of an emphasis on quality in Japanese products.

The technological phase of growth was directed by a newly created agency, the Ministry of International Trade and Industry (MITI). Widely known by the initials of its English name, even in Japan, MITI was somewhat similar in function to the U.S. Department of Commerce. Its mission reflected the strong commitment of the government to make Japanese industries competitive in the world. MITI assembled information, maintained its own research institutes, and made critical judgments on markets in which Japanese business was apt to be competitive. It also financed the Japan External Trade Organization (known in the United States as JETRO).

Aspects of the Growth Economy

In the postwar growth period, the Japanese economy benefited from what has been called "a very accommodating labor force." This meant that a large proportion of workers entered industry directly from rural areas, where traditional norms such as discipline, obedience, and respect for superiors were highly valued. So long as it could be tapped, the pool of workers provided by the traditional side of the dual structure also played a significant role in the supply of mobile and relatively cheap labor.

In the process of growth the modern sector not only absorbed all the increases in size of labor force (and there were some resulting from the postwar baby boom), but also drew substantial numbers of workers out of agriculture and small-scale industry. In the decade 1955–65 the proportion of the labor force in primary pursuits fell from 40 percent to 25 percent. By the early 1970s it fell below 20 percent (in 1975 it was 14 percent). Meanwhile, the proportion of the labor force engaged in secondary pursuits rose from 23 percent to 32 percent between 1955 and 1965. By 1975 it was at 34 percent (see Table 7.1[4]). The share of GNP produced by the primary sector fell from 23 percent in 1955 to less than 10 percent in 1965. Over the same period the share produced by manufacturing increased from 23 percent to over 33 percent. As a result, the end of the dual structure was in sight. Whereas in the 1950s employment as a *sarari man* in a large company with good wages and generous benefits was seen as the privilege of a minority, by the mid-1960s it seemed to be within the reach of everyone.

These are some of the reasons why Kitamura recognized the dual structure as an important factor in postwar growth. Japan was following along the path of developed Western countries, but with a lag of three or more decades. In the early 1960s, for the first time in Japan's history, the demand for and supply of labor came into equilibrium. The other striking characteristic in a kind of telescoped development (to be examined in Chapter 7), was the dramatic increase in the relative importance of the tertiary sector (services, finance, software, information retrieval, and such).

Japan's growth economy of the 1960s was characterized by the relatively high proportion of GNP devoted to fixed capital formation, as compared with other developed nations. Within the manufacturing sector, the biggest gains were made by heavy industry—for example, engineering, automobiles, chemicals, and electronics.

Emphasis on status in the GNP race illustrates the strong Japanese sense of hierarchy. Close attention to status in the outside world also has tended to distort the condition of various parts of the economy inside Japan. Thus, although Japan may have forged ahead in various industries in the advanced sector (like steel, shipbuilding, and automobiles), as late as the 1970s, overall per capita productivity in Japan was still only half that of the United States and about two-thirds that of West Germany. Moreover, the obsession with fixed capital formation produced the counterpart of a steadily declining relative share of national product devoted to personal consumption

Production Lines for TV Sets: Matsushita plant, Ibaragi.

Yawata Industrial District, Kita-Kyūshū: Including the Yawata steelworks.

and benefits. Public outlays on collective services (social security, education, and care of the aged) have remained relatively modest in relation to capacity.

One aspect of this dynamic, booming economy proved to be politically significant in the early 1970s. The location of capital-intensive industry on a relatively small, rather fragile land area resulted in an incredibly high-density economy. Overcrowding in cities and environmental disruption were not unrelated to the system of management under which growth took place. The conservative governments eventually would have to come to grips with this shadow on growth.

Throughout the period of growth there were also imbalances and shortages that acted as fiscal brakes consciously applied to achieve slowdowns, spot scarcities of labor, and rising living costs. The latter deprived the Japanese of full participation in the gains, and some referred to the income doubling plan as "the price doubling plan." A medium-term economic plan (1965) tried to ease some of the pressures by paying more attention to the improvement of efficiency in agriculture and in small business. It also aimed to reduce strains in public housing, transportation, and social services. These developments represented the beginning of the Japanese consciousness that growth itself had limits.

To repeat, a dual structure inherited from earlier times guaranteed, on the one hand, an elastic labor supply and, on the other, relatively low wages. As far as distributive shares of manufacturing output were concerned, the proportion distributed to labor in Japan was significantly lower than the corresponding international standard. One effect was a relatively low consumption ratio. Put the other way around, there was a bias in favor of the maximization of private capital. As economist Martin Bronfenbrenner observed, this was one of the "contradictions" in the Japanese economic miracle. The standard of living of the ordinary Japanese, although it must have risen quite substantially over the growth years, nonetheless never matched the high pitch of economic growth.[5]

Foreigners, too, played significant roles in Japan's growth. They provided needed technical assistance (as they had in the nineteenth century) and supplied direct and indirect investment in order to fill the gap between necessary imports and available exports. The steady growth of exports fulfilled two needs: it matched an increasing demand for raw materials (coal, iron ore, and particularly petroleum products), and it met the increasing Japanese demand for imports of consumer goods. Between 1962 and 1971, exports rose more than fourfold in current prices.

In the early 1970s, before the oil shock of 1973, Japan's remarkable growth, rising level of exports, and balance-of-payments surplus began to arouse hostility abroad. After the 1973 energy crisis, of course, Japan's problem appeared to be in the realm of deficits rather than surpluses. The shortfalls, however, were soon displaced by towering surpluses. Japan came to represent to nations abroad the need to accommodate to a shift in world economic relationships.

Toward the end of the 1960s, Japan, like any other advanced country, began to come to grips with problems inherent in rapid growth. From the early 1970s on, it became apparent that the postwar international financial system, based on the overwhelming superiority of the United States, was heading for transition, if not breakdown. Especially in the United States, there was a temptation to link the Japanese accumulation of foreign exchange with U.S. balance-of-payments problems and the decline in the value of the dollar. Therefore, the Japanese were subjected for the first time to intensive pressures: anti-dumping measures, special quotas, and what were euphemistically called "voluntary export restraints." This was the period, too, in which negative images were called forth: the Tokyo management as "Japan, Inc.," the businessmen overseas as "ugly Japanese," and all of the people of the island nation as "transistor salesmen," "economic animals," and "workaholics."

NOTES

1. Though not an economist, I had the privilege of reviewing an excellent and succinct analysis: Hiroshi Kitamura, *Choices for the Japanese Economy* (London: Royal Institute of International Affairs, 1976). The study was an extremely helpful guide in preparing this chapter.

2. Once again, I am grateful to have had the survey of a colleague and coauthor: E. S. Crawcour, "The Modern Economy," in Arthur E. Tiedemann, ed., *An Introduction to Japanese Civilization* (New York: Columbia University Press, 1974), pp. 487–513.

3. See the proceedings of a conference hosted by the East Asian Institute of Columbia University, held March 24, 1978: Edward J. Lincoln, ed., *Japan's Changing Political Economy* (Washington: United States–Japan Trade Council, 1978).

4. Please note that the figures given in Table 7.1 are for numbers of persons (out of the total gainfully employed). Thus there were 16.1 million in primary pursuits (out of a labor force of 39.3 million) in 1955; only 11.7 million (out of 47.6 million) in 1965; and 7.4 million (out of 53.1 million) in 1975. By way of comparison, the total number in secondary pursuits increased from 9.2 million (1955) to 15.2 million (1965) and to 18.1 million (1975) out of the totals for the labor force in respective years. Also note that by 1975, the total number in tertiary (service) pursuits (27.6 million) exceeded the totals for primary and secondary combined (25.5 million).

5. Martin Bronfenbrenner, "Economic Miracles and Japan's Income-Doubling Plan," in William W. Lockwood, ed., *The State and Economic Enterprise in Japan* (Princeton: Princeton University Press, 1965).

7

The Postindustrial Society

The industrial revolution, which was in fact a prolonged evolution, unleashed a set of forces that vastly changed traditional societies. Economies became diversified, populations migrated to the cities, new classes and political alignments appeared, and standards of living rose. It has most often been identified as happening in England from the middle of the eighteenth century to the late nineteenth century, a little later in France and Germany, after the Civil War in the United States, and in the early twentieth century in Japan.

SOME MODELS OF CHANGE

The literature of the nineteenth and early twentieth centuries was full of attempts to analyze the changes arising out of the industrial revolution, to evolve a science of history, and to prescribe how societies should respond to change. Then the establishment of new states after World War II stimulated countless new attempts to understand the patterns of change, now frequently termed modernization or development. Japan has presented a special case in this literature as the first non-Western state to become a major industrial power; this section will therefore briefly survey the development of modernization theory and its application to Japan.

Older Models

Sliding over for the sake of simplicity certain preliminary stages of history (marked by gathering, primitive, and slave societies), earlier explanations of development usually began with the *traditional society*, which was defined as having rested on a subsistence, usually agrarian, economy. In traditional societies, legal authority and political rule were legitimized by religious or secular tradition. Traditional political culture was parochial. It demonstrated a low level of countrywide mass involvement. Social integration was tenuous, except in primary groups. There was also a low level of education.

After World War II, theorists attempted to apply concepts of change to so-called non-Western societies and to further unravel the tapestry of development. Thus emerged an image of the *transitional society*. Transition was marked by instability of the traditional order and, according to Samuel Huntington, "political decay" of traditional authority. Lucian Pye spoke of the "crisis of identity" in transitional, non-Western states.

In older models, the *modern society* was assumed to be a highly industrialized and integrated unit. Descriptions ran well beyond the economic and technological, however, and embraced social organization, the role of the individual, and the ethos. Subjects or citizens were actively involved in a political system through integrating interest groups, political parties, and (particularly in democracies) elections. The decision-making process was described as being rational and sometimes accountable to the people. The role of the individual, previously rooted in familial status, was now increasingly determined by achievement. Often these criteria of merit conflicted with a growing egalitarian spirit bred in a modern society. All members of the modern society did not engage equally in making decisions. Stability was sustained, however, by the appearance of the characteristics listed above, in what Gabriel Almond and Sidney Verba called a "civic political culture."[1]

An impertinent question, one which challenges the surety of the ideas in modernization theory, inevitably emerges from older models of change. To paraphrase Marx, will the modern condition be historically marked by the withering away of change? Newer theories, to which the Japanese experience contributes valuable data, seem to indicate that development can move beyond modern (if by that term is meant the familiar industrial society of the twentieth century).

Contemporary Models

Contemporary models of development pick up certain constructs from the older models. Thus at the *primary stage* of development the mode of production is usually rooted in agriculture, forestry, and fishing (the primary pursuits). The *secondary stage* is a product of the industrial revolution. (The labor force is engaged mainly in industry, that is, in secondary pursuits.) The *tertiary stage* is characterized by the emergence of employment in highly skilled tasks and services (tertiary pursuits).

According to contemporary theory, when the surplus from industrial output rises to a certain point, there is a parallel shift of demand and supply into services. The service sector, including trade, transportation, finance, insurance, management (both government and business), real estate brokerage, information retrieval, and the like, accounts for most of the output and absorbs most of the labor force. Thus, the primary stage is distinguished by a labor-intensive economy; the secondary, by a capital-intensive economy; and the tertiary, by a knowledge-intensive economy. The third stage has also been labeled the postindustrial era, but there are many other indicative names.

The term *postindustrial* was coined rather casually in the late 1950s in an analysis of work and leisure. Reshaped and applied by Daniel Bell, it came to be used in a much wider context. Whereas much of development theory had hitherto been drawn from, and applied to, Western experience, the ideas of Bell and of some who followed his theoretical path extended the analysis to the unusual case of Japan.

Zbigniew Brzezinski, for example, described in essence three Americas: first, the preindustrial society of Appalachia, of the sharecropper and of the migrant worker; second, the industrial world of the highly unionized blue-collar worker; and third, the "technetronic" realm of the technician, information retrieval specialist, and scientist. As a member of the Trilateral Commission (which includes delegates from Japan, the United States, and Western Europe), Brzezinski devoted six months to study and writing in Tokyo. He found the "sudden blossoming" of Japan—its emergence from traditional, graduation from modern industrial, and entry into postindustrial society—to be something very "fragile."[2] By this he meant to indicate that the Japanese were uncertain as to their mission at this stage of development.

Most studies of advanced industrial societies, however, still concentrated on the experience of Western Europe and North America. The old industrial societies had undergone sufficient alteration to justify viewing the results as something qualitatively different. The range of terminology reflected the search for clues. Some observers spoke of "the technological society." Others called it "the temporary society." Still others referred to "the postmodern, active society." With a little more specificity, John K. Galbraith (who has been widely published, read, and heard in Japan) wrote about "the new industrial state." Samuel Huntington was the first to describe "postindustrial politics." Two authors carried the concept one step further by analyzing policy in a "postwelfare state." Martin Heisler studied political structures and processes in Western Europe, concentrating on "postindustrial democracies."[3]

Japan: Traditional, Modern, and Postmodern

Meanwhile, in the period just before Japan's explosive growth in the 1960s, there was a certain ambivalence to be found in descriptions of Japanese society. It was recognized as highly industrialized and affluent, something like its advanced Western counterparts. Japan's economy still suffered from a dual structure, however, marked by the coexistence of traditional and modern elements. The Japanese political process remained somewhat unfamiliar and therefore not quite modern (as presumably Western political processes were). A distinguished Japanese sociologist referred to Japan as "an open society made up of closed components." It was, moreover, a highly stratified society with mutually exclusive group loyalties—a social structure that had been little changed by industrialization and Western imports.[4]

There was other evidence of the effective admixture of traditional and modern, of the coexistence of preindustrial mores and behavior and the values of an industrial age. These characteristics will be summarized in Chapter 8 after first examining here the results of the variable forces of Japanese tradition, of modernization, and of contemporary transition.

In the 1960s, when Japan plunged into high-speed growth, social critics began to notice that the nation had a highly literate, skilled labor force, attuned to the media, which could be described as an information society (*jōhō shakai*). Other analyses of Japanese society, although they sought to treat various aspects of change, most often began with the narrowly technological or the more broadly economic. In his evaluation of Japanese politics, for example, Taketsugu Tsurutani selected three cross-national criteria.[5] First, in the postindustrial society a majority of the labor force is engaged in the tertiary or service sector. Since 1973 Japan has had 55 percent or more of its workers involved in trade, finance, management, and the provision of what is called software (see Table 7.1).

Second, in the postindustrial society the service sector generates a larger proportion of the gross national product than do the primary and secondary sectors combined. In Japan, the proportion of GNP provided by the tertiary sector has been above 50 percent since at least 1963.

Third, the postindustrial society demonstrates a capacity for very high levels of production, annual national income per capita, savings, and investment. Japan's astounding record on these fronts has been noted previously and is fairly well known as a "miracle," but the figures still remain startling. In 1955 Japan recorded a net GNP of about $20.3 billion (7.3 trillion yen, the total adjusted for inflation and figured at the then-current value of the yen, ¥ 360=U.S. $1). By 1965 the Japanese economy had joined members of the exclusive world's club of $100 billion–GNP nations and by 1970 the GNP had reached $200 billion. Five years later in 1975 the GNP had passed the next mark, $300 billion. In March 1978 Japan's GNP stood at $448 billion (106.49 trillion yen, then at the value of ¥ 237=U.S. $1). Technological progress, economies of scale, organizational skills, and qualitative improvements of capital and labor had contributed an unparalleled share of the output and helped to account for the geometric increases in GNP.

Up until two or three centuries ago the annual income per capita in most societies was below $200. The Japanese had a per capita income of $200 (in 1965 dollars) in 1920. A generation ago, before the impact of inflation was felt worldwide, it

TABLE 7.1
Japan: The Postindustrial Society

Item:	1934-36 annual	1947	1950	1955	1960	1965	1970	1975
1. Population (million persons)	69.3	78.1	84.1	90.1	94.3	99.2	104.7	111.9
2. Gainfully occupied population (millions)	31.2	33.3	35.6	39.3	43.7	47.6	52.6	53.1
3. Population by sector (millions) Total	31.2	33.3	35.6	39.3	43.7	47.6	52.6	53.1
Primary	14.5	17.8	17.2	16.1	14.2	11.7	10.1	7.4
Secondary	6.8	7.4	7.8	9.2	12.8	15.2	17.7	18.1
Tertiary	9.9	8.1	10.6	13.9	16.7	20.7	24.3	27.6
4. Consumer price index (1934-36 = 100)	100.0	109.1	219.9	297.4	328.0	443.2	577.9	988.8

Source: Nakamura Takafusa, "The Need for Continued Growth," trans. from Sengo no Nihon (Tokyo: Kodansha, 1978). Japan Echo (Special Issue, 1979), p. 70, Table 1.

was thought that the highest form of industrial society was attained when the annual per capita income reached $2,000, which was the threshold of the mass consumption phase. It was predicted (about 1965) that the postindustrial stage would be entered when the annual per capita income passed $4,000.

Japan did not reach the industrial level until 1967 (about twenty-five years later than the United States). Within five years, however, the country was hurled into the mass consumption phase. Meanwhile, in 1970, Herman Kahn predicted that Japan would reach the postindustrial stage late in the 1970s. Japanese were tremendously excited over Kahn's predictions that their nation would attain superstate status before the end of the century.

Very high income levels (in March 1978 the annual per capita income of Japanese stood at $7,167, as compared with $9,150 for Americans) provided the potential for higher levels of expenditure (as compared with those of the past) and relatively high levels of savings (compared with those of the other postindustrial nations). Between 1961 and 1970, Japanese gross savings out of GNP averaged 37.5 percent (more than twice the U.S. rate, see Table 6.2). Almost 97 percent of all Japanese households held savings in postal accounts, stocks, and bonds. Holdings averaged about 1.6 million yen per household (or $6,000 at the then-current exchange rate). Such a savings rate made possible high levels of investment not only in fixed capital, but also in sophisticated service networks, advanced software, and extremely high levels of information.

These, then, are the basic economic characteristics of the new society: a majority of the labor force in the tertiary sector; services contributing a larger proportion of GNP than do primary and secondary sectors combined; and high levels of production, income per capita, expenditures, and savings. The characteristics are, however, both cause and effect. The economy is but a subsystem in a total societal structure, and other aspects of the postindustrial phase are equally significant.

ASPECTS OF THE POSTINDUSTRIAL SOCIETY

Perhaps most important of all, Japan's celebrated insularity was being steadily eroded in the 1970s, as the nation entered the postindustrial stage. Kunihiro Masao, a professor who also served as host of a nationally televised program of news and commentary, coined the ingenious phrase "intermestic age" to describe this phenomenon (see Chapter 9). The phrase suggests that whatever happens on the *inter*national front has an effect on a world power at home, and that a major nation's do*mestic* events inevitably affect world affairs.[6]

At the domestic level, the contemporary postindustrial society is bigger than it has ever been: there are more things, more people, more places. What was called "psychic mobility" in the modernization process is now named "the eclipse of distance" by Daniel Bell.

The postindustrial society's component organizations are more complicated: they organize more and more people, they come to dominate the society, and they offer a paradox. Belonging to a new organization may be less encompassing a matter than earlier foci of loyalty (for example, in the single-cell agrarian Japanese village). Moreover, the individual becomes skeptical of strong attachments to causes or organizations. And yet the individual in the postindustrial society is far more involved in regional and national organizations than was the member of the traditional society.

Members of the new society are, or at least soon expect to be, richer in material goods. With the eclipse of distance, the poor are nearer to the rich in lifestyle. The ideal becomes the way of the suburban, white-collar, salary man. In economic terms, everyone is optimistic (whether they are justified or not). On the other hand, there is skepticism on the political front.

The postindustrial society may appear to be easier to live in because of the achievements of advanced technology and the expansion of leisure time, but these advances also create some anxieties. According to public opinion polls, while the Japanese are proud to realize that they are on the threshold of the five-day work week, traditionally socialized to hard work they are quite uncertain as to whether they can effectively use the increased leisure time.

The Political Economy

Modern capitalism at the postindustrial stage turns out such wealth that the economic factor is the central factor in producing a wide political consensus. (The connection tends to frustrate Marxist critics.) Growth is not only extremely rapid but also diffuses, or seems to diffuse, benefits widely.

There is a widespread optimism that the postindustrial society can increase its wealth indefinitely and also distribute the fruits of growth equitably, *if* it has wise leaders and uses the right tools. This feeling allows an increase in public management of economic systems, in mixed—that is, semicapitalist, semiplanned—societies as well as in planned socialist societies. Even under conservative leadership, there is an extension of the welfare state. Again there is a paradox here. An annual increase in income per capita is taken for granted; so the postindustrial seems to be the affluent society. On the other hand, the society has already admitted the precedent of rather strict planning. Often, free individual desires clash with public need.

The high level of production and relatively wide distribution result in a society with a large middle class and a low level of status polarization. A network of active secondary associations makes its appearance. Pluralism, according to one strain of Western political thought, provides the foundation for a stable democracy. Yet there is no reason why the postindustrial might not be a socialist society.

Certainly Japan of the 1960s well illustrated many of the political characteristics listed. The Establishment laid out plans for the mixed economy. The majority LDP was the reconnaissance party, which constantly pierced new frontiers of growth. Affluence altered even the platforms of the progressive opposition into pragmatic, moderate, centrist programs.

In Japan, as in most postindustrial societies, labor-management conflict was not eliminated, but it was better institutionalized. It might be argued that Japanese collective bargaining rights were won by fiat in the MacArthur constitution rather than on the picket line. The advent of advanced technology improved the quality of labor and increased its productivity. Although wages increased at a faster pace than did labor productivity, the share of national income accruing to labor did not increase as fast as did Japan's GNP. Nonetheless, Japanese labor also came to expect more money, more consumer durables, more luxuries, and more leisure. In this context, the worker was (or soon hoped to be) a property owner with a more family-centered life and paid vacations. He was a member of a laboring class that was no longer motivated by nor interested in militant political activity that might challenge the system. Other subtle aspects of the change into the new society demand further analysis of the economy.

The Economy

Japan's growth in the early 1960s was immeasurably aided by the dual structure of the economy. Fully 90 percent of entrants into the labor force came directly out of junior high school; many of these migrated from rural areas. By the late 1970s, however, some 95 percent of Japanese youth was going on to senior high school (a rate about the same as that in the United States; the Japanese dropout rate was, however, lower than the American). Moreover, the proportion of Japanese young people entering college or university was rising steadily (to between 35 and 40 percent in 1978). Such changes had an effect on the mobility of youth. The future of the lifetime employment system came to be openly discussed. The labor force also made new demands: reward commensurate with performance; avoidance of overtime (without extra payment); and longer periods of leisure. Nevertheless, Japanese labor has remained relatively accommodating. Minor recessions of the mid-1970s and Japan's only prolonged severe recession (1978–79) in the postwar period moderated the stridency of labor's voice.

As was the case with advanced, postindustrial nations of the West, by the late 1970s the Japanese economy was feeling the effects of rising relative labor costs and a higher energy bill. The result has been a shift in the very structure of the economy. For example, Japan has suffered a loss of comparative advantage, particularly in labor-intensive industries, where Japanese wages are high as compared with those of developing countries. Certain industries that had been competitive at one time are no longer so: nonferrous mineral smelting, refining, and processing as well as petrochemicals, textiles, and consumer electronics.

Such adjustments of the basic economic structure have created conflicts within the celebrated but by no means monolithic Establishment. Ministry of International Trade and

Industry bureaucrats were among the first to visualize a medium-growth economy, one would be complemented by those of developing neighbors in Southeast Asia, in Korea, and on Taiwan. Those areas now enjoy a comparative labor advantage. Thus the effort would be to move out of black-and-white television in favor of color and out of textiles into refined industrial processes. MITI's response to the oil shock of 1973 was to try to reduce energy-intensive in favor of knowledge-intensive industries. Leaders of large and entrenched industries organized in Keidanren were opposed to the plan. Well represented in the LDP, such interests had kept Japan in largely protected industries—where effective trade barriers were quite high—for example, in smelting and refining of raw materials, in textiles, and in food processing (the most heavily protected of all). These were also the points where international friction was felt.

Enough has been said about levels of income to realize that what might be called the religion of members of postindustrial societies has been consumerism. Japan of the 1960s shared the faith, but in an unusual manner. Most Japanese continued their high rate of savings, but the funds were dedicated to eventual expenditure on consumer durables. (Unlike Americans, many Japanese avoided installment debts except—at a mature age—for the expenditure on a house.) About one-third of all households acquired automobiles. Virtually every house had a refrigerator, a color television set, and an electric washing machine (the three imperial treasures of the 1960s). Durable consumer goods narrowed the lifestyle differences among metropolitan areas, smaller cities, and even villages. In 1962, some 76 percent of all Japanese respondents to a survey considered themselves to be members of the middle class; by 1969 over 90 percent saw themselves in this status.

Contrary to many predictions, in Japan the savings rate remained high into the late 1970s, but the purposes of thrift were different. Whereas in the 1960s savings were made to finance purchases of consumer durables, in the next decade public opinion surveys revealed marked concern for income in old age. Faced with greater difficulty in getting a job after retirement (conventionally at age fifty-five) and with as yet relatively low levels of social security benefits, Japanese continued to save—for survival.

Despite this dedication to consumer durables, one characteristic of Japan's pattern of growth has been that the level of consumption is low relative to the nation's capacity to produce. One reason is the Japanese individual's penchant to postpone expenditure until the total price of an item can be paid. Another is the national bias toward application of surplus to investment in fixed capital. As the per capita income level has approached that of the most advanced countries, the per capita stock of social overhead capital in Japan—parks, recreation facilities, hospitals, and the like—has lagged behind private investment in additional production. The per capita stock of housing is even lower.

In May 1979 the sensitive Japanese were stung by a description emanating from a European Community report, which described them as "workaholics living in rabbit hutches." They ruefully admitted that they suffered confined living quarters called *apāto* ("apartment," which is the general term, or "mansion," an almost ludicrous euphemism). During the Golden Week string of holidays that May, some 61.5 million Japanese (according to the National Police Agency) took refuge on the road to escape their cramped living conditions!

The insufficiency of welfare-related expenditures is at the root of the serious strain that afflicted the rapidly urbanizing society of the 1970s. Despite contributions from the private sector, overall social security still remains woefully inadequate, particularly in services for the elderly in which Japanese performance lags behind international standards.

The Society

In the typical postindustrial society there is a noticeable decrease in *vertical* status polarization (in socioeconomic terms, the society is more egalitarian). But there is a concomitant increase in *horizontal* social stratification: the society is also more complex, with lateral specialization and division of labor in a diversified economy and an emphasis on a myriad of services.

As of October 1, 1978, Japan's population had practically stabilized at 115 million. The annual rate of increase was only 0.89 percent, the lowest rise in eighteen years. Equally significant were changes in location and the subtle shift in structure.

Although population losses suffered by rural areas had eased off from 3.4 percent annually in 1971 to only 0.6 percent in 1978, a white paper issued by the National Land Agency (1978) reported that there were 1,093 villages, towns, and even cities (34 percent of all communities) that could be categorized as "depopulated areas." More specifically, the report indicated a drop of 20.7 percent among children up to fourteen years of age in the depopulated areas (the overall national figure climbed 8.3 percent); the fifteen to sixty-four-year-old group declined by 6.1 percent (as against a 5.1 percent rise nationally). Meanwhile, in depopulated areas the number of persons sixty-five years of age or older increased by 9.8 percent. One could not avoid the image of a rural society of elders deserted by the city-bound younger generation.

The postindustrial society has been created by, and further encouraged the expansion of, education. Education becomes the great socializer. In their study of civic culture, Gabriel Almond and Sidney Verba have linked education, political attitudes, and democracy. Theoretically, education promotes certain specific attributes: a great tolerance for ambiguity, increased deviation from parental (traditional) beliefs, and sophistication in political choice. The general effects are to increase a person's tolerance and support of civil liberties and to decrease prejudice and a tendency to authoritarianism.

The Japanese case bears out all of these attributes by and large, but it is at least doubtful whether education has increased the Japanese sense of political effectiveness. Rates of political participation (in elections) remain high, but this tendency may be as much a product of tradition as of education. And the rates are declining slightly, as skepticism of parties and leaders spreads.

According to UNESCO standards, Japan's literacy rate (99.9 percent) is the highest in the world. The total number of Japanese educational personnel, including research and development (R&D), ranks second (after the United States) in the world. Since the Japanese are highly literate and are voracious readers, public media and mass communications (*masu komi*) are all the more important. This is in sharp contrast to the prescriptive hierarchical oral tradition that operated one-on-one in primary groups. The media can be used for open, liberal education or for mass forced-feeding and indoctrination. Many will consequently become more knowledgeable and even skeptical, but the influence of *masu komi* tends to reinforce, rather than to challenge, the going consensus.

Mass society has most often been pictured as leading inevitably to alienation of individuals and eventual collapse of the social structure. There is a kind of nostalgia for the old unified traditional society. The Japanese case certainly supports the observation that although rapid urbanization gives rise to geographic and social mobility, it has concomitant disintegrating effects on isolated rural (and in that sense, traditional) society. Just as Oscar Lewis has found a marvelously intricate new pattern of social ties in the urban settlements of San Juan and Spanish Harlem in New York City, so observers of the Japanese urban scene have found complex admixtures of traditional and modern in the wards of Tokyo.[7]

Built into the affluent society is a generation of young people who have grown up with almost no exposure to scarcity and want. They constitute the new youth culture and extend it into adulthood. Since the 1960s Japanese youth have possessed an acute awareness of the lifestyle and attitudes of their counterparts throughout the world. The appearance of a youth culture in Japan, as in other postindustrial environments, raises an interesting query: although change moderates the effects of ethnic, class, and regional origin, does it at the same time create another gulf between generations? The end of the Pacific war is a demarcation point between groups of Japanese. As of March 1977, slightly over 50 percent of all Japanese had been born since 1945.

Rising levels of education and the society's need for trained personnel have helped expand the role of intellectuals (*interi*) in postwar Japanese society. More and more often, because of the demand for software in the service society, they have been coopted into the system managed by a permanent, routinized bureaucracy. The bureaucracy is in turn responsible to a conservative oligarchy (the Establishment in Japan). A decreasing number of *interi* step out of the society to be carping critics. They find it hard to combat the fundamental optimism of the middle class.

Perhaps the most important feature of postindustrial society is the continuing migration of people to great urban centers. Thus, whereas in the 1960s planners thought in terms of *industrial deconcentration* from cities, in the 1970s and 1980s they are forced to face further *postindustrial concentration* because of neotechnical growth. Skilled users of computers, transceivers, presses, photocopiers, and software find it necessary to be close to one another. The tertiary stage of industrial development encourages concentration, and concentration has produced the vast conurbation that stretches, with a few rural interruptions, between Tokyo and Kita Kyūshū (see Figure 7.1). Here has developed a pattern of megalopolitan settlement woven from strands of high-speed communication and transportation.

The Graying of Japan

By the end of the 1970s, one aspect of Japan's postindustrial society was becoming so important as to warrant special attention in the press. Japanese referred to the phenomenon

Bullet Trains (*Shinkansen*): Maximum speeds, 125 miles per hour.

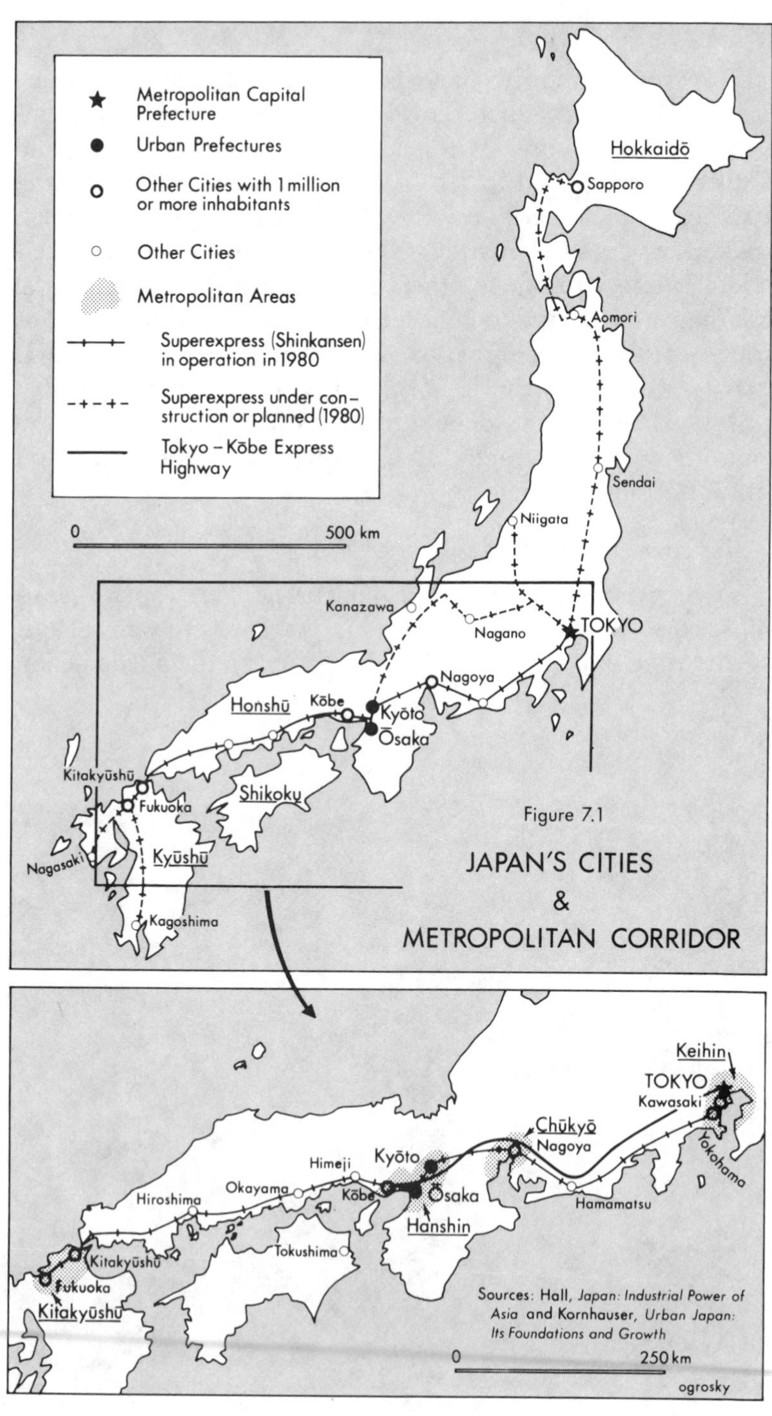

Figure 7.1

JAPAN'S CITIES & METROPOLITAN CORRIDOR

as "the graying of Japan," sometimes as the "twilight of Japan" (*Nihon no yugure*).

Of Japan's total population of 115 million in 1978, the number of elderly (sixty-five years of age or older) numbered almost 10 million, or 8.6 percent (as compared with Sweden's 15.4 percent, West Germany's 14.7 percent, England's 14.3 percent, and France's 13.3 percent). Of even greater interest were the projections made by a statistics bureau of the Prime Minister's Office that predicted that the total number of elderly could reach 25 million in the second decade of the twenty-first century (see Figure 7.2). If it did, the elderly group would then account for 18 percent of Japan's total population, a rate which would probably surpass those of other advanced industrial nations in the year 2015. The implications for social structure and policy are profound.

Experts listed three factors in accounting for this demographic development. First was the postwar baby boom, which provided the original population base. Second was the subsequent sudden drop in the birthrate, a decrease which naturally raised the percentage of elderly in the total population. Third was the extension of average life expectancy in Japan. In January 1979, the Ministry of Health and Welfare estimated that the average lifespan had increased to 72.69 years for males and 77.95 for females, overall the longest in the world.

Such figures reflected the significant impact of structural change on the traditional Japanese family system. There was a sharp increase in the number of nuclear families consisting only of the elderly. The 1978 White Paper on National Welfare reported that the number of such units had increased from 680,000 (2.7 percent of all families) in 1963 to 1.9 million (5.6 percent of the nation's households) in 1977. About three-quarters of Japan's over-sixty-five population were still sharing homes with their married children (as compared with about one-third in either Europe or the United States). Japanese observers, however, have referred to "quasi-household sharing," where the older live with the younger family members in the same house but with strictly separated living space and household accounts; and to "quasi-household separation," where the elders live separately but at a distance short enough to allow daily contact.

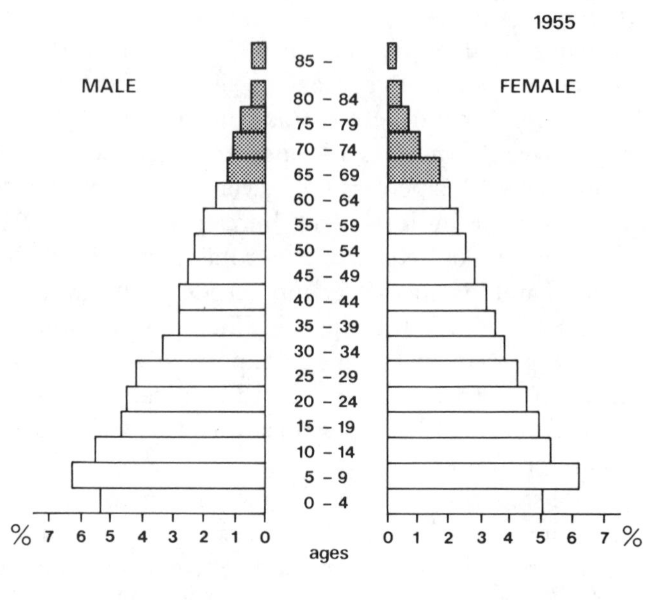

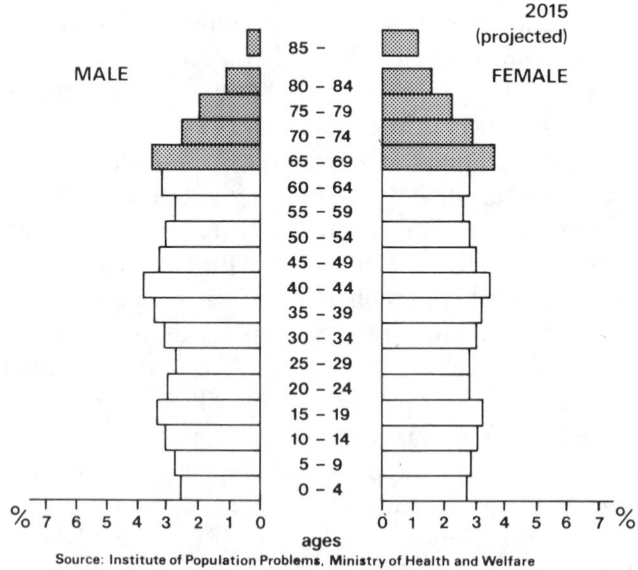

Source: Institute of Population Problems, Ministry of Health and Welfare

Figure 7.2: Shift in Age Structure of the Japanese Population

In one case of quasi-household sharing, a young wife commented, "The privacy of each family is well guarded. I'm free from psychological warfare with my mother-in-law."

Demographers and economists have agreed that the graying of Japan has come at the very worst time, when the nation is adjusting to medium or slow growth. Management has preferred to await attrition rather than to engage in arbitrary dismissals or layoffs. As a result, according to Kuroda Toshio of Nippon University, one of every five productive-age workers (ages fifteen to sixty-four) is now over fifty-five years of age. Nonetheless, unemployment and underemployment are overwhelmingly concentrated in the older age group. The aging has forced companies to review their personnel policies—for example, the tradition of lifetime employment, treatment of the older staff, increases in personnel costs, clogged channels for promotion, and sagging morale among younger workers.

Tradition and Transition

From the results of surveys on attitudes (see also Chapter 8), we can surmise that Japanese entered the 1970s not unalterably committed to any ideology. The emerging contemporary culture contains substantial elements of traditional beliefs: emphasis on the family, the group, and the nation-family, rather than on the individual; stress on discipline and duty, rather than on freedom; reliance on distinctions of status (measured by merit as the Japanese define it), rather than on social equality.

Although the end of the famous dual structure was in sight in the early 1970s, it had not entirely disappeared. At the top were the big, highly rationalized corporations with an organized labor elite. At the bottom were small enterprises with poorly organized workers, who earned marginal salaries and lacked fringe benefits. In the late 1970s, more than half of Japanese laborers were still working in firms that employed fewer than forty employees.

An illustration of the combination of tradition and transition is the seniority system (*nenkō joretsu*), which fixes basic status in a firm or in a ministry according to age. In the first decade or so of service, advancement is according to seniority;

in the middle years, merit and achievement may affect status. An interesting variant of the seniority system is the persistence in higher positions of university cliques (*gakubatsu*) made up of individuals graduated from prestigious institutions. *Gakubatsu* members receive status within the clique according to date of graduation. In the bureaucracy above the rank of bureau chief, 141 of 169 positions (83 percent) are filled by Tōdai (University of Tokyo) graduates. In 124 of 303 giant corporations (5 billion yen capitalization or more), management is presided over by Tōdai graduates. The political parties, including even the Socialists, are led by (public) national university graduates.

On the other hand, research on postindustrial Japan of the 1970s also yielded much evidence of change. The younger generation was more scientifically inclined and better educated than the graying generation. Young Japanese were creating what was doubtless the world's most egalitarian society. This does not necessarily mean that all Japanese have participated equally in decisionmaking. Rather, it signifies that the majority came to feel that all were treated and most were managed equally. Ever since the war's end, in fact, labels like "democracy" and "liberalism" have evoked favorable responses among Japanese. But in the 1970s what often puzzled visiting Americans, who had faith in Japan's "conservative" leadership, was that "socialism" was viewed with favor, whereas "capitalism" was almost universally held in low esteem. And "individualism" was regarded as selfishness.

It may be too early to jump to the conclusion that today's Japanese, like residents of other advanced industrial societies, are witnessing what has been dubbed "the end of ideology." Nevertheless, it is intriguing to speculate on future developments of a relatively open society with republican institutions surrounded by a high degree of affluence and marked by a newly emergent, white-collar, urban middle class that tends to be intensely pragmatic, even apolitical. What sort of political institutions are appropriate at this stage? This interesting question remains to be answered both in Japan and in the Western industrial democracies.

NEW ISSUES IN THE POSTINDUSTRIAL SOCIETY

Historically viewed, the salient issues of the preindustrial society revolved around the choice of elites and relevant questions of political justice. The preindustrial society was vertically fragmented. At the industrial stage, the salient issues revolved around management of the economy and questions of economic justice. Thinkers wrestled with problems of production (capitalism and laissez-faire) and the ideas of Adam Smith and Social Darwinism or with problems of distribution (socialism and communism) and the ideas of Marx, Lenin, and Mao. The industrial society tended to be horizontally fragmented.[8]

In the transition between late industrial and early postindustrial society in Japan of the 1960s, a certain residual behavior was apparent. In a kind of cultural lag, many leaders (for example, the Establishment led by the LDP) continued to emphasize production and growth. Others (the progressive opposition, for instance) continued to hammer on issues of equitable distribution. All groups have been both vertically and horizontally fragmented. Most important, salient issues have come to transcend management, labor, class, and even political party.

The Japanese Response in General

Members of the Japanese Establishment may appear to be slow to move and overly careful. One recent prime minister is said to have been so cautious that he would have tapped his way with a cane over a stone bridge. Yet Japanese conservative leaders have not been slow to detect subtle changes in public mood. In one of his first interviews after becoming prime minister, Ōhira Masayoshi remarked to an *Asahi Weekly* magazine reporter:

> We can no longer expect the kind of high economic growth we have had until recently. . . . Depending on the circumstances, we cannot entirely rule out the possibility of having negative growth in the future. We have to restructure our industries, our life-style and so on. Everyone should be aware that there exists a life worth living to

> cope with the new age. Economic success should not necessarily be the primary consideration in life; there should, I believe, be more valuable things.[9]

As a matter of fact, by the mid-1970s the question of how long the Japanese economy could, and indeed should, engage in unbridled growth was being asked even in the slick weekly magazines of opinion read by commuters. The key questions were beginning to be stated in philosophical terms and were tending toward matters of moral development. The Japanese public dimly perceived that once modern man fulfills material wants, he then confronts difficult ethical choices. Japanese began to ask, Growth for what? and, with or without the gadgets of technology, Who are we Japanese?

Opinion surveys in the 1970s clearly revealed a shift: Japanese had come to look toward a less strenuous and more leisurely way of life. It is true that attitudes may have changed faster than behavior: there was still a high motivation for work, as indicated by the very low absentee rate in Japan (2.12 percent in a February 1973 poll). And although making money was no longer the goal of life, wage levels were still important concerns for workers at all ages. The young expected more leisure. The middle aged wanted a house with some land as a hedge against inflation. Senior workers were more concerned about health care, retirement benefits, and welfare measures. Such subtle alterations in points of view were the raw materials from which the major issues in the Japanese postindustrial society were manufactured.

Economic Issues

Opinion surveys demonstrated that Japanese had come to recognize problems along the path of development in the 1960s. Although the standard of living had improved, many felt that the level of well-being of the average Japanese had not risen as fast as the gross national product. The lower levels of the dual economy having been absorbed into middle and upper levels, labor shortages and the demand for higher wages were inevitable. Moreover, the backlog of technology imported from abroad was not inexhaustible; so other advanced nations were coming into competition with Japan. The very strength of the economy had begun to build up opposition abroad, and Japanese realized that they would henceforth have to exercise restraint.

Paradoxically, the real purchasing power of Japan's currency began to decline on the domestic front, resulting in a widening disparity between the externally strong and the internally weak yen. As was the case in all advanced industrial nations, the oil crisis toward the end of 1973 (in effect quadrupling the price of crude oil) added to the gravity of the situation in Japan. In the first quarter of 1974, the annual rate of inflation leaped to a height of 25 percent in consumer prices (35 percent in wholesale prices). By the mid-1970s, "price restraint" carried a higher priority than "political participation" among respondents in public opinion surveys.

Japan of the 1970s was beginning to illustrate very well the principle that in the postwelfare state scarcity is no longer a major economic issue (a problem of production). It may remain a social or political problem (a question of distribution). Economists pointed out that Japan's future development would require public policy to establish new priorities in order to guide the economy away from the dictates of the free market and toward matching social needs. Otherwise the gap between flows of private and public goods would continue and would seriously jeopardize "social balance," according to U.S. economist John Kenneth Galbraith, who was widely known in Japan. Surprisingly, the role of government would have to be expanded to correct the disparity. (We say surprisingly because observers abroad firmly believed that government and business in Japan were already closely intertwined.)

Even as early as 1972, Japanese began to recognize what they called "the shadows of growth." Private consumption in Japan as a proportion of GNP was running around 52 percent (as against 60 to 61 percent in the United States and in Western Europe). The gap in public consumption was even greater: Japan was putting a little more than 8 percent of the GNP in this sector (as compared with 15 percent in Western Europe and 20 percent in the United States). What Americans refer to as "the free ride" in the area of military security accounted in part for the low level, but the disparity was still on the order of

$24 billion per year. Furthermore, had Japan been willing to invest less of its savings in fixed capital and to accept a slightly lower growth rate (something like those of other advanced nations at about 5 percent), it would have had another $45 billion or so to spend per year. The total, almost $70 billion per year, would have purchased a lot of welfare and social overhead.

Finally, there were domestic byproducts of Japan's rise to international superpower status. In effect, the average Japanese was working hard to subsidize exports. These brought huge balance-of-payments surpluses to Japan's credit. Such profits, however, were as often as not plowed back into further expansion of fixed capital. It began to dawn on Japanese that they should demand some of the rewards for diligence *now*, in place of further investment in industry for returns *later*. Towering trade surpluses were also bringing Japan into disfavor abroad.

Proposals that the Japanese government reenter the economy for purposes of redistribution of income might seem to imply a kind of socialist collectivism. Such an agenda, however, can be lifted directly from a rather early official document, the *Economic Survey of Japan, 1971–72*. In 1971, a semipublic body, the Council on Industrial Structure, drafted a scheme whereby pollution-prone and resource-hungry heavy industry would give way to knowledge-intensive projects that could economize on energy resources. Again in 1973, a private group of economists projected a drastic industrial reorganization to be carried out through 1985. They proposed that steel production be limited to meeting domestic demand and that the construction of oil refineries and petrochemical plants be slowed down. In 1974, the Council on Industrial Structure again prepared its long-term vision of industrial structure within a revised growth plan. The report expected the economy to grow at an average annual rate not exceeding 6 percent.[10]

Since government planning has been a logical consequence of the mixed (public-private) economy, such ideas were soon reflected in Japan's new official economic and social plan for the period 1973–77. At least the rhetoric of policy objectives was altered to fit apparent changes: to create "a rich and balanced environment," to guarantee "affluent and stabilized living conditions," to stabilize prices, and to contribute to international harmony. Admitting that these were highly subjective concepts, nonetheless government planners were trying to reach a consensus reflecting the shift from obsession with GNP to emphasis on what was increasingly called "net national welfare" (NNW).

The direction of planning again had to be readjusted in 1978 as Japan's only severe recession in the postwar period continued unabated. As Hugh Patrick pointed out, in the macroeconomic sense the root cause was operation of the economy at about 10 percent below capacity. This cost Japan about $50 billion per year in output not produced. (The same problem existed in Western Europe and in the United States.) At the microeconomic level, the recession showed itself in the low level of corporate profitability. Nakamura Takafusa, head of the Economic Research Institute, identified another weakness, the low net-worth ratios of Japanese firms. In other words, the percentage of total capital that a company owns (out of owned plus borrowed capital) has been unusually low in Japan. The consequent heavy reliance on borrowing was manageable during high growth and ill suited to a period of low growth.[11]

Meanwhile, two sharply divergent views emerged in the conservative Establishment. One, entertained by the Ministry of Finance and the Bank of Japan, was that the era of high growth was over. A 4 to 5 percent rate of growth would be quite respectable and would meet the threat of inflation. The other view, held by MITI bureaucrats and some big-business leaders, favored continued high growth. Such a course was still safe and would bring full employment, they argued, providing Japanese were willing to put up with inflation. Representative of large industries, MITI and Keidanren were delighted with the U.S. pressure on Japan (on the eve of the 1979 Tokyo summit) to maintain a higher, that is a 7 percent, growth rate.

Ministry of Finance bureaucrats opposed such stimulative policies since, in their opinion, the country was undergoing a significant change in demographic structure (the graying of Japan). Eventually the elderly would constitute a drain because of transfer payments (in the form of social security benefits), and any tax reduction would make later increases in tax rates difficult. Finance planners were also concerned over the steady rise in internal debt. In 1978 the total had reached about

20 trillion yen (general accounts deficit, 11 trillion; prefectural and local deficits, 5.6 trillion; national railway and public corporation deficits, 3 trillion) or about $85 billion at current exchange rates (compared with the U.S. federal deficit of about $60 billion and the states and municipalities deficits of about $30 billion).

Growth policies were to be settled in the arena of politics. By 1978 the combined opposition had come to outnumber the majority LDP, which had been identified with high growth. In the House of Representatives Budget Committee, for example, the progressive parties blocked all legislation until the LDP administration agreed to a tax cut. Some commentators identified the poor showing of the LDP and Prime Minister Ōhira in the October 1979 lower house elections with Ōhira's support for national tax increases. The prime minister withdrew the proposal for a tax increase. After the summit of 1979, it was apparent that Japan would have difficulty in maintaining the previously pledged 7 percent growth rate.

Political Issues

Postindustrial transition not only reframed the economic issues but also provided a subtly different environment for political decisionmaking. In surveys conducted during the 1970s there was evidence of a measurable change from traditional submissiveness to authority to demands for participation in politics and even active protest.

In 1953, a majority of Japanese over twenty years of age were still prepared to leave the settlement of issues to "competent politicians." By 1973, a majority explicitly disagreed with this traditional attitude (51 percent disagreed; only 23 percent agreed; and 15 percent sidestepped the issue by urging a case-by-case approach).[12] Here, by the way, was a significant mixture: not only increased knowledge, a product of the information explosion, and increased participatory motivation, a product of the new politics; but also decreased trust in institutional channels (political parties and elections), a byproduct of sophistication and skepticism.

Such political trends were in line with the change in attitude toward growth itself. On the macropolitical level, priorities decisively shifted toward more balanced growth and improvement of welfare. Henceforth the realm of public policy would be clearly separated from the realm of private economic activity. On the micropolitical level there was a transition from Establishment politics of industrial growth to the coalition politics of postindustrial transition.

The previously ignored costs of growth had become politicized. Moreover, the effects of heavy industrialization—inflation, pollution, traffic accidents, neglect of housing, and such—were indiscriminate, cutting across class boundaries. Their impact was felt in egalitarian fashion. This was because income and costs were more equitably distributed and because information about the effects was widely disseminated.

There were countless illustrations of these trends in Japan during the 1960s and 1970s. The media so widely advertised the problem of environmental disruption (*kōgai*) that Japanese leaders found it necessary to devote parliamentary attention to the issue.[13] One legislative session became known as the Pollution Diet (1970). Women found themselves fighting pitched battles over the major issues: inflation as it affected household accounts; traffic accidents as they affected children; and housing as it provided the cramped environment for family life. Women were among the first to see—distinctly—a disjunction between their status and increasing national wealth.

Then there were the extremists, who seized upon the disarray of transition and engaged in political action for the sake of expression rather than for the purpose of influencing decisions. At one extreme was the celebrated Red Army, which engaged in a kind of red romanticism and nostalgia for the old class struggle. At the other was the Society of the Shield (formed by Mishima Yukio), a group that was seized with nostalgia for traditional "basic Japan." Somewhere between was the coalition of forces that steadily opposed the construction and disrupted the expansion of the new Narita International Airport.

Boredom with growth combined with unwillingness to give up its fruits—paradoxical products of skepticism and widespread advertising—led to myriad public demands that simply could not be met, particularly if consumers continued to expect all the private services of an advanced society. So, equipped with one of the world's finest public transportation networks, the average

Japanese, like his American counterpart, insisted on the inalienable right to drive an automobile while denouncing the rising levels of photochemical smog in Tokyo.

One effect of the changed political environment was the steady decline in popularity of the majority Liberal Democratic Party (LDP), which had identified itself with growth. In the twenty-eighth general election (held just after the conservative merger in 1955), the LDP had garnered 57.8 percent of the popular vote. By the thirty-first general election (1967), the LDP vote had dropped to 48.8 percent, below the 50 percent level for the first time in two decades. In the election for the lower house held in October 1979, the LDP garnered 44.6 percent of the popular vote. In the unprecedented election for both houses, held June 22, 1980, the LDP swept back to a majority (284 seats in the lower house, 136 in the upper house). Observers listed the sympathy vote over Premier Ōhira's death (June 12), a desire for stability, and the high electoral turnout (74.5 percent) as reasons for the triumph.

In the mid-1960s, when the torque of growth was being felt, prospects for the Socialists seemed to be bright. By the 1970s, however, the JSP had also declined in influence. For a time, the Kōmeitō, the Communists, and the Democratic Socialists harvested a slightly larger share of the votes. By the late 1970s, all the parties felt insecure, however, because a large number of voters in the big cities (with educational levels and nonpartisan orientation high) constituted an unpredictable floating vote.

The flood tide of this floating vote came with the rise of citizens' movements (*jūmin undō*), which in turn produced what were variously called the "urban communes" or reformist (*kakushin*) local governments. The best example was the reelection of Minobe Ryōkichi to a second term as governor of Tokyo in 1971. He was backed by a coalition of independents and rolled to a landslide victory, garnering the largest number of votes cast for any single candidate in the election history of Japan. Governor Minobe remained popular with women consumer advocates, environmentalists, and welfare supporters. (In April 1979, at age seventy-five and after three terms as governor, Minobe chose not to run again.)

The conservatives were not, of course, deaf and blind. Often they seized postindustrial issues more quickly than did the opposition parties. By Tanaka Kakuei's second cabinet (1972–74), voters had begun to express uneasiness over the distortions of rapid growth. Prime Minister Tanaka responded by writing *Building a New Japan,*[14] which soon became a best-seller. His plan for the remodeling of the Japanese archipelago was scuttled by speculation, inflation in land prices, and his own involvement in a corruption trial. It was the oil shock of 1973, however, with its attendant inflation and recession, that led all Japanese seriously to reconsider high growth policies.

Miki Takeo (prime minister, 1974–76) represented the last attempt to stave off the decline of LDP majorities, which had traditionally depended on continuing growth. The Lockheed scandal of February 1976 (an affair that directly implicated former Prime Minister Tanaka in bribes connected with aircraft procurement) convinced many Japanese that high growth had structural political weaknesses. As a result, the LDP suffered its first election debacle, maintaining a bare majority in the lower house and then only with the aid of independents.

Prime Minister Fukuda Takeo (1976–78) was the first to try to maneuver conservative policies through a Diet in which LDP and opposition strengths were evenly matched. His policy was a compromise, balanced between LDP demands for further growth and opposition desires for limits to growth. For example, he advocated a pattern of "permanent residential zones" interspersed with industrial areas to ease the housing shortage.

The first Ōhira cabinet (1978–79) marked a major milestone as Japan played host at the Tokyo summit of June 1979. At the same time, Japan felt the domestic pressures typical of the postindustrial stage. Ōhira's "pastoral cities" plan (the idea of creating a network of medium-sized cities in sparsely settled regions) had to be abandoned by his second cabinet (1979–80), which was formed with a narrow margin of support. After Prime Minister Ōhira's visit to the United States, Mexico, and Canada in May 1980 and after his untimely death in June, LDP leadership used its newfound majority to form a cabinet around Suzuki Zenko, a 69-year-old veteran compromiser among the LDP factions. As Japan entered the 1980s it was quite apparent that the nation had not escaped from the orbit of change.

Japanese carried with them across the postindustrial frontier certain fitted and durable clothes, the raiment of tradition. Prewar precedent had prepared the way, and several postwar decades of conservative rule had seen the new constitution, the parliamentary system, the habit of elections, and certain civil liberties become thoroughly entrenched. On the one hand, there was a rising demand for participatory democracy, not only in theory but in practice. On the other hand, all the political parties were feeling the effects of public disillusion—a lack of faith in the ability of the political process to solve a whole new range of problems.

By 1980, it had become apparent that neither the familiar theories of the right—those that justified capitalism—nor the equally familiar theories of the left—those that criticized capitalism—were entirely appropriate to contemporary Japan. This may be because many of those theories were culture-bound, having been developed within the parameters of Western societies. These theories had also emerged from a former age of industrialism and growth. A new era demanded fresh ideas and by and large they were not available. For this reason, postindustrial problems have seemed intractable, both in Washington and in Tokyo.

NOTES

1. Gabriel A. Almond and Sidney Verba, *The Civic Culture: Political Attitudes and Democracy in Five Nations* (Boston: Little, Brown, 1965).

2. Zbigniew Brzezinski, *The Fragile Blossom; Crisis and Change in Japan* (New York: Harper & Row, 1972), Introduction, p. xii.

3. Martin O. Heisler, ed., *Politics in Europe: Structures and Processes in Some Postindustrial Democracies* (New York: McKay, 1974).

4. Chie Nakane, *Japanese Society* (Berkeley, University of California Press, 1970), p. 149.

5. Taketsugu Tsurutani, *Political Change in Japan; Response to Postindustrial Challenge* (New York: McKay, 1977), especially Chap. 1.

6. Masao Kunihiro, "The Intermestic Age," *PHP* 10, no. 6 (June 1979):7. (The title of the journal, *PHP*, stands for peace, happiness, prosperity.)

7. See, for example, the excellent study of the emergent politico-

religious group by James W. White, *The Sōkagakkai and Mass Society* (Stanford: Stanford University Press, 1970).

8. See Tsurutani, *Political Change*, pp. 33–34.

9. "Japan's Changing Outlook" (Interview with Ōhira Masayoshi, prime minister of Japan), *PHP* 10, no. 7 (July 1979):7.

10. *Sangyo kozo no choki bijion* [Long-term vision of industrial structure] (Tokyo: Council on Industrial Structure, September 1974).

11. Nakamura Takafusa, "The Need for Continued Growth," *Japan Echo* 6 (Special Issue, 1979):71.

12. Watanuki Jōji, *Politics in Postwar Japanese Society* (Tokyo: University of Tokyo Press, 1977), pp. 32–33.

13. In the summer of 1970, I participated in a series of miniseminars on the subjects of pollution and environmental disruption (*kōgai*) held with metropolitan desk editors of the media at sites ranging from Sapporo in the north to Fukuoka in the south.

14. First published in Japan as *Nippon rettō kaizō-ron* (1972), the volume appeared in an English-language edition the following year: Tanaka Kakuei, *Building a New Japan; A Plan for Remodeling the Japanese Archipelago* (Tokyo: Simul Press, 1973).

8

Kokuminsei: *Who Are the Japanese?*

There are those who argue strenuously against any further use of the term *national character*. Critics of the concept claim that Japanese have used this vague idea to exaggerate the unique in their lifestyle. Many Japanese have gone on to imply that foreigners can never really understand their way of life.

Toward the end of the Pacific war and immediately thereafter, national character studies of the Japanese belonged in the field of pathology. In good Freudian and post-Freudian style, foreign analysts took (secondhand) clinical findings related to Japanese individuals and lifted them to the status of national averages in order to account for puzzling traits (of the enemy). They then arrived at policy recommendations for victory, occupation, and so forth. Thus, to cite extreme cases, it was said that the Japanese adult personality was warped by earlier strict toilet training (just as Russian character was once said to emanate from the practice of swaddling the infant in the fields, and the American personality was said to be indelibly marked by timed breast-feeding in babyhood). Yet the formulas thus derived and applied to Japanese perhaps made more sense than the assumptions behind the policy of unconditional surrender, in which Japanese were treated as subhumans.

Unfortunately, national averages always obscure individuation. Whether national character studies belong in the soft or the hard sciences, they are certainly persistent and subjectively important. Consider, by way of example, the following images sketched by foreign observers and by the Japanese themselves.

SOME PORTRAITS

The pictures that follow are not so much snapshots, catching the Japanese at work or play, as very preliminary sketches for full-scale, three-dimensional portraits. They can, however, be grouped under various headings.

Japanese at Work

In 1970, I had to visit a friend working at the headquarters of OECD in Paris. I arrived there just as a plenary session had come to an end. Streams of people were pouring out of the big meeting hall—all types, all nationalities, all languages, but no Japanese. I looked into the hall. There were the Japanese gathered in a corner, actively sharing comments among themselves, but so clearly separated from all the others; a small Japanese island in the sea of OECD.

(*Robert J. Ballon*)

Sato Taro has been described as bright and conscientious, a salary man who works in a research laboratory for the Company. He has just made a technological breakthrough. For this triumph he is given some credit, but his abilities will not be valued far above those of his coworkers. Messrs. Suzuki, Takahashi, and other workers in the field earned enough profits for the Company to finance the successful research. Sato-*san* owes a great deal to those who assisted in the lab. It is assumed that he achieved the breakthrough by means of cooperation from all, including blue collar workers in the Company. Credit also goes to Personnel, the office that assigned him to the project, and to his Director, who supervised his work. If Sato-*san* comes to assume that it was *his* accomplishment and he speaks out in this vein, he will elicit so much hostility as to be uncomfortable remaining with the Company. No matter how outstanding, he probably cannot get a job with the Other Company, which certainly does not want a troublemaker. If Sato-*san* strikes out on his own, he will receive no help from the Company and no researchers are likely to join him.

(*adapted from Takeuchi Hiroshi*)

For these reasons, good communications between Japanese and Americans seldom take place. Americans leave a conference with disappointment while the Japanese are relieved that it is over. There is little achieved at such conferences in terms of real communication or agreement on future conduct. The Japanese will say, "That was a good conference," because it is something they feel obligated to say. An unperceptive American might say to himself, "It was not bad after all," despite his own disappointment.

(*Mochizuki Kiichi*)

Japanese at Play

In 1979, newspapers estimated that there were 200,000 video computer games called *inbeedaa sakusen* in Japan. Introduced only in July 1978, the "space invader campaign" threatened to displace pachinko as the national diversion. It cost 100 yen (about 50 cents) to declare war on the machine and the player could continue without additional fee until a loss was suffered. The player faced a mob of invaders from space, five lines of mutated crabs on each line. They moved to the right or to the left, making a sound of "voom . . . voom . . . voom, . . ." and dropping missiles on the earth. Suddenly a UFO flew in above the advancing crabs, making a sound of "whui . . . whui . . . whui. . . ." Shooting down a UFO with a missile launcher was worth many more points than for a downed crab. Some of the space invader machines played a passage from the Beethoven Ninth to signal the end of the war.

(*The Japan Times Weekly*)

In summertime, Japanese who like beer swarm to what are called "beer gardens." These are usually set up on the roofs of department stores and office buildings. . . . Funny thing about beer gardens is that they are not "gardens" at all in the ordinary sense. You have a few potted plants around to create a garden atmosphere, but no more than that. . . . These days the beer gardens are attracting more and more female customers. In fact, beer is almost like a "soft drink" in modern Japan.

(*Okamoto Kokichi*)

Japanese Women

The two things that have become stronger since the end of the war are women and nylon stockings.

(*postwar saying*)

Ichikawa Fusae has maintained an image of integrity that she has built up over half a century. By now she is a proven part of the nonaligned "progressives," but affiliated with no party (and opposed by most). She has had difficulty because she has chosen to act on her own terms and because she is a woman. She has not only survived longer than any other women in Japanese politics (in 1979 she was eighty-six years old), but has become the symbol of an unfinished struggle for social equality.

(*Patricia Murray*)

"Good wives" exacted revenge by rendering husbands and offspring psychologically and emotionally dependent on them. "Good wives" inflated the husband's ego by relaxing tensions produced by a structured, duty-conscious society. They became excellent servants solicitous of every comfort, and as skillful home economists added a further dimension of male dependence. "Good wives" imitated men by being high-handed toward inferiors; daughters-in-law became favored targets. "Wise mothers" elicited praise from men by train-

Food Preparation on TV.

ing sons in their rights and daughters in their duties. In making themselves indispensable havens of nurturance Japanese women in a sense emasculated their men.

(*Hazel J. Jones*)

In General

Kawabata Yasunari, Japan's Nobel prize-winning novelist, once said that the Japanese communicate through quiet understanding, a kind of telepathy, since for them the truth lies in the implicit rather than in the stated. They have a word for it: *ishin-denshin*, "communication by the heart."

(*John K. Emmerson*)

The American scholar, once affiliated with the Michigan Center for Japanese Studies located in Okayama, now faced a dilemma. He did not like the idea of even passing through the city without at least informing the retired liaison officer, who had been the link between the Center and the *kenchō* [prefectural office]. When the American did let the Japanese know, no matter how early the hour nor how brief the stop, the old Japanese gentleman was on the train platform. "It's too early and I'm only passing through, . . ." the American would protest. "But it's my duty," the Japanese always responded. ("Now then, is he *happy* doing this? does he really *like* me?" the American wondered and then realized that such questions were quite irrelevant in the Japanese context.) The Japanese was *content* only when duty was done.

(*adapted from a journal*)

Rice is still the Japanese staple food (despite a general notion of a switch to bread). Even for breakfast (the hurried meal), some 71 percent of the respondents said they eat rice; for lunch, 77 percent; and for dinner, 96 percent. In fact, only 17 percent responded that they have bread as a staple for breakfast. For lunch, some 9 percent take noodles. About 41 percent replied that they frequently eat fish; two out of three of all respondents complained about the rapid rise in prices of seafood.

(*1979 poll, Office of the Prime Minister*)[1]

The problem inherent in these intriguing portraits is that they are highly impressionistic. Moreover, the lines between attitudes and behavior have been drawn in fuzzy fashion. Fortunately, there are more objective, reliable data—much compiled by the Japanese. First, it will be convenient to observe some guidelines in order to sort out the data into meaningful patterns.

SOME GUIDELINES

Kano Tsutomu, editor of a useful English-language journal that serves as a window to Japanese thinking, has referred to the "state of questioning among Japanese themselves that is recently so relentless as to constitute a national identity crisis." In 1972 alone, the editor remarked, more than forty new books were published in Japan on the general theme, "What is 'Japanese'?" The discussion of identity (*Nihonjin-ron*) has been dubbed an "introspection boom."[2] By and large the Japanese search has led to impressionistic answers. Japanese authors have been self-conscious and ambivalent, and the literature has often confused such subtly different aspects of national character as modal personality, culture, ideology, attitudes, and behavior.

Perhaps the most measurable among these are attitudes revealed in surveys. More specifically, the patterning of attitudes has been called *kokuminsei* (national character) by the most skillful Japanese pollsters.

Attitudes

Certainly for "attitudes, or ways of thinking, of a people" we now enjoy a wealth of data, thanks to Japan's Institute of Statistical Mathematics of the Ministry of Education. Every five years over the period from 1953 to 1978 the institute conducted a survey in depth, a total of six polls. In each survey respondents have been a random sample of 5,400 persons chosen from some 300 cities, towns, and villages throughout the country.

The institute has pointed out that revealed attitudes lend themselves to various interpretations. For example, one can identify those points of view that Japanese share with citizens of other postindustrial countries. Such an approach might strengthen what sociologists call the "convergence thesis," namely, that because of universal historical experiences, the stages of economic growth, and the impact of advanced technology, Japanese will soon resemble their counterparts in other developed nations. More often, however, the tendency is to concentrate on differences between Japanese and non-Japanese. This is called the *cross-societal dimension*.

Beginning with the surveys conducted in the 1970s, the institute added a control, data drawn from surveys of Japanese-Americans (*Nikkeijin*) in Hawaii. One of the striking features uncovered by the 1973 survey was the breadth of Japanese-American attitudes (indicating widely individual outlooks) compared with clusters of Japanese attitudes (indicating the importance of the group even in a period when outlooks are in transition). These different configurations led one institute observer to conclude, "Japanese-Americans are not Japanese," but "We Japanese are Japanese!"

Another approach looks at opinion distribution among the Japanese. This produces a map of the topology of national character known as the *intrasocietal dimension*.

Yet another view results from a look at opinions and attitudes that a majority of the Japanese hold. This is called the *modality dimension*. In the surveys conducted by the Institute of Statistical Mathematics, a "majority" consists of not only two-thirds of the total sample of respondents, but also two-thirds across-the-board regardless of distribution according to sex, age, or level of education. The institute has identified a few key attitudes held by such a majority in five surveys (1953–73).

Such findings suggest one last approach. The institute has been interested in the degree and direction of change in attitudes (including no change) over time. For the purpose of identifying national character, obviously opinions that remain relatively persistent are significant. This aspect the institute labels the *constancy dimension*.

The institute's approach, then, is not too different from the "national character" defined by Alex Inkeles, but perhaps it is more precise. He has stated that national character "refers to relatively enduring personality characteristics and patterns that are modal among adult members of a society." By way of comparison, the institute concludes, "Therefore, it is reasonable to define the study of the (Japanese) national character as the search for those attitudes which satisfy constancy, homogeneity, modality, and cross-societal difference."[3]

Behavior

Interestingly enough, in light of the flurry of activity in the behavioral sciences in the postwar period, the link between attitude and action is at best tenuous. There is no invariate connection between orientation, ideology, or national character and behavior. Often, of course, national character *has* been described in terms of certain striking behavior emanating from orientation. The connection, however, has not been empirically demonstrated and what we think we know so far is based on instinct.

Anthropologists have put the equation in negative terms: a social organization (and social behavior) in order to be viable in the long run must complement—not clash with—basic systems of belief shared by the society. Social scientists have gone one step farther: national character, it has been argued, forms the substratum that nurtures, shapes, and supports the political regime of a nation. From there, doctrine has on occasion wandered into the swamp of generalization. By way of illustration, it was once fashionable to say that relatively open, individualistic, egalitarian, and autonomous personality types were supportive of stable democracies (like the United Kingdom and the United States); that closed, rigid, aggressive, and hierarchically oriented personality types were equated with authoritarian regimes (like Nazi Germany and prewar Japan). Such a quantum leap from individual personality clinically observed to national characterization is too great.

Specifically, what shall we do with post-treaty, postindustrial Japan? If some attitudes are relatively open and egalitarian, but not individualistic and autonomous; if others reveal a more closed, rigid, and hierarchically oriented but not aggressive stance, will the resultant behavior be stable and democratic or authoritarian?

Middle-level linkage, short of such broad generalization, is far safer. In the case of Japan, we can connect certain salient and persistent attitudes with certain specific practices. The former seem to nurture the latter. Three examples are dealt with in some detail later in this chapter.

SOME PATTERNS

Doubtless the most important finding in surveys conducted by the Institute of Statistical Mathematics and by other polling agencies is evidence in Japan of a clear reassertion of traditional elements in national character. Understandably, the turmoil of total war, devastating defeat, and brainwashing by the Occupation (even though it was benign) all served to throw into doubt the validity of any previous orientation. The latest poll (December 1978) available at the time of this writing demonstrates that Japanese are continuing to regain self-respect and to view their own traditions and culture without the prejudice that so often marked postwar attitudes.

Although the prewar dogma of the superiority of the Yamato people has subsided due to scientific enlightenment, an implicit racism (if not racial arrogance) survives in the belief that racial differences do exist and are socially important. Nonetheless, contemporary Japanese nationalism is less virulent than the prewar variety. It is spun out of Japan's insular location, formidable language barrier, and a cultural gulf between Japanese and outsiders, particularly Westerners. Continued use of the notorious term *gaijin* ("foreigner") stems not so much from feelings of mythical superiority as from ignorance. Insular feelings are enhanced by the tightly knit homogeneity of the Japanese. This attitude explains why the OECD Japanese delegation found it necessary to confer alone. If there are to be any people about whom generalizations in terms of national character will be made, it will be the Japanese.

The Group

As one might expect, attachment to the group has remained an attitude shared by the majority in all six surveys conducted by the institute. Ezra Vogel, the Harvard sociologist, has referred to this phenomenon as "a continuing value consensus." Even in the earliest surveys taken immediately after the Occupation (1953), among 68 percent of the respondents individual Japanese contentment was contingent on the eventual success of Japan.

Japanese group consciousness, however, has not been all that simple to describe. What may seem like something of a paradox is the continued vivid interest in merit and achievement as a measure of status. The Japanese sense of personal satisfaction in achievement is generated in relation to groups (the family, the firm, or the ministry), which are the objects of devotion and determine the rewards for personal activity. It is in this context that the breakthrough of Sato-*san*, within and for the sake of the company described above can be understood.

In the 1973 institute survey respondents were given hypothetical situations: The president of a firm is to hire a person and, on the qualifying examination, the highest grade is won by an unknown; the second highest, by a relative of the president. It is made clear that either candidate will perform satisfactorily in the position. Whom should the president hire? Almost three-quarters of the respondents advised hiring the candidate with the higher grade. Respondents were given another choice: you may have a department chief who sticks to the work rules, who seldom demands overtime, but who does nothing in matters not connected with the job; *or* you may have a chief who is much more flexible about rules, who occasionally demands overtime work, but who also looks after you personally in matters not connected with the job. Over 80 percent preferred the latter kind of department head. Put in slightly different fashion, about three-quarters of all respondents in the fifth (1973) survey indicated a preference for a firm "with a family-like atmosphere."

This is not to say that Japanese never feel a certain malaise because of membership in the group. Indeed they often do, and they recognize that discontent arises from the pressures of conformity and from the tight web of obligations to the group. It is one reason why the executive cited in the portrait section of this chapter finds nostalgia for his early working days and release from present pressure in the beer gardens on the rooftops of Tokyo.

Conformism and Hierarchy

Stories embracing Japanese tradition, Kabuki theater, and even contemporary literature are sprinkled with descriptions of the group-centered society in which human feelings (*ninjō*) and bonds of moral obligation (*giri*) are central concerns. It is widely believed even in Japan that in the postwar period such traditional norms, along with filial piety (*oyakoko*), suffered notable declines among attitudes shared by Japanese. It is often pointed out that there has been a shift from elaborate relationship-oriented pronouns of address to the more neutral "you" and even "I." Results of surveys conducted in the 1953–58 period, however, show that although a healthy majority (some 60 percent) were using such new language, they still preferred traditional modes of address.

The 1970s saw a remarkable resurgence of traditional values. In the 1973 survey, given a multiple choice among various values, respondents most often singled out filial piety (which appeared on 63 percent of the replies) and the need to repay a moral debt (*ongaeshi*, a value which appeared on 43 percent of the replies). In the 1978 survey, these traditional precepts again ranked first and second (filial piety favored by almost three-quarters, and the compulsive feeling of gratitude by almost half the respondents).

The trend can be explained in yet another way. In the first five of the institute's surveys (1953–73) those Japanese who believed that it is best to conform to society's established mores accounted for no more than about one-third of the respondents. In the sixth survey (1978) the total soared to 42 percent. In parallel, the immediately postwar norm of respect for individual rights and freedom remained relatively strong (from 40 to 45 percent of the replies) through the early 1970s. Such respect, however, ran far higher (60 percent in 1973) among younger respondents (the twenty to twenty-four-year-old group). In 1978, to the amazement of the pollsters, respect for individual rights among the younger folk plummeted (to 46 percent) and remained at a level below that for some of the older Japanese (the thirty-five to thirty-nine-year-old group). The trend of opinion was apparently on the way to offsetting the fear among elders in the 1960s that the younger generation was widely infected by privatism (called *mai homism*—"my home-ism"—by the Japanese).

The Family

Observers generally agree that there is no society in the world in which family life has been regarded with such satisfaction as in Japan. In the institute's 1973 survey, some 80 percent of all respondents expressed contentment with the Japanese family as an institution. In the 1978 survey, the total reached 86 percent. Significantly, the level of satisfaction with Japanese society at large was much lower—37 percent; yet this marked an improvement over the 1973 level of 26 percent.

Even Japanese men would readily admit that the stability of the family depends in large part upon the attitudes and actions of women. Although the Japanese female is socialized to be content and her behavior is supposed to accommodate to the wishes of the male, the lot of the woman in Japan is not enviable in the opinion of a resident expert, Iwao Sumiko of Keiō University. She finds that Swedish women have a status higher than that of their American sisters and French females rank some-

Japanese Wedding: Exchange of nuptial cups (*sansankudo*).

where between women in the United States and those in Japan. And yet, to the despair of outside feminist observers, many young Japanese women when asked "If you could be born again . . . ?" seem quite willing to be reborn as females. Iwao offers three possible reasons for this attitude. First, women are wary of outside world's pressures to which Japanese men are subjected. Second, they share the satisfaction of most Japanese with the high status of the family in Japan. Third, they truly enjoy the child rearing, if not the housework.[4]

There is a tendency, particularly among middle-aged Japanese women, not to want the husband's help around the house. Much of the work is drudgery, but this is the wife's domain. Within that realm she has control of the budget and is also primarily in charge of the crucial planning for the children's education. In the extreme division of labor, she regards herself as the center of the household enterprise. It should be added that the Japanese woman, once having satisfied herself about the care of her children, is increasingly interested in an outside career. Nor is the nuclear family regarded as viable over the whole lifespan: a large proportion of women expect to live with or close to their children and eventually to become the central figure in an extended family.

In any case, Japanese women's attitudes toward the female status is yet another indication of the steady shift back to traditional standards. Responses have been sought by the institute to the query: "If you could be born again, would you rather be a man or a woman?" In 1958, only 27 percent of the female respondents wanted to remain a woman. The proportion rose steadily to 36 percent in 1963, to 48 percent in 1968, and to a majority of 51 percent in 1973. It would be equally accurate, of course, to state that only half of Japanese women would choose to be women again. (In the 1973 survey, 89 percent of the men responded that they would prefer to remain male.)

Religion

The literature on modernization is rich in generalizations on the transitional status of Japan as it shifts subtly away from the traditional. This is evidenced in the emphasis on achievement as opposed to ascriptive status and on rationality (science) as opposed to religion (or myth). In the Tokugawa period Japanese began to move toward a more secular, highly pragmatic outlook. Modern, and particularly postwar, Japanese attitudes have moved steadily toward pragmatism and scientism. Yet an interesting aspect of all postindustrial societies is the continued search for transcendent truth. The present Japanese society offers no exception. For example, when confronted with the blunt question, "Do you have any personal religious faith?" three out of four Japanese responded (1973) that they did not. In the same poll almost 80 percent replied that a "religious attitude" is important! Data indicated that Japanese, like other people, grow more religious as they grow older. On the other hand, information on younger Japanese has been startling: in the twenty to twenty-four-year-old group (in the 1973 survey) only 8 percent of the respondents were religious-minded; in 1978 the portion doubled to 17 percent.

Nature and Aesthetics

In a somewhat similar vein, we have come to think of modern man as one who can and will conquer the forces of nature. However, what has been regarded as a traditional and an Oriental outlook—namely, the need for man to adjust to nature—has been gaining popularity steadily in a postindustrial Japan that has become sensitive to pollution and acutely aware of the limits of growth. In the 1978 institute survey, one-third of the respondents advocated subservience to nature and only 16 percent advocated its continued conquest.

Certainly, in at least one related attitude the Japanese have remained confident. Shown a picture of a Japanese garden and at the same time a picture of a Western garden, almost 80 percent of 1953 survey respondents chose the native style (perhaps the remaining 20 percent thought it was "smart" to choose the exotic formal garden). By 1973, nine out of ten respondents came down on the side of the traditional Japanese style.

The Modern Society

Although some of the traditional norms have remained firm or have been revived in Japanese minds, there were also changes in attitudes detected by the institute, and these by and large had to do with daily lifestyle. Because of the rising level of material well-being in the 1960s, it is not surprising that Japanese have become more conservative. Their conservatism does not just apply to the political arena and, as was indicated in Chapter 5, does not necessarily imply support for a specific party.

In 1979, for example, although more than 90 percent of all Japanese considered themselves members of the middle class, three out of four who did differentiated the ideal from the reality. According to a life insurance survey, they defined middle-class status as an individual family in a separate house with a small garden and an annual income of 5 million yen (about $22,725). Many Japanese did not have the house, the garden, or the requisite salary.

The rosy outlook generated by the era of high growth nevertheless had not yet eroded in the 1970s. Despite lingering recession, as of 1978 almost half the Japanese thought the future looked bright (compared to 38 percent in 1973).

Paradoxes in data about the attitudes of the postindustrial society are to be expected. Thus, in the Japanese case, a preference for acquiring wealth as life's goal, which has never been startlingly high (about 17 percent of the respondents from 1958 to 1969), has actually declined (14 percent in 1973 and 1978). "To live according to one's own taste"—this would seem to be a form of individualism to the outsider—has become the top goal (almost 40 percent in 1978). "Acquiring fame" has ranked low in Japan (about 2 percent in 1978). Perhaps this attitude reflects the firm belief shared by Japanese that real power always resides behind the screen.

There has been an increase in the desire for participatory politics, an increase in the understanding of political issues, and also an increase in distrust of political leaders. In child rearing within the family, however, traditional attitudes have shown strong retentive power.

Finally, it will be of interest to hear some Japanese responses to the question, "Which of the following adjectives do you think describes the character of the Japanese people?" Respondents could list as many words as they wished. In order of occurrence, these were used (1973 survey): "diligent" (66 percent); "persistent" (52 percent); "polite" (37 percent); "kind" (31 percent); and on less than one-third of the lists, "idealistic," "matter-of-fact," "rational," "free," "cheerful," and "original." In comparing themselves with others, Japanese ranked peoples according to whether or not they were "superior." Distributions and percentages or appearances were revealing (1973): first, Japanese (60 percent); second, Germany (36 percent); third, Americans (25 percent). Russians ranked second to last (5 percent), just ahead of Indians (3 percent). Other surveys have shown that, when Japanese were asked (somewhat differently) whom they *liked*, Americans regularly ranked first.

SOME EFFECTS

It is a long step from these rather careful surveys of attitudes to generalizations on behavioral patterns in Japanese society. In Japan, as in other countries, a specific pattern of values unique to the particular society is generationally transmitted through enculturation. As Nobuo Shimahara has pointed out in his study of education in Japan, such norms "are tenacious, persistent, superorganic principles that resist pressures for changes brought about by the institutional transformation of such a society."[5] Certainly through education, as well as through the family, Japanese values have been passed along, demonstrating that training, as a behavioral pattern, is linked to attitudes. Education has also played a crucial structural role in bridging the traditional and the modern Japanese societies.

College Entrance Examinations

On January 13 and 14, 1979, over 325,000 high school seniors and graduates took uniform college entrance examinations, which were held at 225 universities and testing places throughout Japan. The first battery of tests covered Japanese language and general science; the second battery–English, mathematics, and social studies. In March, successful candidates then sat for supplemental examinations at universities of their choices. It would be difficult for outsiders to grasp how much these examinations had dominated the lives of the youngsters (and their mothers) since nursery-school days.

Morning Assembly, Elementary School.

The entrance examinations and the education geared toward them have demonstrated adaptive efficiency in fitting together certain traditional, particularistic (Japanese) norms and certain modern, universalistic (worldwide) orientations essential to behavior in the postindustrial era. The examination system has above all been instrumental in the recruitment of the Japanese elite. Studied in the context of city life in the early stages of the growth era (Tokyo in the 1960s), arduous preparation for the entrance examination was identified as a kind of rite de passage through which a young person (usually a man) proves that he has the qualities of ability and stamina necessary to become a "salary man."[6]

The examination system has played an even wider role, too. The impact of the entrance tests has been felt not only by the select elite, who finally succeed, but by *all* Japanese, who are all educated in schools geared to the college entrance examination. The system thus identifies early the future white-collar leadership and also sorts out the necessary technicians, accountants, foremen, blue-collar laborers, and unskilled help. It has been suggested that prolonged socialization and schooling (the tone for which is set by the entrance examinations) contribute to adolescents' development of particular patterns of orientation functional to the perpetuation of existing social, economic, and political systems. In this sense, the educational system conserves a relatively unaltered pattern of values, even though education itself has contributed a great deal to change in the social structure. Japanese education can therefore be termed conservative.

The entrance tests, often denounced as the "infernal examination hell," in fact turn out to be key devices for socialization. Emphasis during the adolescent years on universalistic achievement orientations–mastery of mathematics, acquaintance with modern science, familiarity with languages–gives way in adulthood to particularistic norms–loyalty to the group, a sense of hierarchy, the desire to conform. The great divide is the college entrance examination.

Lifetime Commitment

The second illustration of a behavioral pattern linked to basic attitudes has to do with the group. Japanese cultural historians trace the contemporary concern for the good of the group back to its ancestry in the traditional household (*ie*) developed during the Tokugawa period. (They also point to the group of households in the countryside, the *dōzoku*, and its urban equivalent, the *iemoto*.) Especially in its reincarnation in Tokugawa towns, the group tended to blend ascriptive factors such as place of birth, kinship, and status with new criteria such as ability, perseverance, and achievement. These "pseudo-kinship" groups came to embrace a variety of bands of those dedicated to such traditional pursuits as the tea ceremony, Kabuki theater, *sumō* wrestling, flower arranging, *koto* playing, garden design, cooking, and (in our day) photography, architecture, and certain academic disciplines. Key to the guildlike structure was the fictitious household (*ie*) with its master-disciple relationship, wherein the experienced elder (*sensei*) offered training, support, and protection in return for followers' permanent obligation (*on*).

The group in contemporary Japan is, of course, a far more complicated structure (guildlike bands still exist in traditional arts and crafts). It mixes a heritage from the Confucian ethic and modern practices of managerial familism. The Japanese anthropologist Nakane Chie has identified the process whereby individuals with different "attributes" become members of a group, which exerts lasting pressure to conform to its "frame."[7]

This insight into the society of attributes as contrasted with the frame society is best understood by means of an everyday illustration. At the Stonier Graduate School of Banking at Rutgers University, American in-service trainees respond to introductions with name followed by profession. The American is a "banker," and it is only later that one learns that he is a product of the Harvard Business School, a former intern at the Bank of America, and now an employee of the First National City Bank. In summer institutes for Japanese bankers, who have on occasion been at Rutgers to learn about U.S. business and to upgrade their English conversation, the trainee usually responds to introductions with family name followed by affiliation with a firm. The Japanese is a "Sumitomo salary man," a product of the University of Tokyo, and only later does one surmise that he performs duties connected with the banking profession. The American is from a society of attributes, whereas the Japanese is from a frame society.

In Japan, orientation and behavior come together in a system of lifetime employment found in large corporations. We must be careful here, for recent studies have claimed that such lifetime commitment has been exaggerated in terms of its spread through Japanese society or even through the business world. It is true, however, that most Japanese still at least think of loyalty to one university and to one firm and of the security that comes with permanent affiliation.

In large firms, institutional practices underline the ideal: employees are recruited directly from schools, with an emphasis on their adaptability and willingness to conform. They receive a variety of group benefits: bonuses paid twice a year equal to regular salaries for three to five months (these are the sources for much of household savings), company housing in the early stages of a career, and family benefits (for education, marriages, child care, illness, and deaths).

The characteristics of Japanese groups, aspects of a lifestyle that has become fairly familiar to outsiders, can be summarized as follows. First, individuals seem to strive to become homogeneous members of the group. Second, once they belong to the group, they are protected regardless of their position. Japanese firms lean more toward reward for longevity of service than for individual achievement. Third, relations within the group are mostly vertical; Japanese are famous for a lack of horizontal, collegial relationships. (There are exceptions: members of a given college class and those of the same age cadre may maintain informal contacts across departments, bureaus, and branches of a firm and even among different private and public organizations.) Fourth and finally, Japanese groups (as well as the nation-family) are exclusive. One's own group is conceived of as close, intimate, and protective; the outside group as comparatively alien, potentially unkind, and probably hostile.

There are numerous examples of vertical group orientation in organizations other than the firm. The clique (*-batsu*) is a well-known phenomenon and shows up in the form of a political party faction (*habatsu*), finance circle (*zaibatsu*), and the bureaucracy (*kambatsu*), particularly in the higher civil service. One can also detect layers running horizontally across the vertical frames made up of school cliques (*gakubatsu*), the most famous being made up of graduates of the University of Tokyo.

It is now almost trite to say that Japanese are found to be hard working and diligent people. They exhibit resilience to hardship, toughness of character, and almost compulsive perseverance. There is a great deal more insight in saying that such energies are channeled through groups, in which Japanese seek personal satisfaction.

The Rule of Consensus

A third example of a pattern of behavior in Japan has now received rather widespread attention. The distinctly Japanese method of decisionmaking can be linked to the basic Japanese orientation. Persistent attitudes that highlight the group and emphasize the principle of collective responsibility lead quite naturally to a decision-making process of circulation and consensus.

In the Japanese system, it is necessary that leaders (the "legitimizers") obtain all the views of subordinates and constituents before announcing a final decision. The respected elder leader is precisely where he is because he has come to know and trust his subordinates. The objective of the system is to retain harmony within the group. The mode is mutual reliance ("interpenetration") on horizontal levels, and the style is of the patron-client relationship in a vertical chain. It has been recognized that the middle level in such a system is in a critical position, strategically located to accommodate different views from the lower half, to transmit them to the upper half, and then to relay ideas on the implementation of policy from top to bottom.

To offer an illustration drawn from politics, in the postwar era the Japanese prime minister, though an important figure, has probably been less powerful than a determined and energetic U.S. president. The prime minister must seek consensus among powerful elites (a traditionally recruited bureaucracy, various LDP factions, and components of the world of finance—*zaikai*) and at the same time avoid too frequent and outright confrontation with the opposition. The ideal is a public consensus, not a decision resting on a majority of 51 to 49 after a division.

Thus President Richard Nixon could in a flash overrule the U.S. bureaucracy, make an abrupt change in policy, and announce normalization of relations with Chinese authorities in Peking (the event, incidentally, caused the "Nixon shock" in Tokyo). In taking his first cautious steps into "independent diplomacy," Prime Minister Tanaka Kakuei had to devote six months to consensus-building before Tokyo could normalize relations with Peking. The diplomatic historian Hosoya Chihiro has concluded, "The Japanese Prime Minister seems to perceive his role in the accommodating of different views of the various leaders and agencies concerned, so as to secure their maximum support, rather than asserting his own priorities in order to lead his nation in a certain direction."[8]

It has been argued that the Japanese system is in one sense more democratic than its American counterpart in that the views of a variety of members of the society are taken into account ahead of time. The American example of Ambassador Andrew Young publicly taking a position different from that of his administration in 1979 is almost inconceivable in Japan. On the other hand, Japanese consensual decisionmaking has been called less democratic than the U.S. counterpart in that it is more deficient in terms of interaction and feedback between the decisionmakers on the one side and the Diet, the interested public, and various interest groups on the other.

Most often, shortcomings in the Japanese system have been identified with an elaborate documentary process called *ringisei.* The exercise includes a system (*-sei*) rooted in a habit of what is called "reverential inquiry" (*rinshin*) into the intentions of a superior. The byproduct is a circulatory memorandum (*ringisho*), which is painstakingly disseminated from a desk up to a bureau chief, then down to another desk and up to another bureau chief, until all the bureaus have been covered. The document then proceeds to division level, across-and-up, across-and-up to departments, and eventually to the government minister or firm president. Any amendment, of course, requires a filtering through the whole process again. At best, the process guarantees an eventual consensus and guards against any nasty surprises. Japanese have roundly denounced the process as dominated by a "feudal lord system" (*tonosama hōshiki*) at its worst and, when a horizontal veto is absolute, as marred by the interference of "compost emperors" (*hiryō tennō*). An equally colorful figure of speech has been applied by Maruyama Masao to the academic world to describe its extreme compartmentalization according to specialties and relative lack of collegial relationships. He says this helps produce "our octopus-pot culture."

Somewhat more seriously, it will now be understood why a meeting between Japanese on the one side and Americans on the other will, as often as not, produce a minor crisis rather than an agreement. The American side will be somewhat blunt, impatient, openly adversarial, and expressive of the wish to reach a decision quickly and go home. The Japanese side will be circumspect (more often called "devious" by Americans), expressive of the wish to reach a lasting compromise, polite in offering another cup of tea to break the silence, and quite willing to prolong the exchange until a sound human relationship (if not a decision) is reached. Additional comments on these interesting and yet puzzling cultural exchanges will be given in the concluding chapter.

NOTES

1. All these portraits are faithful copies of authentic originals. Among the "photo credits" are the following: (OECD) Robert J. Ballon, "A European Views the Japanese; Thirty Years in Tokyo," *the wheel extended* (Toyota organ, special supplement no. 2, summer 1978); (Sato-*san*) Takeuchi Hiroshi, "Keys to Corporate Resilience" (trans. from *Jūkōzō no Nihon keizai* [Tokyo: Asashi Shimbun Sha, 1978]), *Japan Echo* 6 (Special Issue, 1979):29–39; (conference) Mochizuki Kiichi (manager of corporate planning, Nippon Steel), "The Problems of Japanese-American Verbal Communication: A Personal Footnote," in *The Role of American and Japanese International Corporations in a Changing World Economy: A Dialogue* (Boston: Fletcher School of Law and Diplomacy in cooperation with Keiō University, November 20–21, 1974), p. 37; (*imbeedaa sakusen*) *Japan Times Weekly* (International Edition), June 9, 1979; Okamoto Kokichi (executive managing director, Hotel New Otani, Tokyo), "Beer Garden," *PHP* (Peace, Happiness and Prosperity) 8, no. 8 (August 1977):56; (postwar saying) as is; (Ichikawa Fusae) Patricia Murray, "Ichikawa Fusae and the Lonely Red Carpet," *Japan Interpreter* 10, no. 2 (Autumn 1975); ("good wives") H. J. Jones, "Good Wives–Wise Mothers and *Pan Pan:* Notes on the Position of Japanese Women," *Asian Profile* 3, no. 6 (December 1975):627; (Kawabata) John K. Emmerson, *Japanese and Americans in a New World in a New Age* (New York: Japan Information Service, Consulate General of Japan, 1974); (Okayama) the American was the author; the Japanese was the late Ueda Chikao, whom the Michigan team recalls fondly; (rice) *Japan Times Weekly* (International Edition), January 20, 1979.

2. Kano Tsutomu, "Introduction: Why the Search for Identity?" in Japan Center for International Exchange, ed., *The Silent Power; Japan's Identity and World Role* (Tokyo: Simul Press, 1976).

3. The analysis of the surveys draws heavily on the notes I took at an invitational seminar with members of the Nihonjin Kenkyūkai, held at Japan House in New York, on March 14, 1977. Notes have been buttressed by a detailed *Text of the Seminar on "Changing Values in Modern*

Japan" (Tokyo: Nihonjin Kenkyūkai (NK), n.d. [ca. 1976]). The quotation is from the lead article by Hayashi Chikio, "Changes in Japanese Thought During the Past Twenty Years," Appendix I (Kokuminsei Survey), p. 36.

4. Remarks by Iwao Sumiko at seminar, 1977; also Iwao Sumiko, "A Full Life for Modern Japanese Women," *Text of the Seminar*, pp. 95–111.

5. In the comments on education that follow, I have drawn heavily on the insights of my colleague, Nobuo Shimahara (whom I visited in Nagoya, 1976–77), and on his published results: Nobuo K. Shimahara, *Adaptation and Education in Japan* (New York: Praeger, 1979).

6. Ezra Vogel, *Japan's New Middle Class* (Berkeley: University of California Press, 1965), p. 40; see also Shimahara's comment, *Adaptation*, p. 82.

7. Chie Nakane, *Japanese Society* (Berkeley and Los Angeles: University of California Press, 1970).

8. Hosoya Chihiro, "Characteristics of the Foreign Policy Decision-Making System in Japan," paper prepared for delivery at the 1972 meeting of the International Studies Association, Dallas, March 14–18, 1972, p. 21.

9

Japan in the World

Perhaps no country has offered the fascinating variety of international experience that Japan has enjoyed and suffered in modern times. Rapid, often urgent, shifts in international status have left deep impressions on Japanese images of the outer world.

THE VARIOUS JAPANS

Reared as a kind of distant younger cousin of the great Middle Kingdom of China within the venerable Confucian family of nations, Japan was the first member of that family to modernize and to seek status in the Western nation-state system on its own terms. Thereafter the Japanese did not completely forget the sinic tradition. Even before the 1978 normalization of relations with mainland China, it seemed inevitable that Japan would seek to return to some of its main roots, which were Chinese.

In the early 1940s, the Greater East Asia Coprosperity Sphere was, in its more idealistic aspects, an attempt to reject the Western nation-state system, to rebuild a hierarchical family of nations, and to construct a new order for Asia, in which Japan would play the self-appointed role of elder brother. Some have said that what the Japanese had previously failed to accomplish by force, they brought about in the postwar period by economic clout.

In the late 1940s Japan was prepared, with U.S. aid, to return to the peaceful life. Since the Japanese were among those with the most vivid experiences about the horrors of war, they had come to believe conclusively in the idea—before it was incorporated in their new constitution—that they should renounce force as an instrument of national policy. In the 1950s, 1960s, and 1970s, largely with the help of the United States, they were reintroduced to the harsh realities of diplomacy and force. A Japanese observer sadly expressed the idea that his people had moved from a prewar fear of dependence to a postwar fear of independence.

In the era after the peace treaty, Japan's diplomacy has been denounced for being pragmatic. It could equally be praised for pursuing what Japanese call an omnidirectional course, unencumbered by the need to press for any dogma or ideology. Japan has been a pioneer in an experiment to try to conduct diplomacy within a multistate system without large components of force. This effort will doubtless fail, unless the world system is changed radically, but the ideal can scarcely be faulted.

Meanwhile Japan, although it was still *in* Asia, began to feel less and less *of* Asia. The island nation had been the first to emerge from the old Confucian tradition, the first from East Asia to pass through the threshold of modernity, and among the first in the world to enter the postindustrial stage. (Taiwan and South Korea are not too far behind; the People's Republic of China promises an even more explosive transformation in the twenty-first century.)

Consider for a moment the claim often made by Japanese that their nation remains an Asian power. Certainly this is the broadest kind of generalization. More specifically, Japan is the first member of the Confucian family to test the process of modernization with tools inherited from the old orders in East Asia. Even more specifically, today Japan is an island nation anchored in Northeast Asia. As such it is a regional power with political, economic, and security concerns directed to the continent and to the Korean peninsula. Japan is located on the western edge of the Pacific basin (a link to the West) and on the northern edge of Southeast Asia (the nearest link to the developing world). Tokyo is now a world city. Its connections are aerial routes, mapped on great circles (the fastest links to the developed world). Japan is an American ally—sometimes regarded as reliable, sometimes as reluctant—with bonds forged from security links, trade, and educational and cultural exchange.

As an advanced industrial power, Japan has grown economically closer (both in cooperation and in competition) to the industrial democracies of the West. In June 1979, it hosted the first summit conference of advanced industrial nations to be held in Asia. Japan had joined those nations that account for about 55 percent of world economic activity.

ECONOMIC PROBLEMS AND TRADE

It is interesting to note that when the media in Japan discuss major divisions in the world, they describe not the East-West gap of the 1950s, but the widening gulf of the 1960s and 1970s between what they call the North (the developed world) and the South (the developing world). The terminology is borrowed from United Nations documents and often shows up in summit communiqués, especially those emanating from Tokyo. The difficulty is that the labels are often used loosely so as to exclude from the North rapidly developing areas (like Taiwan and South Korea) and to include in the South oil-rich areas (for example, members of the Organization of Petroleum Exporting Countries, OPEC) with the effect that quite disparate nations are commingled (for example, impoverished Bangladesh and rich Kuwait). In any case, as far as most of the world is concerned, Japan is now definitely part of the developed world, and Japanese continue to hope, usually in vain, that they can serve as a bridge to the developing world.

Japan's International Trade

Perhaps patterns of trade, better than any others, are the best indicators of Japan's ties throughout the world. Because Japan has had to sell abroad in order to pay for vitally necessary imports of raw materials and food, exports have played a key role in the country's economic policy of growth.

Data on import sources have been revealing. In 1977, for example, ranking after the United States (which was the source of 18 percent of Japan's imports), the chief countries of origin for imports were Saudi Arabia (12 percent), Iran (6 percent), and Bahrain (5 percent). Thus, in trade terms, Japan's vital contacts were not with neighboring East Asia, but with North America and the Middle East. Japanese have been quietly negotiating contracts with the oil-producing nations, agreements which indirectly exchange technical assistance for black gold. Japan's other major import sources were in the Pacific basin: Australia (8 percent of Japan's imports) and Indonesia (7 percent).

Statistics on export destinations and categories have also been indicative of Japan's pattern of world economic relations. In 1977 the United States absorbed 25 percent of Japan's exports. Major items in the nation's total exports included: machinery (25 percent), motor vehicles (19 percent), iron and steel (15 percent), and completed ships (10 percent). The balance of trade surplus in manufactures (including automobiles) was a particularly sensitive issue in the United States and, as we shall see, gave rise to political pressures on the U.S. government for protectionism.

The second most important destination for Japanese exports was the Republic of (South) Korea (accounting for 5 percent of the total). In this sole case, Japan was interacting with a traditional neighbor (and former colony) in East Asia. Immediately after normalization of relations between Tokyo and Peking on August 12, 1978, China loomed large in Japan's hopes for future trade and export of technical assistance. In 1979, however, Japanese grew cautious as Chinese leaders put a rein on ambitious schemes for development. After Prime Minister Ōhira's visit to Peking late in 1979, hopes were revived. Trade between China and Japan was expected to expand steadily.

After the oil shock of 1973 and through the continuing recession of the late 1970s, many Japanese urged consideration of an alternative strategy in place of a continuing aggressive export drive. They argued that Japan could settle for a lower rate of growth and could reassign energies previously devoted mainly to exports to improvements in social welfare at home. When Prime Minister Ōhira adopted a modified version of this strategy, however, he found himself at odds with President Carter, who wanted a higher Japanese rate of growth in order to boost imports of U.S. goods.

In the middle and late 1970s, Japan's international trade was substantially affected by the state of the world economy. A major feature was the continued slow rate of recovery of the industrialized nations from the 1974–75 recession, the worst worldwide economic slump since the 1930s. Lack of resilience was due in part to steadily increasing energy costs as OPEC countries exercised their pricing power. Slow growth, sluggish investment, excess productive capacity, and persistently high levels of unemployment reduced the growth of international trade and nurtured protectionist attitudes and policies. With divergent rates of inflation and real growth, such developments widened trade and payments imbalances and increased instability in foreign exchange markets.

The Japanese were concerned about many aspects of their international status other than economic, and later in this chapter these matters (security policy, foreign aid, and cultural relations) shall receive attention. As in the case of relations with the world at large and with industrialized nations in general, Japan's ties with the United States were dominated by problems of international trade and economic issues. The year-to-year details served to obscure the significant fact that these allies were engaged in the largest volume of cross-ocean commerce in the history of the world.

The Japan–U.S. Balance

The Japanese might well be forgiven for their confusion over the various U.S. positions with regard to Japan's economic performance. In the great growth era of the 1960s, Washington complained to Tokyo about excessive growth rates and aggressive export drives. In the slower growth era of the 1970s, Washington urged Japan to maintain a higher growth rate in order to stimulate imports from the United States. In the late 1970s, although Japan's huge balance of trade surplus had begun to decline, Americans remained irked by Japan's commercial policies. A senior business counselor, former Undersecretary of State George W. Ball, described U.S. attitudes toward these policies in wry fashion. They were symbolized, he said, not only by the huge trade balance in Japan's favor but also by the components of U.S. exports to Japan, which made the United States appear as an undeveloped country. Japan had been taking U.S. food and raw materials, but manufactured goods accounted for only two-fifth of Japan's imports from the United States.[1]

In such a climate, specific differences tended to exacerbate the more general trade problem. In the early 1970s, its focus was on textiles, a politically sensitive issue to Japanese. Later it was the U.S. steel trigger price mechanism (a trade barrier thinly disguised by Washington's claim that it was a measure to prevent dumping). The net result, Japanese quietly argued and some economists openly argued, was to minimize foreign competition by operating the U.S. steel industry at costs higher than those found elsewhere in the world. Then in 1979, just before the summit in Tokyo, Japanese allowed a dispute to escalate by slow, deliberate negotiation, thus endangering the success of President Carter's visit and the outcome of the world conference itself. The issue had to do with procurement–specifically, purchases made by Japan's public corporation, Nippon Telegraph and Telephone (NTT) and reciprocal access to the Japanese market by American companies (for example, American Telephone and Telegraph– AT&T). At the eleventh hour, Japanese and American negotiators in Tokyo hammered out an agreement based on principles of reciprocity.

During the fiscal year 1978-79, one paradox in the world economy involved the relatively early and rapid recovery of the United States from the recession of the mid-1970s. The more buoyant U.S. economy created a demand for imports that Japanese exporters were well qualified to satisfy. Because of lagging recovery abroad, however, a reciprocal demand for U.S. goods did not develop. There were additional reasons for the poor American record in Japan: various subtle barriers to imports, the difficulty of access to Japan's market, a weak U.S. export effort, and in some cases, the inferior quality of U.S. products.

By 1978, U.S. efforts to increase exports and Japanese attempts to increase imports–together with dollar-yen exchange rate fluctuations–gave promise of a movement toward equilibrium. But the shifts were long range and selective, and the Americans were impatient. Measured in dollar terms, Japan's exports to its largest overseas customer increased, but at a decreasing rate during the four quarters of 1978. Similarly, Japan's imports from its main supplier accelerated during the year (an average of 42.5 percent in the fourth quarter). Yen-denominated purchases from the United States turned around to a 7.8 percent increase in the October-December period (after a series of decreases in the first three quarters). In summary, as a result of these movements, Japan's trade surplus vis-à-vis the United States (measured in either dollars or yen) peaked in the second quarter of 1978 and then fell during the remainder of the year.

Much of Japan's 1978 imports from the United States consisted of agricultural products and primary raw materials, but even purchases of U.S. manufactures advanced in 1978, climbing 29.8 percent to a total of $6.1 billion. Nevertheless, the relative U.S. position in manufactures eroded, falling from 31 percent of Japanese imports of manufactured goods in 1976 to 28.8 percent of total Japanese imports in 1978. Most of this loss was to the European community, from which Japan managed to raise its share of purchases of manufactures, even though European currencies depreciated less against the yen than did the American dollar. Thus, although the Japan–U.S. balance had begun to improve, both Tokyo and Washington remained concerned over the volatility of trade relations.

To the Summit

Beginning in 1974, efforts had been made in the Organization for Economic Cooperation and Development (OECD) and the International Monetary Fund (IMF) to encourage a greater awareness of the linkages among the economic policies of the industrialized democracies. The first steps were taken at the Bonn summit in July 1978. All the countries with a balance-of-payments surplus—Japan, Germany, France, Italy, and the United Kingdom—pledged to achieve somewhat higher growth rates. Japan was to attempt, at the same time, to reduce its large global trade surplus. The United States, the major deficit country, was to give priority to reducing inflation, to promoting exports, and to developing a domestic energy policy that would reduce its demand for imported oil. All these powers failed to reach their goals during 1978.

Despite the fact that in June 1978 OECD members renewed their 1974 pledge to avoid trade restrictions, measures to restrict or to cartelize trade proliferated. Protectionist measures and import quotas adopted by the United States were of particular concern to Japan. The European Community also increased restrictions on the import of steel and electronic products. Japan undertook no new import restrictions but continued to be severely criticized for failure to pursue more vigorously liberalization of trade. By the end of 1978, the amount of world trade under some sort of restriction was higher than the proportion the year before. It had reached a total of 3 to 5 percent of the total trade (estimated at from $30 to $40 billion).[2]

For the Japanese, the conference of leading industrial democracies, which met June 28–29, 1979, was like a semicolon in a long sentence. The first clause described how the Japanese, over the course of a century, had struggled to modernize and, over three postwar decades, had worked hard, sacrificed, and saved in order to become members of an exclusive group. Japan had attended such conferences before, but the 1979 meeting was dubbed the Tokyo summit. It was the first held outside the Western world. The second clause, beyond the punctuation, began to describe the dangers of becoming an economic superpower. Certainly for Japan, the Tokyo summit was an historic turning point marking a shift from one set of problems—those of development and modernization—to another set of problems—those of the postindustrial era.

It was immediately apparent that Japan did indeed belong to the elite group of nations. Nevertheless, the Japanese delegation, boasting a national economy larger than that of West Germany, for example, was less confident than the Germans. A closer look at Japan's status may explain the ambivalence.

On the eve of the Tokyo summit, Japan enjoyed the highest annual rate of growth. (The rate of 9.1 percent shown in Figure 9.1 was an estimate, a projection from the unusually active first quarter of 1979 to an annual basis, in nominal terms not adjusted for inflation.) To the outside world, this growth was still geared to a relatively high rate of exports, which resulted in a record trade surplus exceeding that of all the members of OPEC combined. The Japanese feared trouble from the

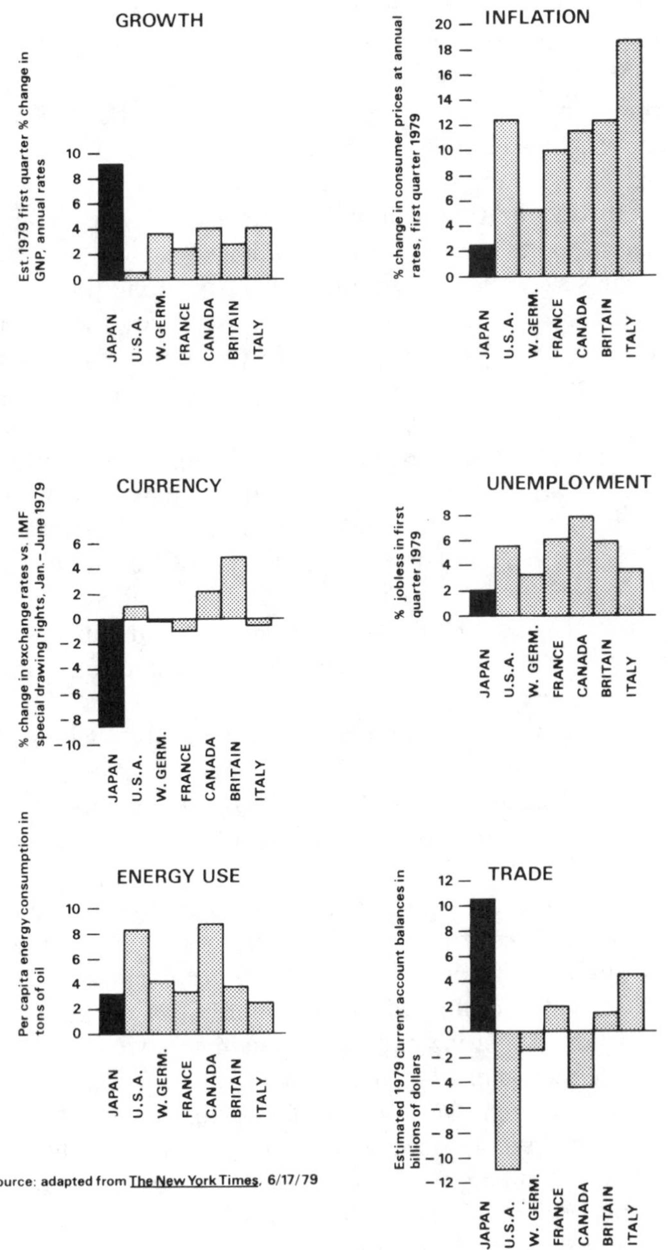

Figure 9.1: Major Powers at the Tokyo Summit (1979)

Western powers and felt vulnerable on this account.

Among the summit powers, Japan was the second-lowest consumer of energy (measured by per capita use of oil). Japanese were using less than half the energy consumed by the profligate Americans and yet felt far more vulnerable. About 99 percent of Japan's supplies of petroleum products had to be purchased abroad, the total bill in 1978 accounting for 30 percent of Japan's imports (or about $23.4 billion).

Japan's was the lowest inflation rate among those of the seven summit nations. Like the West Germans, the Japanese preferred to avoid overheating their economy. This strategy brought criticism from the Americans, who wanted a higher growth rate in Japan. Despite the relatively low *rate* of change, the *level* of prices in Japan was already high. The consumer price index was evidence, according to the Japanese, of an internally weak yen as compared with an externally strong yen. Though the strength of the yen abroad reflected the truly remarkable growth of productive capacity, its weakness at home demonstrated that the real purchasing power of Japanese currency continued to decline because the consumption standard was kept relatively low.

The lowest unemployment percentage also belonged to Japan, but because of Japanese management practices, this rate was a poor indicator of the level of business activity. A stubborn recession continued and underemployment of personnel was widespread.

By far the most sensitive issue at the Tokyo summit was the reaction of Western partners to Japan's towering trade surplus. In 1978 this favorable balance had been translated into a current account surplus of $16.6 billion (on an IMF value basis). Although floating currency adjustments were leading to long-range equilibrium, Japan still came to the summit in June 1979 with a current account surplus estimated for 1979 at $10.5 billion (as compared with an estimated U.S. deficit of $11 billion). Although such balances were perhaps only temporary, their effects were volatile, for they indicated a profound shift in the structure of the international economy.

The Japanese carefully prepared for the important, but routine, conference scheduled for June 1979. The planned agenda included issues of growth, inflation, employment, trade, relations between the North (developed nations) and South (developing nations), and currency equilibrium. Then on June 26, the very eve of the summit, the OPEC powers met in Geneva and announced higher oil prices. The effect, particularly on Japan, was electric. In a flash the Tokyo conference became the energy summit.

In their final communiqué, the summit powers denounced the oil policies of OPEC, which had imposed a terrible toll on both the developing and the developed world. (Interestingly enough, the OPEC nations were not explicitly included in either camp.) Higher oil prices would feed inflation, which would curtail growth in all sectors of the world. A complex arrangement among subunits of the summit group was planned to manage oil imports and handle the energy crisis. Japan for its part pledged to do its "utmost to reduce oil imports through conservation, rationalization of use, and intensive development of alternative energy resources in order to move toward lower figures" (item 2). The energy summit underscored slowly evolving Japanese-American cooperation in joint research and development of alternate energy resources.[3]

Meanwhile, on the domestic front it was apparent that Japan had already entered a lower growth era. In January 1978, in response to prompting by its Washington delegation, Japan had made a public commitment to the United States to achieve a 7 percent growth rate. Fukuda Takeo (prime minister at the time) argued that the figure was a "goal," not a "commitment." By the end of 1978, when Ōhira became prime minister, it was obvious that real economic growth in fiscal 1978 would be about 6 percent. On June 30, 1979, immediately after the summit, Ōhira told a national press conference that despite the OPEC oil price increase, Japan should be able to achieve its revised goals of a 6.3 percent growth rate and an inflation rate of less than 5 percent. In August 1979, Japan's Economic Council offered a new seven-year plan (1979–86) calling for an inflation-adjusted growth rate of 5.7 percent per annum.

Japan and Official Development Aid

The Tokyo Declaration, issued at the close of the June 1979

summit, addressed the need for interaction between the North and the South (item 8):

> Constructive North-South relations are essential to the health of the world economy. . . . We recognize, in particular, the need for the flow of financial resources to the developing countries to increase, including private and public, bilateral and multilateral resources.

The Japanese delegation had taken the lead in pressing for such a statement, arguing that their country was now most suited to serve as a bridge between the developed powers and the less developed countries (LDCs). Once again, leaving aside the rather sweeping categories (North and South), one can identify Japan as a leading economic power that can and perhaps will play an important role in offering official development aid (ODA) to the developing world.

To those desiring aid, Japan's record, at least up to the 1970s, had not been impressive. In the immediate postwar era, Japan had shrewdly arranged reparations agreements with nations in Southeast Asia. These arrangements practically guaranteed a flow of exports and subsequent technical services to this region.

In August 1977, Prime Minister Fukuda completed a thirteen-day, six-nation tour of Southeast Asia by unveiling the so-called Fukuda Doctrine in Manila. Alarmed by the growing animosity displayed by peoples of the region to the "ugly Japanese," the prime minister pledged that Japan would never again engage in military aggression. Japan was determined to foster mutual trust among Southeast Asian nations and to cooperate with them as mutual partners. On the same trip, in Kuala Lumpur, Fukuda had committed $1 billion in assistance for five planned industrial projects to be jointly sponsored by members of the Association of Southeast Asian Nations (ASEAN) and Japan. At the same time, the prime minister called for peaceful coexistence between the non-Communist ASEAN and the Communist nations of Indochina.

On May 10, 1979, Prime Minister Ōhira addressed the opening session of the United Nations Conference on Trade and Development (UNCTAD) in Manila. The significance of his appearance lay in the fact that he was the first leader of an industrial power to speak to the UNCTAD forum, where developing nations regularly aired their demands for aid from the developed world. Ōhira reminded the UNCTAD delegates that, as the leader of an Asian nation that had within the last century undergone the development process, he wanted to serve as a channel for presentation of the developing nations' views to the summit nations scheduled to meet later in Tokyo.

The prime minister reported that, in 1977, Japan's ODA amounted to a little more than $1.4 billion. In 1978, Japan had provided assistance of $2.2 billion, a 56 percent increase over the previous year's level. He assured the UNCTAD delegates that by 1980 Japan would certainly be able to achieve its target of $2.8 billion in aid, thereby doubling its 1977 level of assistance. Moreover, as Ōhira remarked, 64 percent of Japan's bilateral aid in 1978 went to developing countries with a per capita GNP of less than $400.

Despite Ōhira's promises—and his continuing emphasis on the development of "human resources"—it was obvious that a radical change in Japan's priorities would be needed in order to increase the proportion of public funds devoted to technical assistance. These sums accounted for an extremely low share of Japan's ODA in comparison with the general pattern in other donor countries. A disproportionately large part of Japan's ODA had been given in the form of direct bilateral loans, in which the major consideration was to favor commercial exports from Japan.

SECURITY PROBLEMS AND THE DEFENSE ISSUE

In light of the nettlesome trade problems between Japan and the United States, it is rather remarkable that the Washington-Tokyo security axis has remained unbroken and, legally at least, unaltered. It has been in Japan's interest (or at least in the interest of Japan's conservative governments) to continue the agreement, for the presence of the U.S. defensive umbrella has made possible the unprecedented security of Japan. It has permitted a succession of conservative cabinets to concentrate on unprecedented economic growth instead of on defense. Japan has meanwhile spent a smaller proportion of GNP on security than has any comparable great power. One disadvantage is apparent: under the arrangement, Japan has suffered a feeling of dependence, since security policy for Japan literally emanated from Pearl Harbor. Another disadvantage began to appear in the late 1970s: after the Vietnam debacle of the 1960s, Japanese widely commented on successive U.S. diplomatic defeats and the apparent withdrawal of U.S. power from the western Pacific.

The U.S.–Japan Security Agreements

The U.S.–Japan security treaty was adopted in 1951 along with the peace treaty. (Some said that the security pact was the price paid by Japan for the peace treaty.) Both were supplemented in 1952 and 1954 by administrative and mutual defense assistance agreements with the United States. Paradoxically, although the security pact slowly won increasing Japanese support, the U.S. presence in the form of military bases in Japan under the mutual administrative agreements remained unpopular.

All through the 1950s and, to an only slightly lesser extent, in the late 1960s, the Washington-Tokyo security axis provided the major point of difference between the LDP and conservative administrations on the one hand, and the progressive parties and opposition forces on the other. Renewal of the treaty, in the summer of 1960, threatened to tear up the delicate roots of democracy transplanted to Japan after the war. Automatic renewal of the treaty in 1970 was something of an anticlimax, owing in part to the U.S. decision to revert Okinawa to Japanese administration.

More recently, the opponents to the security treaty—those who had spent much of their adult lives warning against a revival of militarism under U.S. auspices—were amazed by the position taken by the Chinese who had previously also opposed the treaty. During his visit to Tokyo in October 1978, Deputy Premier Teng Hsiao-p'ing let it be known that China supported the U.S.–Japan security arrangement, the U.S. presence in Japan, and even the existence of the Japanese Self-Defense Forces (SDF).

Problems lay not in the security treaty in general, but rather in specific issues and subtly different interpretations by the two parties. Some Americans persisted in referring to "Japan's free ride" under the treaty. Indeed, the Japanese pact was, among agreements with the United States, quite different from any similar pact. Under the treaty, the United States agrees to come to the aid of Japan if the latter is attacked. The agreement did not, however, provide that Japan would come to the aid of the United States. Other Americans, among them President Carter and his aides, have made it clear that the United States is not interested in a rearmed Japan. Conversations have continued to revolve around a policy to upgrade the quality, not the quantity, of Japanese forces. The Russians and the die-hard opposition in Japan have chosen to ignore the joint statement made by Deputy Premier Teng and President Carter that a massively rearmed Japan is not in the interest of either the United States or China.

Then there have been the differences in interpretation of the treaty. For example, the U.S. normalization of relations with mainland China had been welcomed in Tokyo. In fact, Japan soon followed suit by playing its "China card." Immediately, however, a technical issue arose. The Japanese foreign minister publicly assumed that Taiwan would thereafter be excluded from "the Far East" in the words of the security treaty. (In the past, the pact had been justified, not only for the defense of Japan, but also for its contribution to "peace and security in the Far East." So far as the Americans were concerned, the treaty had included Korea in the 1950s and Vietnam in the 1960s.) The Japanese interpretation was distinctly different from that of the U.S. government, and particularly of Congress. Japan and the United States agreed to postpone a decision on this matter, leaving in doubt whether or not U.S. forces in Japan could be deployed to protect Taiwan as part of "the Far East."

The Japanese saw other problems. The *Asahi Shimbun*, one of Japan's great newspapers, began to refer to the "creaking Japan–U.S. axis." By the late 1970s the Japanese press treatment of U.S. intentions had grown quite gloomy. The newspapers said the trend had begun with the Nixon Doctrine enunciated in Guam, whereby Asians would be expected to defend Asians. The U.S. withdrawal of forces from Vietnam had followed. Then there was President Carter's campaign pledge to withdraw U.S. forces from Korea. Of significance to both the United States and Iran, the collapse of the Shah Pahlevi regime (and subsequent disorder in Iran) constituted another setback. With such defeats in mind, Japanese argued, the American "free ride" thesis was evidence that the United States would not, in a major showdown, come to the defense of Japan.

Meanwhile, it remained quite clear to the Japanese that Washington had enunciated a Europe-first strategy. Knowledgeable columnists and TV commentators openly discussed the "one-and-a-half-crisis" defense policy of the United States, under which Americans were prepared to deal with one big and one small challenge at a time. For the first time since World War II, Japanese wondered if their country could remain secure within such a strategy.

On the other hand, the Japanese were relieved to observe a shift in U.S. intentions toward Korea. After the Tokyo summit in 1979, President Carter went on to visit Seoul and made clear that the announced withdrawal of U.S. forces would be indefinitely suspended. Although Washington joined Tokyo in privately expressing misgivings about violations of civil rights by the regime of President Park Chung-hee, when the South Korean leader was assassinated late in 1979, U.S. forces were deployed in and near the peninsula as a warning to North Korea not to try to capitalize on the disorder in Seoul. Tokyo was satisfied that once again the security of Japan was linked to stability in the Korean peninsula.

The Issue of Defense

Obviously, the revived issue of Japan's defense capability was closely related to developments on the U.S.-Japan security front. As long as the U.S. commitment was entirely credible, the Japanese needed merely to provide support and supplemental forces. When the U.S. defensive umbrella appeared to be leaking, the Japanese increasingly and reluctantly turned to considerations of more self-reliant capability. Moreover, Japanese appeared to be ready to debate the defense issue, but only if and when external threats to Japan's security emerged from the possible into the probable.

Despite some claims to the contrary, up to the 1980s all evidence has pointed to a Japanese determination to build only *defensive* capability. For example, legally and politically, Japan has been in no position to contribute forces to even a U.N. peace-keeping assignment. And thus far, every government and every Japanese leader has been explicit in upholding the three nonnuclear principles: not to produce nuclear weapons, not to possess them, and not to allow such weapons to be brought into Japan. (There is every reason to believe that the United States has occasionally and surreptitiously ignored Japan's sensitivity in these matters by bringing nuclear weapons into or passing them through Japan without formal consultation.)

In the last two or three years of the 1970s, a psychological change in Japanese public attitudes became evident. An apparent U.S. withdrawal from Asia and the clear Soviet military buildup in the region awakened the public to the gravity of the defense issue. There were other ominous problems: the two Koreas constituted a flashpoint, any explosion from which would profoundly affect Japan; the Sino-Soviet tension mounted; and Communist powers began to attack their brethren (Vietnam against Cambodia and China against Vietnam). Japanese began to reconsider the status of their Self-Defense Forces.

In a government-sponsored public opinion poll conducted in 1979, those who agreed with the statement "The SDF is necessary" rose to a record 86 percent. Even more remarkable was the fact that 82 percent of the rank-and-file members of the Japan Socialist Party (JSP) had come to support this statement. This was true despite the fact that JSP leaders officially maintained an anti–U.S. security, anti-SDF, and unarmed neutrality stance.

Beyond these general trends in public attitudes, a number of different views on the defense issue have been articulated, and Japanese journals of opinion continued to contribute to a lively debate. For some (for example, the majority Liberal Democratic Party) the argument has remained relatively unchanged: the LDP has contended that the constitution never intended to waive the inherent right of self-defense. The party has therefore advocated a gradual buildup of the SDF. Similarly unchanged, the opposition JSP has officially urged unarmed neutrality. Magazine articles claiming that the existence of the SDF violates the constitution have decreased in number, but they have not entirely disappeared. The influential journal, *Sekai*, for instance, has been consistent in adhering to such an editorial line.

In the 1950s, many articles that expressed sympathy for Communist nations opposed the U.S. security arrangement and demanded the abolition of the U.S.-supported SDF. They argued further that surely no country would invade Japan, an island nation with a peace constitution. In the 1960s and 1970s, with wars in the Middle East, a Sino-Indian border conflict, instability in Southeast Asia, and a cold war between the People's Republic of China and the USSR, articles denying the possibility of invasion grew scarce. Some argued that even if invasion were theoretically possible, the nation should rely on U.N. peace-keeping forces stationed on Japanese soil. Still others urged Japan to respond to any aggression through non-military means, such as nonviolent popular resistance and general strikes.

In any case, Japanese and outsiders alike began to realize the significant facts: although the proportion of Japan's GNP devoted to a defense budget remained relatively low, the total so expended had become impressive. In 1978, Japan devoted 5.5 percent of its national budget, or about $9.5 billion, to defense. Over the previous decade, Japan's defense expenditures had increased 8 percent annually (NATO spending rose only 2 percent annually). Japan's security costs thus ranked sixth in the world (after those of the Soviet Union, the United States, China, Western Germany, and France).

IDENTITY AND THE PROBLEM OF COMMUNICATION

So varied has Japan's modern international experience been, it is no wonder that Japanese are often puzzled in the search for their identity and their world role. The terms that outsiders have on occasion applied to Japanese international behavior have been so harsh that the sensitive Japanese have responded by additional agonized self-appraisal.

The Criticism

Japan has been described even by Japanese as an endogamous society in which intuitive, not verbal, communication is used. It is the sort employed by family members living under one roof. The style is nurtured by the dominant loyalty to the group described in Chapter 8. Japanese are thus awkward in relating to outsiders and poorly equipped to engage in modern international relations.

Sometimes described by observers in even stronger terms, Japanese are psychologically "other-directed," insecure, and uncertain of their identity unless they can clearly define relationships with others around them. They have a tendency to be obsessed with what others think and with their own appearance. Such attitudes create a national hypersensitivity to international reputation and world image.

Some Japanese have gone so far as to say that their society, viewed from the outside, must appear like a black hole in the sky of the world. Culturally shrunken to the point of maximum density, Japan does reveal tremendous surges of energy, but without any transmittal of signals. It is a "receiver," not a "transmitter," civilization. The balance, in the realm of international educational exchange and cultural communication, has been unfavorable. One outsider has referred to the silent trade of Japan: Toyotas, Trinitron television sets, and Panasonic transistor radios flow out and inundate the world, but communication with Japan is blocked. Japan is "the silent power."[4]

A checklist of weaknesses can be continued indefinitely: Japan's conservative bureaucracy inhibits innovation; consensual decisionmaking within Japan guarantees delay; "the ugly Japanese" overseas are cliquish and project the image of "economic animals"; and so forth. Serious doubts have been expressed within and outside Japan about Japanese ability to function effectively in international diplomacy.[5]

The Response

Certainly such perennial doubts, even those expressed by the Japanese, constitute exaggerations. It may well be that

Japanese are poor linguists (as are Americans) and that all but their most skilled diplomats are tongue-tied in international negotiations. In the realm of culture and art, however, Japan has not been a silent power. Japanese artists have spoken clearly and directly to all the world. In some of the world's finest and greatest novels, garden masterpieces inspired by Zen, simple pots distinguished by *shibui* taste, colorful woodblock prints, the introspective "I-novel," Kurosawa's motion pictures—all of these Japanese productions have spoken eloquently to outsiders. Houses and gardens throughout the Western world have felt the impact of Japanese architectural style. Even Japanese food is to be found in all the major cities of the world.

One can only wonder at the resilience of the Japanese and guess at its source. No other major power in the modern world (except perhaps for Israel) has been so poorly endowed with natural resources. Perhaps no other society has engaged in such a wide pattern of trial and error to fulfill social needs, ranging from settled agrarian (a modified sinic form), through feudal (strikingly like the familiar European form) and industrial (a universal form), to postindustrial (a new form). Through all the changes, Japanese have succeeded in remaining distinctly Japanese. Their problem is not so much one of identity as perhaps one of communication.

THE CASE OF JAPAN

In May 1979 in his address to delegates from the developing world gathered in Manila, Prime Minister Ōhira had Japan's image abroad and the problems of communication faced by Japanese very much on his mind. In offering a sizable package of aid, he added that Japan was prepared to begin making its contribution of about $10 million to the ASEAN cultural fund. This activity in Southeast Asia paralleled the country's worldwide effort mounted through the Japan Foundation, which was concentrating on educational and cultural exchange.

At the UNCTAD meeting in Manila the prime minister also staked out an interesting claim for Japan. As leader of the only Asian nation that had successfully gone through the development process in the past century, Ōhira argued that Japan could serve as a model of modernization for many nations that remained economically underdeveloped. He went on to say that the key to successful development, judged from Japan's experience, was the development of skilled human resources.

Assuming that Prime Minister Ōhira was correct in his identification of the crucial element in development, it remained to be seen whether most, part, or none of the modernization mix in Japan was transferable abroad. Ōhira's thesis, however, was part of a trend to use Japan as a case study in a manner that was earlier unheard of as a way of looking at the history and social development of the island nation.

Japan Follows the World

Prior to Japan's re-emergence as a great power in the postwar period, the nation's development was most often judged against principles of history derived from experience outside Japan. Societies inevitably went through certain stages of development: slash-and-burn, primitive, slave, feudal, warring states, imperial, and so forth. For the longest time, Japanese believed that the clearest expression of universal truths about civilized man was to be found in the history of China. Japanese had, it is true, always adapted Chinese learning to their own needs; but the more they adjusted, the greater the authority of the Chinese model.

According to the Chinese classics, individual fulfillment was best achieved within a group; the most important group, the one that provided the most intimate experience, was the family. And thus the Confucian ethic was subtly woven into the Japanese lifestyle. Japanese followed the Chinese physiocratic bias: agriculture alone was productive; other pursuits like trade, commerce, and industry resulted in socially unearned increment. If Japanese society on occasion strayed from the Chinese exemplar, it was because Japanese social development was, if not distorted, unique. It never occurred to Japanese scholars to challenge the outside propositions.

So, even as in the nineteenth century Japan emerged from the old orders of the Confucian family of nations, the postwar society was being judged in terms of principles derived from non-Japanese situations. The first assumption, made by outsiders and often by the Japanese themselves, was that what happened after 1868 was the Westernization of Japan. On some occasions sophisticated Japanese promoted this idea (through the ballroom societies of Tokyo and the brick-clad Ginza) in order to enable Japan to escape from the Western-imposed unequal treaties. Though such Japanese appeared to adopt the West as a model, they were fiercely protecting the essentials of Japanese lifestyle.

Two subtle applications of Western propositions to the Japanese experience have been reviewed. First, some observers found in feudalism the preconditions for Japan's successful adoption of modern culture. It was admitted that feudal institutions had evolved independently in medieval Japan and were not the product of culture transfer. But the whole construct of feudalism, and much of the terminology, faithfully followed the Western model. Japanese institutions were remarkable because they were found to be similar to those in Western Europe. The converse was never suggested: that certain Western European nations were successful because they evolved from institutions similar to those found in Japan. The Japanese carried on the tradition of testing their country by measuring it against outside models; they did not test the models against Japanese experience.

Second, modernization theory was certainly enriched by the inclusion of data from the Japanese experience. Strive as they did to use unfamiliar ("non-Western") experience to universalize their disciplines of history and the social sciences, the modernizationists assumed a kind of convergence thesis. Japan alone in the non-Western world, they argued, was successful in moving into modernity. Once again the construct and much of the terminology were derived from a model historically and culturally structured from Western experience. Transition from ascriptive status to position judged by merit and accomplishment; political involvement of citizens in the modern, administrative state; the appearance of political parties that integrated new interests; the emergence of a civic culture—all of these were propositions derived from the political sociology that mainly emphasized Western civilization.

The World Follows Japan

In the period just after the peace treaty of 1952 and before the explosive growth of the 1960s, for the first time it was suggested that the Japanese experience might be useful to parts of the world outside Japan. The nation, often called a "late developer" (as compared with nations of Western Europe and North America), might serve as a model of modernization for even later developers. Most often mentioned were nations in neighboring Southeast Asia. Prime Minister Ōhira sounded the same theme in his Manila speech.

Japan certainly can give valuable technical assistance. Its small overseas youth corps plays a role similar to that of the U.S. Peace Corps (or somewhat like that of the foreign employees in Meiji Japan a century ago). It is doubtful, however, that Japan itself can serve as a model for the later developers. The roots of development were planted in Japan well over a century ago in the postfeudal, protomodern Tokugawa era. Underdeveloped countries in today's world would probably not agree to wait a whole century to reap the fruits of dedicated effort, to allow (much less encourage) unequal income distribution, to nurture oligopolistic commercial organization, and to postpone consumption. The state of world communications, even in the developing world, is such that expectations rise too rapidly to brook delay.

Conditions in present, underdeveloped nations have really been quite different from those found in premodernized Japan. From the Meiji oligarchy to the income-doubling economists of the post-treaty period, Japanese leadership rarely had to pause in order to take into account sharply competing interests. The new states have often suffered from a lack of national identity, have been burdened with politicized religious feuds, have been handicapped by shortages of experienced business leaders and of skilled labor, and have plodded along with low levels of education.

It is a moot point whether military demands inevitably accompanied Japan's early urgent defensive modernization. Certainly military mobilization eventually led Japan to disaster.

Nonetheless, in the Japanese case it did help to build capital (which was lost in the wars) and skills (which were not). It is very doubtful that today's developing states would want to run such a high risk.

More recently, it has been suggested that contemporary Japanese experience might prove to be useful to economically advanced parts of the world. The way was paved by futurologists who, writing in the early 1970s, predicted the emergence of the Japanese superstate by the 1980s. Some claimed that the twenty-first would be the Japanese century.[6] Japanese were at first unbelieving, then puzzled, and then pleased to have their nation so advertised. The soothsayers were confounded by the unforeseen oil shock of 1973, which Japanese recognized as growth-limiting.

Once again in the late 1970s, Japanese became excited over the appearance of a book by a Harvard University professor, who traced Japan's extraordinary development into what he nominated as the world's most effective industrial power. With a title that intrigued Japanese—*Japan as Number One*—and caused them to overlook the subtitle (*Lessons for America*), the translated version quickly made the best-seller list in Japan alongside a few other works by outsiders like Galbraith and Reischauer.[7] Ezra Vogel offered a masterful analysis of Japan's continued modernization long after postwar reconstruction, the country's effective organization, its skill in adapting technological imports, its patience in marketing, and its disciplined work force. A good deal more dubious was the assumption once again that Japan could serve as a model, this time for other postindustrial powers. Specifically, it was felt that Americans could learn a lot from Japan's success if they were only willing to pay attention.

It is now quite clear that the West of the nineteenth century did not provide a completely transferable model for the modernization of Japan. Despite the penetrating influences emanating from the United States, Japan did not become Americanized during the Occupation in the 1940s. In similar fashion today, Japan cannot supply a transferable template for the modernization of later developers. Nor are the factors in Japan's success in achieving postindustrial superpower status readily adaptable in other superpower countries like the United States. The differences in size, location, history, ethnic composition, and ethos are obvious.

This does not mean, of course, that experiments in model-building have been useless. Whether factors in successful development are transferable or not, speculation has drawn attention to the fact that it is high time to view Japan's history and experience as valid standards for testing propositions in history, political organization, social structure, and economic development. Japan can be compared not only with Asian, African, and Latin American countries but also with the advanced industrial democracies that gathered at the Tokyo summit. With such a balanced perspective, Japan offers an interesting and potentially rewarding case study.[8]

One difficulty is that Japan has been described as post-industrial with the same surety as social scientists discuss primitive, settled agrarian, feudal, or modern industrial societies. The major features of the postindustrial stage have been identified, and certainly Japan enriches the comparison among societies at that level of development. Some of the effects of this stage have been apparent in Japan: shift in economic emphasis, qualitative changes in social structure, political issues that transcend class lines of the industrial age and traditional political parties. Many of the effects have yet to be felt.

The Magic Mirrors

In the nineteenth century, foreign scientists working in Japan became intrigued with what were called magic mirrors. When held at one angle, the burnished metal surfaces offered perfect reflections of faces or objects in front of them. When light struck them at a slightly different angle, they projected different images on the wall. The scientists were quick to come up with a logical explanation: deep and shallow impressions sculpted into the back of the mirror by the artist created reverse impressions on the seemingly smooth front of the mirror. Japan may be more a magic mirror than a model. Sometimes the mirror offers a subtle Japanese image. At other times, in the mirror we see ourselves.

NOTES

1. *Japan, the United States, and the World; A Conversation with George W. Ball, Robert C. Christopher, and Fuji Kamiya* (New York: Japan Information Center, June 1979), p. 8.

2. Although the United States–Japan Trade Council in Washington, D.C., acts openly as a registered agent of the Japanese government, it has also objectively provided the interested public a valuable range of data and analysis on Japan's international trade position. For example, the council has begun to publish a new series of reference books, including the first edition of the *Yearbook of U.S.–Japan Economic Relations 1978* (Washington: United States–Japan Trade Council, March 1979). Much of the review of Japan's status in 1978, as the nation approached the summit, is based on the *Yearbook*.

3. In May 1978 in Washington, Prime Minister Fukuda had proposed joint U.S.–Japan research on and development of alternative energy resources. In May 1979, during Prime Minister Ōhira's visit to Washington, a $1 billion plan was initialed for joint research and development in coal liquefaction (in which West Germany was also to participate).

4. Such interesting if gloomy views were contained in a volume of ten essays written by leading Japanese social scientists and selected from *The Japan Interpreter*; see Japan Center for International Change, ed., *The Silent Power; Japan's Identity and World Role* (Tokyo: Simul Press, 1976).

5. See Michael Blaker, ed., *The Politics of Trade*, Occasional Papers of the East Asian Institute (New York: Columbia University Press, 1978), especially the preface, p. vii.

6. Herman Kahn, *The Emerging Japanese Superstate: Challenge and Response* (Englewood Cliffs, N.J.: Prentice-Hall, 1970).

7. Ezra F. Vogel, *Japan as Number One: Lessons for America* (Cambridge: Harvard University Press, 1979).

8. One of the first volumes of essays to make an attempt to compare other countries with Japan is Albert M. Craig, ed., *Japan, A Comparative View* (Princeton: Princeton University Press, 1979).

Annotated Bibliography

In the postwar era and especially in the last decade, there has been a veritable explosion of excellent books—written in, or translated into, English—about Japan. The following list, with entries annotated, contains standard and recent studies that have proved useful in the development of the topics indicated.

AN INTRODUCTION: JAPAN AND THE JAPANESE

Hall, John W., and Beardsley, Richard K., eds. *Twelve Doors to Japan.* New York: McGraw Hill, 1965.

Essays designed for upper division and graduate students.

Reischauer, Edwin O. *The Japanese.* Cambridge, Mass.: Belnap-Harvard University Press, 1978.

An authoritative analysis, arranged by topics, by the former U.S. ambassador to Japan.

Tiedemann, Arthur E., ed. *An Introduction to Japanese Civilization.* New York and London: Columbia University Press, 1974.

A series of eighteen essays written by scholars and designed for lower division students; nine devoted to the chronological history of Japan and another nine to various aspects of Japan's culture.

Varley, H. Paul. *Japanese Culture, A Short History,* rev. ed. New York: Praeger, 1977.

An introduction, with emphasis on Japan's cultural contributions to the world.

LANDSCAPE AND SETTLEMENT

International Society for Educational Information, ed. *Atlas of Japan; Physical, Economic and Social.* Tokyo: International Society for Educational Information, 1970.

A series of seventy-five maps of comparable scales, reproduced in color; with accompanying text (English, French, Spanish).

Isida, Ryuziro. *Geography of Japan.* Tokyo: Kokusai Bunka Shinkōkai (distributed by the East West Center Press, University of Hawaii), 1961.

A topical survey of geography, extensively illustrated with maps and photographs.

Kornhauser, David. *Urban Japan; Its Foundation and Growth.* London and New York: Longman, 1976.

An introduction to Japan's geography with emphasis on contemporary urban settlement, but with ample attention as well to the historic and rural background.

HISTORY: TRADITION, TRANSITION, AND MODERNIZATION

Dore, R. P. *Education in Tokugawa Japan.* Berkeley and Los Angeles: University of California Press, 1965.

A British scholar analyses the preconditions for, and one of the major factors in, Japan's rapid modernization.

Dower, John W., ed. *Origins of the Modern Japanese State: Selected Writings of E. H. Norman.* New York: Pantheon Books, 1975.

An annotated reproduction of the work of a pioneering Canadian historian; the editor's notes provide a kind of rebuttal to the "modernization" approach.

Hall, John Whitney. *Japan from Prehistory to Modern Times.* New York: Dell Publishing Co., 1970.

With special emphasis on ancient and early modern (Tokugawa) history.

Hall, John Whitney, and Jansen, Marius B., eds. *Studies in the Institutional History of Early Modern Japan.* Princeton: Princeton University Press, 1968.

Emphasizes the dynamic rather than the dormant aspects of the Tokugawa era; see especially Hall's analysis of feudalism and the "new look" of Tokugawa history.

Jansen, Marius B., ed. *Changing Japanese Attitudes Toward Modernization.* Princeton: Princeton University Press, 1965.

The first volume (and the history volume) in the six-volume series, "Studies in the Modernization of Japan," published by the Conference on Modern Japan of the Association for Asian Studies.

Morley, James W., ed. *Dilemmas of Growth in Prewar Japan.* Princeton: Princeton University Press, 1971.

One of the six-volume "Modernization" series; devoted to the resultant tensions of growth.

Sansom, G. B. *Japan, A Short Cultural History*, rev. ed. New York: Appleton-Century-Crofts, 1943.

The classic one-volume survey of Japanese history and culture.

Silberman, Bernard S., and Harootunian, H. D., eds. *Japan in Crisis: Essays on Taishō Democracy*. Princeton: Princeton University Press, 1974.

A companion to, and in a sense a criticism of, the "Modernization" series; U.S. and Japanese scholars explain how the earlier drive to development changed between 1900 and 1945.

CULTURE: ART, LITERATURE, AND THOUGHT

Seidensticker, Edward G., trans. *The Tale of Genji.* New York: Alfred Knopf, Inc., 1976.

A modern rendition of one of the world's earliest novels, written by Lady Murasaki.

Shively, Donald, ed. *Tradition and Modernization in Japanese Culture.* Princeton: Princeton University Press, 1971.

One of the six-volume "Modernization" series; the volume devoted to thought and culture.

Tsunoda, Ryusaku, deBary, W. Theodore, and Keene, Donald, eds. *Sources of Japanese Tradition.* New York: Columbia University Press, 1958.

Original Japanese sources translated into English; selections tell what the Japanese thought of themselves and of their culture across history.

Waley, Arthur, trans. *The Tale of Genji.* Boston: Houghton Mifflin, 1925–33.

The older, classic rendition of the novel by Lady Murasaki.

Warner, Langdon. *The Enduring Art of Japan.* New York: Grove Press, 1952.

Japan's history as seen through its art.

POSTWAR POLITICS

Burks, Ardath W. "The Government and Politics of Japan." In *Far Eastern Governments and Politics*, ed. by Paul M. A. Linebarger with coauthor, Djang Chu. Princeton: D. Van Nostrand Co. (rev. ed), 1956.

Modern Japanese political institutions within a setting of political history and compared with those of China.

Kishimoto, Kōichi. *Politics in Modern Japan; Development and Organization.* Tokyo: Japan Echo, 1978.

An institutional survey (distributed by Japan Information Center, New York City).

Pempel, T. J., ed. *Policymaking in Contemporary Japan.* Ithaca, N.Y.: Cornell University Press, 1977.

Nine original essays devoted to the process of decisionmaking; written in a comparative framework.

Scalapino, Robert A., ed. *The Foreign Policy of Modern Japan.* Berkeley and Los Angeles: University of California Press, 1977.

A series of essays by Japanese and U.S. scholars, contributions originally made to a conference sponsored by the Social Science Research Council.

Tsurutani, Taketsugu. *Political Change in Japan; Response to Postindustrial Challenge.* New York: David McKay, 1977.

Institutional change and political issues in the contemporary Japanese society.

Ward, Robert E., ed. *Political Development in Modern Japan.* Princeton: Princeton University Press, 1968.

One of the six-volume "Modernization" series; the political science volume.

Watanuki, Jōji. *Politics in Postwar Japanese Society.* Tokyo: University of Tokyo Press, 1977.

Essays that were prepared over a decade by a Japanese political sociologist.

POSTWAR ECONOMY

East Asian Institute of Columbia University. *Japan's Changing Political Economy 1978*, ed. by Edward Lincoln. Washington, D.C.: United States–Japan Trade Council, 1978.

Proceedings of a conference chaired by Robert S. Ingersoll, former U.S. ambassador to Japan.

Hollerman, Leon, ed. *Japan and the United States: Economic and Political Adversaries*. Boulder: Westview Press, 1979.

Japanese and U.S. contributors discuss economic and political controversies between the two countries.

Kitamura, Hiroshi. *Choices for the Japanese Economy*. London: Royal Institute of International Affairs, 1976.

A succinct economic analysis with emphasis on shifts in priorities from growth to welfare.

Lockwood, William W., ed. *The State and Economic Enterprise in Modern Japan*. Princeton: Princeton University Press, 1965.

One of the six-volume "Modernization" series; the economics volume.

United States–Japan Trade Council. *Yearbook of U.S.-Japan Economic Relations*. Washington, D.C.: U.S.-Japan Trade Council, March 1979– (annual).

A survey of U.S.-Japan trade problems, with up-to-date statistics on Japan's economy.

POSTINDUSTRIAL SOCIETY AND NATIONAL CHARACTER

Almond, Gabriel A., and Verba, Sidney, eds. *The Civic Culture: Political Attitudes and Democracy in Five Nations*. Boston: Little, Brown, 1965.

A comparative study of modern industrialized integrated societies and their political life.

Bell, Daniel. *The Coming of Post-Industrial Society: A Venture in Social Forecasting*. New York: Basic Books, 1973.

An early identification of the postindustrial phenomenon.

Brzezinski, Zbigniew. *The Fragile Blossom: Crisis and Changes in Japan*. New York: Harper and Row, 1972.

Theory of the "technetronic" society applied to Japan.

Huntington, Samuel. "Political Development and Political Decay." *World Politics* 16 (1975).

One of the first attempts to measure the political implications of the emergence of the postindustrial society.

Japan Center for International Exchange, ed. *The Silent Power; Japan's Identity and World Role*. Tokyo: Simul Press, 1976.

Ten essays by leading Japanese social scientists, selected from *The Japan Interpreter* by its editor, Kano Tsutomu; devoted to *Nihonjinron* (the "introspection boom").

Nihonjin Kenkyūkai (NK). *Text of the Seminar on "Changing Values in Modern Japan."* Tokyo: Nihonjin Kenkyūkai, in association with the Japan Society, New York, n.d. (ca. 1976).

Summary and interpretation of data collected over a period of two decades (1953-73) by the Institute of Statistical Mathematics, Tokyo; including the essay by Iwao Sumiko, "A Full Life for Modern Japanese Women."

Nakane, Chie. *Japanese Society*. Berkeley and Los Angeles: University of California Press, 1970.

Authoritative analysis of the "frame" social structure of Japan.

Shimahara, Nobuo K. *Adaptation and Education in Japan*. New York: Praeger, 1979.

A field study of Japanese education and particularly of the college entrance examinations; a case study of the socialization of youth.

Vogel, Ezra. *Japan's New Middle Class*. Berkeley and Los Angeles: University of California Press, 1965.

The salary man and his family in a Tokyo suburb.

White, James W. *The Sōkagakkai and Mass Society*. Stanford: Stanford University Press, 1970.

Urban life, alienation, and new religion as a buffer.

JAPAN: SOME COMPARISONS

Craig, Albert M., ed. *Japan, A Comparative View*. Princeton: Princeton University Press, 1979.

Japan and Japanese culture as equally valid standards for comparisons; a series of essays by Western and Japanese scholars.

Vogel, Ezra. *Japan as Number One: Lessons for America.* Cambridge: Mass.: Harvard University Press, 1979.

Japan as an organizational object lesson; the Japanese translation was a best-seller in Japan.

Index

DATE DUE